D0204059

Quilt Culture

Quilt Culture

Tracing the Pattern

Edited by

Cheryl B. Torsney
and Judy Elsley

University of Missouri Press
Columbia and London

Copyright © 1994 by
The Curators of the University of Missouri
University of Missouri Press, Columbia, Missouri 65201
Printed and bound in the United States of America
All rights reserved
5 4 3 2 1   98 97 96 95 94

Library of Congress Cataloging-in-Publication Data

Quilt Culture : tracing the pattern / edited by Cheryl B. Torsney and Judy Elsley.
   p.   cm.
   Includes bibliographical references and index.
   Contents: Everyday use: my sojourn at Parchman Farm / Cheryl B. Torsney—A history reduc'd into patches: patchwork and the woman novelist / Audrey Bilger—Reading lessons / Anne L. Bower—Sisters' choices: quilting aesthetics in contemporary African American women's fiction / Margot Anne Kelley—The color purple and the poetics of fragmentation / Judy Elsley—Fabricating a reading of Toni Morrison's Beloved as a quilt of memory and identity / Cathy Peppers—Butor's scissor marks: quilts and origins in Mobile / Page R. Laws—Census, consensus, and the commodification of form: the NAMES Project quilt / Van E. Hillard—Quilt-value and the Marxist theory of value / Nora Ruth Roberts—A quilt is an art object when it stands up like a man / Susan E. Bernick—Preserving the social fabric: quilting in a technological world / Susan Behuniak-Long.
   ISBN 0–8262–0963–7 (alk. paper)
   1. American fiction—Women authors—History and criticism.   2. Quilting in litera-
ture.   3. Women—United States—Social life and customs.   4. Women and literature—
United States.   5. Quilts in literature.   6. Quilting.   7. Quilts.   I. Torsney, Cheryl B.
II. Elsley, Judy, 1952–
PS374.Q54Q54   1994
306.4'87—dc20   94–9388
                                                                                                          CIP

∞™ This paper meets the requirements of the American National Standard
for Permanence of Paper for Printed Library Materials, Z39.48, 1984.

Designer: Rhonda Miller
Typesetter: Connell-Zeko Type & Graphics
Printer and Binder: Rose Printing Company, Inc.
Typeface: Baskerville

*For my nieces, Kaela Shepard Stambor, Lucie Rose Stambor,
Meredith Cate Torsney, and Colleen Elise Torsney—CBT*

For Ralph and Marianne Elsley—JHE

♦ Contents ♦

◆ Acknowledgments ◆

One of the myths about quilting that this volume tries to dispel is that because the art is mostly woman-centered, it is thus a non-hierarchical sharing of scraps and experience. On the contrary, hierarchies abound in quilt culture: someone devises the design, which is then performed by others; someone has the final say about whose stitches remain and whose are pulled out. Quilt guilds elect their leaders as officers, who then operate hierarchically. Although power may shift, precedence of one person's ideas over another's may be temporarily established to bring a project to completion; moreover, that authority may be arbitrarily conferred in order to accede to institutional requirement or to personal desire.

Necessity requires that one of our names appear first on the cover of this collection. Once established, such order is often read by institutions as a conventional index revealing the relative distribution of effort expended to bring the work to publication. That information, in turn, is brought to bear on established procedures, such as promotion decisions. The order of names, however, may only fix an artificial and shifting hierarchy. We want to make clear that the order of our names results from our experience of the requirements of academic evaluation rather than from our own sense that one of us put "more stitches" into the final product.

If this book were a quilt, an album quilt, for example, Judy would have scheduled the bee. Of the two of us, she is the real quilt scholar, and the idea for the collection was hers from the start. Because the vision was hers, she announced the project by putting out the call for papers in a variety of folklore, history, and literary journals. The contributors responded by sending us their essays, that is, their individual pieced or appliqué blocks. Some blocks went to Judy in Utah, some to Cheryl in West Virginia, who then conferred through the mails and over the telephone lines, deciding which pieces to stitch together. Cheryl produced the sashing of the introduction and the order of the essays, and hung the frame up at her house because there was more room than at Judy's. In other words, in the last stages of the process, the press and the contributors communicated with Cheryl. Finally, in August 1993, Judy and Cheryl had the opportunity to quilt the collection, take it off the frame together in West Virginia, and admire the product of their labors. That Cheryl's name appears first is a concession to academic interpretive practices.

We have been privileged to work at institutions that value our teaching and scholarship and to be able to rely on the love of friends and family. Cheryl Torsney would like to acknowledge the financial support she has received from West Virginia University, from the Department of English and the Eberly College of Arts and Science. She gratefully acknowledges the other important institution in her life, the Torsney "boys," for their love: Jack (her husband), and Benjamin and Edward (their sons). She would also like to thank Dennis Allen, for his reading of the introduction, and the members of the 1993 Quilt in American Culture seminar, sponsored by the West Virginia Council for the Humanities, for their eager responses to the ideas presented in these essays. She owes a debt not soon to be repaid to Virginia Blanton Broaddus for her work on the seminar, for the bibliography included in this volume, and for her friendship.

Judy Elsley would like to thank her women friends at Weber State University for their love, support, good advice, and good humor. She would also like to recognize Candadai Seshachari, former chair of the Department of English, Weber State University, for his encouragement and support.

Both of us recognize the inestimable contributions to American quilting made by James Thibeault, Director of Cabin Creek Quilts, Malden, West Virginia; and by Fawn Valentine, independent scholar, Lindside, West Virginia. Their commitment to the past and the future of quiltmaking and quilt scholarship inspires us all.

Quilt Culture

◆ Introduction ◆

You want to keep these things in mind: history and family. How they are often inseparable. In the twentieth century you may feel that all those things that went before have little to do with you, that you are made immune to the past by the present day: All those dead people and conflicts and ideas—why, they are only stories we tell one another. History and politics and conflict and rebellion and family and betrayal.

Think about it.

Whitney Otto, *How to Make an American Quilt*

The project of this collection of essays is precisely that—to "think about it," it being the quilt: its mode of production, its value to its makers and owners, its meaning in culture. For some time now, quilts have maintained their status as both art and craft, partaking in both high and low culture, reflecting the provenance of their individual producers and their historical, ethnic, and geographical contexts. Friendship quilts, Baltimore album quilts, temperance quilts, crazy quilts, appliqué quilts—appearing in sources as diverse as documentary films, museum exhibits, children's books, and home decorating magazines, quilts have become the blazon of the national consciousness as well as the balm to our collective guilt over national tragedies. As Elaine Showalter suggests, "The patchwork quilt [has come] to replace the melting-pot as the central metaphor of American cultural identity. In a very unusual pattern, it transcended the stigma of its sources in women's culture and has been remade as a universal sign of American identity."[1] No matter who we are, we all want to wrap ourselves in a quilt, metaphorically speaking. Like those comfort foods of childhood—macaroni and cheese, peanut butter and bananas, tapioca pudding—quilts provide a sensory experience that makes us feel good about ourselves.

But it wasn't always that way. The history of quilts is, in many ways, the history of our country. Women quilted in various war efforts—as Patricia Mainardi reminds us, "Flags are piecework (remember Betsy Ross?)"—and

---

1. "Common Threads," in *Sister's Choice: Tradition and Change in American Women's Writing*, 169.

responding through appliqué quilts to the potential for social and political change, by 1894 Fanny Bergen characterized patchwork quilts as remnants of "bygone times" made only in "out of the way corners" of the country. The influential Oregon feminist Abigail Duniway would have cheered their total disappearance as quilts were, according to her, "primary symbols of woman's unpaid subjection."[2] But quilts in the twentieth century have not become dead cultural artifacts of the past. Rather, as political as well as aesthetic statements, they have taken on lives as texts to be positioned, read, and restitched (or reinscribed).

This reinscription of the quilt in academic culture began rather quietly with the second coming of the women's movement in the late 1960s, the movement's arrival on college campuses as women's studies courses and courses in feminist criticism, and the awakening of interest in quilting by the art world, beginning with Jonathan Holstein's 1971 exhibition "Abstract Design in American Quilts" at the Whitney Museum of American Art, the first exhibition of quilts as art in a major museum. Historians such as Nancy Cott began to reevaluate the rhythms and duties of women's lives, seeing in acts like quilting examples of the "bonds of womanhood": the results of activities that simultaneously unite women socially and politically and restrict their access to other forms of power.[3] Elaine Hedges notes that nineteenth-century women's biographies characteristically open with a memory of the writer's early quilting experience.[4] Interestingly, many of the essays in this volume partake of that tradition, opening with a scene of the tactile experience of fingering a quilt.

Soon twentieth-century writers, Alice Walker for example, began to stitch quilts into their texts, in some of the same ways that Louisa May Alcott and Harriet Beecher Stowe, to name but two writers, had done in the nineteenth century as the premise for larger social commentary in *Aunt Jo's Scrapbag* and "The Minister's Wooing."[5] Walker, in fact, provides the contemporary critic with the Ur-text of quilt criticism in her story "Everyday Use," which focuses on Mrs. Johnson and her daughter Maggie, who, scarred during a childhood accident, remains with her mother in the house, and her other daughter, the educated Dee, who, in those heady early days of black pride and the Back-to-

---

2. "Quilts: The Great American Art," in *Feminism and Art History: Questioning the Litany*, ed. Norma Broude and Mary D. Garrard, 335. Quoted by Elaine Hedges, in Pat Ferrero, Elaine Hedges, and Julie Silber, *Hearts and Hands: The Influence of Women and Quilts on American Society*, 96, 94.

3. See Nancy Cott, *The Bonds of Womanhood: 'Woman's Sphere' in New England, 1780–1835*.

4. "The Nineteenth-Century Diarist and Her Quilts," 295.

5. The groundbreaking essay on quilts in nineteenth-century American women's writing, the article from which we have taken our examples of Alcott and Stowe, is Elaine Showalter's "Piecing and Writing." Showalter reprises much of that argument, adding to it discussions of works by Alice Walker and Bobbie Ann Mason and an analysis of the AIDS quilt in "Common Threads," which appears in *Sister's Choice*.

Africa movement, has adopted the name Wangero.[6] The two sisters represent two approaches to the quilt as artifact. Dee/Wangero wants to treat the quilts as textual representations of her family's past, to hang them in a sort of museum display; Maggie, on the other hand, wants them for "everyday use," for practical rather than aesthetic purposes. As Houston Baker and Charlotte Pierce-Baker write, "Quilts designed for everyday use, pieced wholes defying symmetry and pattern, are the signs of the scarred generations of women who have always been alien to a world of literate words and stylish fantasies." Baker and Pierce-Baker, and other critics of the now famous story, side with Maggie's right to the textiles.[7] But the narrative has offered other readers autobiographical occasions for personal criticism. Cheryl B. Torsney, for example, reads Dee/Wangero's desire for the family heirlooms in light of her struggle with her own past.

Once quilting was redis-"covered," as it were, by the art community and, shortly thereafter, by historians, it took nearly fifteen more years for literary scholars to recognize the relationship of quilting to women's writing and the usefulness of the quilt as a metaphor for textuality. When Elaine Showalter first noted in 1986 that "the strongly marked American women's tradition of piecing, patchwork, and quilting has consequences for the structures, genres, themes, and meanings of American women's writing in the nineteenth and twentieth centuries," many scholars and students found a new tactic to employ in their readings of women's texts.[8] At last, the intimate connection between quilting and writing had been made by a noted literary theorist and critic. Thus, by the time Norma Brady Allen wrote the 1988 "Postscript" to her award-winning *The Quilters: Women and Domestic Art, An Oral History*, she could claim that her text was being used in classrooms at Harvard, Texas Tech, the University of California at Berkeley, and Vassar, in addition to having been scripted for the Broadway play of the same name, which was nominated for seven Tony Awards.[9] Using the quilt as a metaphor, particularly for women's writing, is now so commonplace that some readers have begun to investigate the underside of women's textile traditions. For example, Elaine Hedges, one of the first scholars of quilt culture, has recently moved beyond others who have sentimentalized the relationship between women and their quilts

6. "Everyday Use," in the *Norton Anthology of Literature by Women,* ed. Sandra M. Gilbert and Susan Gubar, 2366–74.

7. "Patches: Quilts and Community in Alice Walker's 'Everyday Use,'" 719. See also Barbara Christian, "The Black Woman Artist as Wayward," *Black Feminist Criticism: Perspectives on Black Women Writers,* 86–87; and Marjorie Pryse, "Zora Neale Hurston, Alice Walker, and the 'Ancient Power.'" In *Conjuring: Black Women, Fiction, and Literary Tradition,* ed. Marjorie Pryse and Hortense J. Spillers, 16–17. For a pro-Dee reading of the story, see Marianne Hirsch, *The Mother-Daughter Plot: Narrative, Psychoanalysis, Feminism,* 186–91.

8. "Piecing," 223.

9. "Postscript, 1988," in *The Quilters: Women and Domestic Art, An Oral History,* ed. Patricia Cooper and Norma Bradley Allen, 156.

to reveal the oppression and ambivalence of nineteenth-century quilters in "'The Needle or the Pen': The Literary Rediscovery of Women's Textile Work."[10]

Marxist critic Jean Baudrillard would attribute this ever-growing twentieth-century fascination with quilting, particularly patchwork, to what he calls "the 'taste' for the bygone."[11] His assessment seems to respond to questions Charlotte Robinson asks in *The Artist and the Quilt:* "Why do so many people prefer the antique over the contemporary? Is it because the quality is higher, the variety greater? Or simply because we revere the old?"[12] In intellectual and artistic circles, Baudrillard sees this taste for the bygone manifested in "the refusal (or ashamed affiliation) of economic status and of the social dimension, a will to situate themselves outside all classes and in order to do so, a digging about in the stockpile of a past prior to industrial production."[13] The taste for the bygone that Baudrillard critiques characterizes the desire of Dee/Wangero in Alice Walker's "Everyday Use," to value the quilts as repositories of signs rather than as warm blankets.

We may well attribute the publishing industry's recent infatuation with quilt patterns—witness, for example, the covers for *Feminisms: An Anthology of Literary Theory and Criticism, A Dictionary of American Proverbs, Sister's Choice: Tradition and Change in American Women's Writing,* and even the *Case Studies in Contemporary Criticism* edition of *The Scarlet Letter*—to the desire of the intellectual elite to "situate themselves outside all classes," as Baudrillard suggests.[14] The pieced, rather than the appliqué quilt, has been appropriated as the metaphor *par excellence* of diversity and political correctness precisely because it stands outside social class. But even the appliqué quilt suggested by the fancy embossed cover of Whitney Otto's *How to Make an American Quilt* appears in "relief," perhaps to suggest the ability of the quilt to allay the pain of alienation and separation.

But new quilting techniques, new patterns, and new motivations have recently fired the imaginations of quilters, leading them to produce texts radically different from those we see on the covers of textbooks. While some quilters have taken to employing fabric as painters use acrylics or watercolors, others have adapted older quilting traditions to contemporary personal purposes. Katharine Brainard, for example, was driven to appliqué a divorce quilt, with blocks

10. "'The Needle or the Pen': The Literary Rediscovery of Women's Textile Work," in *Tradition and the Talents of Women,* ed. Florence Howe, 338–64.

11. *For a Critique of the Political Economy of the Sign.* Trans. Charles Levin, 43.

12. "The Quilt Project: A Personal Memoir," in *The Artist and the Quilt,* ed. Charlotte Robinson, 11.

13. *Critique,* 44.

14. Robyn R. Warhol and Diane Price Herndl, eds. *Feminisms: An Anthology of Literary Theory and Criticism;* Wolfgang Mieder, Stewart A. Kingsbury, and Kelsie B. Harder, eds. *A Dictionary of American Proverbs;* Elaine Showalter, *Sister's Choice: Tradition and Change in American Women's Writing;* Martin Buris, ed. *Case Studies in Contemporary Criticism:* The Scarlet Letter.

depicting, for example, a voodoo doll of her husband full of pins and an unflattering portrait of his lover with fangs.[15] Similarly, artist Faith Ringgold has quilted *Tar Beach*, the story of her girlhood desire to transcend the tar roof of her apartment building in Harlem and take flight over the city.[16]

Of these radically personal quilts, none is more familiar to the country at large than the NAMES Project, commonly known as the AIDS quilt: a pieced textile composed of pieced blocks dedicated to AIDS victims, its size a metaphor for the nature of the tragedy. This special quilt has little obvious connection with the Baudrillardian bygone; however, in many ways it ironically reinscribes our nostalgia for a fictive past. We long for a time when such tragedy was nonexistent, though, in reality, similarly mysterious diseases assaulted us in the past, eluding understanding and claiming victims indiscriminately. It also nods to the tradition of burying loved ones in quilts. In describing quilting customs of the past, quilter Eleanor Munro's comments also speak to the special meaning of the AIDS quilt: "And if quilt-making preceded such events as a housewarming, it also preceded, to negate the 'waste' of, such events as a family's departure from a community or a man's retirement. The quilter's hands and eyes, perhaps even without the collaboration of her conscious intelligence, understood that she was engaged in a process of creation that, as much as literal birth, brought into being a vehicle of human continuity." The almost religious character of the AIDS quilt, the responses of those who experience it, results from what Munro calls "the redemption of those memory-laden bits from the random dispersal that is the sign of decay."[17] Or, as photographer Bridget McGraw has written across one of her series of photographs of the NAMES Project quilt, "Art, love, and compassion are creating a new ritual: quilting together against forgetfulness."

These personal quilts address not only the past, but also the present and the future. Reading texts like the NAMES project quilt, Faith Ringgold's *Tar Beach*, and Katharine Brainard's divorce quilt, we find bits of the personal past rewritten as quilted texts, reflecting our lives in the public context of twentieth-century social history. Thus, lawyer Marie Ashe, for example, reads her grandmother's coverlet as a metaphor for the kind of law that recognizes the truths of "our natural and acculturated bodies": "I would like to give to my own daughter my grandmother's work, this text inscribing her touch and her bodily being, blessed by her eyes, recording the rhythm of breath and heartbeat, the scent of her lap."[18]

15. Susan Baer, "The Picture of Anger," *St. Petersburg Times*, May 28, 1991.

16. Originally a museum quilt, *Tar Beach* has been turned by Ringgold into an enchanting picture book for young children.

17. "Breaking Stars: A Collaboration in Quilts," in *The Artist and the Quilt*, ed. Charlotte Robinson, 46.

18. "Zig-Zag Stitching and the Seamless Web: Thoughts on 'Reproduction' and the Law," 358.

Be it old or new, the quilt is probably the single most compelling metaphor of beauty, domesticity, diversity, and memory currently available. In part because of its long associations with family and ritual, no matter what the national or ethnic background—in addition to the diverse cultural traditions represented here—we received essays on Native American, Chicana, Hawaiian, Japanese, and German traditions—quilts carry meaning and import. Thus, the quilt, what Patricia Mainardi has called "The Great American Art," has become an appealing area for study not only for feminist critics but also for cultural, reader-response, deconstructive, and Marxist theorists. Odd, then, that no single volume has appeared before now treating the quilt as metaphor, the real subject of so much interest in quilts. For the quilt appears both as itself—a covering, a pieced artifact, a family heirloom—and as a representation of something else—class and gender relations, aesthetic theories, readings of democracy—in much current intellectual discourse.

Writing on quilts inevitably, irresistibly employs quilting metaphors. Thus, arguments and quotations are said to be "pieced"; patterns are "traced" to be later "stitched"; "borders" are added. The unavoidability of puns suggests how significant the structural relationship is between the making of a text and the sewing of a quilt. Readers will understand, then, that when we describe this collection as pieced, we are not claiming any originality for ourselves, not even in our choice of metaphor. Rather, as editors we have tried to design a text whose chapters, colorful and various, joys to the intellect in themselves, work together to enlarge our sense of the quilt as a cultural artifact, as a metaphor for various literary, historical, and aesthetic realities. Neither a crazy quilt, nor a pieced quilt with a repeated pattern (like Drunkard's Path), nor a patchwork affair made of worn-out clothing, this volume is more like an album quilt where the contributors have signed their own blocks. We have added only this introductory border for additional context.

The collection opens with Cheryl B. Torsney's essay about her experiences reading Alice Walker's now widely anthologized short story "Everyday Use" in light of her visit to the Mississippi State Penitentiary. This work of personal criticism, which focuses on the quilt as a metaphor for the identities both of its maker and of its owner, raises issues of how quilts function as metaphors not only in private but also in public life. Because quilts are frequently double-voiced, speaking to both private and public questions, this piece serves to introduce the rest of the essays in the first section, which treat quilts as literary metaphors, as well as those in the other sections on political and aesthetic figures.

The other essays in the first section also focus on literary representations of the quilt; significantly, several of the essays in this grouping examine works by contemporary African American writers. To position its topic historically, however, this cluster opens with "A History Reduc'd into Patches: Patchwork and the Woman Novelist," in which Audrey Bilger discusses Jane Barker's 1723 work *A Patch-work Screen for the Ladies*. Only recently rediscovered, this

novel appeared "when the sharpening division between art and craft began to imply a corresponding division between 'serious' and 'frivolous' works." "Only a needleworker," Bilger suggests, "would have noted the resemblance between the patchwork technique of joining miscellaneous fabric pieces and the novel's ability to shape details from everyday life." Jane Barker carefully noted what has become today the privileged relationship between needlework and novel writing, and in *A Patch-work Screen* enlists "what came to be called 'women's work' as an acceptable model for female authorship."

From Bilger's location of the roots of the quilt metaphor in the eighteenth century, we move to Anne L. Bower's essay, "Reading Lessons," which discusses the image of the quilt in poems by six contemporary women, who, in adopting the quilt metaphor, claim "for their work and themselves the durability, beauty, functionality, and warmth of the quilts." This is hardly surprising. Bower points out, however, that the quilting metaphor can also present an occasion for cynicism. For example, Kathleen Spivack and Sandra McPherson, Bower suggests, "rip the quilt off the bed and the body, daring us to read the naked forms within our metaphors; they can undo all the quilters' careful seams, disclaiming the comfort of past communities, domesticity, and the illusion of a neatly patterned happiness."

Margot Anne Kelley's "Sisters' Choices: Quilting Aesthetics in Contemporary African American Women's Fiction" furthers Bower's emphasis on the underside of the quilt metaphor by asserting that black women novelists are "interrogating the prevailing assumptions about the subject, external reality, and representation" through their use of quilting in their fiction. The first essay in a cluster treating African American writers' representations of quilts, "Sisters' Choices" reads Alice Walker's *The Color Purple*, Gloria Naylor's *Mama Day*, and Toni Morrison's *Beloved*, using a cultural studies model that explains how traditional African American quilt aesthetics differ from those aesthetic standards erected by the European American majority and how that aesthetic gets represented in the fiction.

While Kelley's essay describes, in part, the relationship between African American quilt aesthetics and the postmodern, the two essays following, Judy Elsley's "*The Color Purple* and the Poetics of Fragmentation" and Cathy Peppers's "Fabricating a Reading of Toni Morrison's *Beloved* as a Quilt of Memory and Identity," offer close readings of these novels. Elsley muses that the act of tearing initially defines the patchwork quilt: "This deconstructive act is, paradoxically, also one of the quilter's most creative acts—an act of courage, necessity, and faith. Tearing seems a singularly appropriate place for a woman to begin, whether with a quilt or with finding a way to autonomy, because being torn is so familiar an experience for women." Elsley asserts that in characterizing Celie, Alice Walker begins by presenting her as a rape victim, as torn, and concludes by revealing how quilting "is a paradigm for how Celie goes about reinscribing her life."

Peppers's essay presents a self-conscious critic, a self-described "white feminist critic," whose effort is to construct a reading of Toni Morrison's *Beloved* as a quilted narrative informed by black feminist theory. By citing the appearance of the quilt in the narrative itself and by using it as a metaphor for this nonlinear, disconnected text, Peppers is able, despite her compromised position, to participate in the text.

Like Peppers, who is writing across her racial identity, Page R. Laws, in "Butor's Scissor Marks: Quilts and Origins in *Mobile*," is writing across her national and gender identity. Her essay follows the tracings of the French novelist on the Shelburne Museum catalogue *Pieced Work and Appliqué Quilts at the Shelburne Museum* (1957) by Lilian Baker Carlisle, describing how Butor used Carlisle's work in making his own pieced quilt. Laws asserts that because of the quilted nature of *Mobile,* because many of the patches are translated and recyled patches from Carlisle's prose, "to make something out of *Mobile* requires active readers to carefully (sometimes painfully) stitch Butor's proffered patches onto the backing of their own experience."

Quilts figure importantly in political as well as literary narrative. For example, Van E. Hillard's "Census, Consensus, and the Commodification of Form: The NAMES Project Quilt" employs strategies of cultural criticism to explore a specific political quilt. Hillard argues that the AIDS memorial quilt is "a provocative instance of postmodern cultural politics," an appropriation of authentic forms and tradition, transformed to meet present needs of commodification and consumption. Many readers of the NAMES Project quilt may, however, object to Hillard's focus on the quilt itself as an assembled construct operating within a commodity culture, his citing of what Elaine Showalter describes as "the attendant metaphors" of the NAMES Project's promotional literature: "football, sales conventions, and cargo planes."[19] Judy Elsley, for example, prefers "to see the finished quilt, the material product [as] of secondary importance to the process of healing, community and transformation it represents."[20] As Hillard's essay implies, the quilt is nothing if not a democratizing text that offers possibilities for plural readings. His rhetorical approach extends in many ways the argument presented recently by Peter S. Hawkins: "But apart from any of the political uses to which it has been put— to raise consciousness or money—the Quilt in any of its forms is most profoundly about the naming of names: the sight of them on the myriad panels, the sound of them read aloud."[21]

The last grouping of essays moves the metaphor of the quilt from the context of politics to the realm of philosophy. Nora Ruth Roberts's piece on

19. "Common Threads," 172.

20. "The Rhetoric of the NAMES Project AIDS Quilt: Reading the Text(ile)," in *AIDS: The Literary Response,* edited by Emmanuel Nelson.

21. "The Art of Memory and the NAMES Quilt," 760.

"Quilt-Value and the Marxist Theory of Value" remarks that "Marx's use-value definition in and of itself seems inadequate to explain in economic or sociological terms the special value I find in the quilt." Roberts posits a theory of value—quilt-value or heirloom-value—as a new feminine theory of value that challenges the sentimental theory of value established by philosophers such as Adam Smith and John Locke.

Similarly, the topic of value is at the core of the argument Susan E. Bernick presents in her investigation "A Quilt Is an Art Object when It Stands Up like a Man." This essay touches on issues suggested by several earlier essays by implicitly reprising the binary opposition between quilt as art and craft; and by attempting to define what is meant by value when the term is applied to quilts. By classifying various quilting traditions according to their "order of social legitimacy," Bernick argues that the increase in status for some quilts was bought at the cost of women's control over quilting as an art form, the creation, reception, and preservation of their quilts, at the cost of deep divisions between traditional quilters and art quilters, including some feminists that resulted from a splintering of what had been a fairly unified artistic tradition.

The central philosophical question of value—whether it is defined by Marxist theory or by personal experience—is a given in nearly all the essays collected here. What does it mean to value or to e-value-ate, to read, a quilt? Does it matter whether a quilt is pieced by hand or by machine? Does the quilt "read" differently given different points of "origin"? In "Preserving the Social Fabric: Quilting in a Technological World," Susan Behuniak-Long turns to quilting as a metaphor for setting the limits of technology in a society driven by the pursuit of speed, efficiency, and production, since quilts are, especially in a mechanized world, statements about social values and technological limits. "Quilters," she asserts, "use a needle to stitch the line beyond which technology should not tread"—or should we say "thread"—erecting boundaries between themselves and their craft, on the one hand, and technology on the other "based on [their] conception of what it means to create a quilt."

But, as Behuniak-Long well knows, any attempt to establish such fixed boundaries, to arrest aesthetic play, may be destined for failure. Familiar not only with recent poststructuralist literary theory, but also with, say, the differential expression of a traditional quilt pattern like Robbing Peter to Pay Paul or even the simple Log Cabin, we recognize that boundaries are arbitrarily imposed. Or, to paraphrase Henry James, the master of the high art of fiction, "Really, universally, relations stop nowhere, and the exquisite problem of the quilter is eternally but to draw, by a geometry of her own, the rectangle within which they shall happily appear to do so."[22] Because the NAMES project quilt

---

22. In the preface to the New York Edition of *Roderick Hudson,* James states, "Really, universally, relations stop nowhere, and the exquisite problem of the writer is eternally but

has grown so enormous, reflecting the extent of the national AIDS tragedy, it can only be displayed in parts, its boundaries artificially constructed by the requirements of space.

With this collection of essays on quilting as a metaphor in literature, politics, and philosophy, we are attempting to hint at the directions taken by critiques of quilting, to insinuate the theoretical vistas suggested by the points in the Lone Star quilt pattern. This introduction is designed to establish a border we immediately recognize as under erasure. In other words, it is meant both to create a context—to limit—and, at the same time, to explode traditional contexts—to delimit.

Whitney Otto concludes *How to Make an American Quilt* with a final discussion of the *Crazy Quilt:* "Which has so divided the women. Which has so joined the women." "Remember," the narrator admonishes, "you do not need to tell anyone what your contributions mean and it is more than likely they will hold meaning for you alone anyway. Do not explain. This is your right."[23] But quilts, novels, and essay collections about quilting as a cultural metaphor differ. In piecing this collection, we have tried to explain; we think that the essays will hold meaning for us all.

---

to draw, by a geometry of his own, the circle within which they shall happily appear to do so." Henry James, *The Art of the Novel* (New York: Scribners, 1934), 5.

23. *American Quilt*, 179.

◆ "Everyday Use" ◆
My Sojourn at Parchman Farm
Cheryl B. Torsney

October 1991

Today, when autumn colors camouflage the existence of the strip mines in the vertical West Virginia landscape of mountain and hollow, it is hard to remember actually having lived in the Mississippi Delta. What I do recall is that although the area lacks coal, it is rich in other things—soybeans, rice, and cotton—and flat as a quilt pulled tight over an old bed. From my backyard, I could see the water towers of six neighboring towns, not including the cotton boll affair in Minter City, Sunflower County.

In 1983, I, a white northern Jew—an alien by the standards of nearly everyone in Bolivar County, Mississippi—was teaching at Delta State University. It was the height of one of the first job crunches in literary studies, and I was delighted to have that tenure-line position in the state where Goodman's, Schwerner's, and Cheyney's bodies had been found buried in an earthen dam near the ironically named city of Philadelphia. With the enthusiasm of a new Ph.D., I brazenly launched into a program of introducing my students to figures both literary and political, inviting them to reflect on their history and traditions through discussions of sense of place, political agenda, consciousness of race and class: I remember talking about Eudora Welty, Fannie Lou Hamer, Alice Walker. I figured, presumptuously I now see, that since the traditional curriculum silenced many southern voices, I was responsible for telling my mostly white students what I thought they should know about their past, not to mention their present.

At that time, my husband, Jack, was employed as a counselor in the psychiatric hospital at the Mississippi State Penitentiary, the Parchman Farm of so many blues songs. He had heard about a quilter there: one of the female

Cheryl B. Torsney, "'Everyday Use': My Sojourn at Parchman Farm." From *The Intimate Critique*, ed. Diane P. Freedman, Olivia Frey, and Frances Murphy Zauhar, 67–74 (Durham, N.C.: Duke Univ. Press, 1993). Reprinted, with few changes, by permission of the publisher.

inmates, who had pieced a quilt for one of the psychologists at the prison hospital. My teaching of Alice Walker's short story "Everyday Use" and my continuing research on feminist theory and quilting as a metaphor in women's writing were no substitute for firsthand information. I asked my husband to take me to work with him so that I could meet the woman.

Unlike the hospital facility, the women's unit, camp 25, had no parking area. No one from the outside was encouraged to stay. Even guards didn't want duty at 25. We stopped outside the gate, which was open several feet to let some of the inmates out for work detail on the farm. Laughing and clowning with the guards, the inmates, clad in blue-and-white denim, piled into the prison bus like high school kids on a field trip. We left our keys in a wooden coffer, which was then hoisted up to the guard tower. (Many people in Mississippi leave their keys in their cars, a particularly stupid thing to do at Parchman. The administration also does not want to risk a visitor's dropping his or her keys inside the camp gates, or him or her being abducted and keys stolen, though nothing like that had ever happened.)

Inside I met the case manager, a young, neatly dressed black woman; a white inmate with short-cropped hair and sinewy biceps, who was wrestling with an unwieldy box too large for her arms; and finally, the quilter, Lucille Sojourner, who emerged from the residential "Zone" bathrooms, where she had been brushing her teeth and managing stray hairs into place. She wore "A" custody blues, signaling her good behavior and its attendant privileges. Dark-skinned, petite—almost doll-like—the quilter wore very little makeup and clean, slickly pressed prison garb. Lucille Sojourner, #46496, Unit 25, Parchman, Mississippi, 38738: her name reminded me at once of Sojourner Truth. I recalled that, etymologically, the name Lucille came from the same word as *lucid* and *light,* a mythic metaphor of Truth itself, and wondered how she had come to be incarcerated. (I later learned that she had been convicted of murder and given a life sentence.) Her name gained additional resonance when I remembered that B. B. King, the blues legend from nearby Indianola, had named his guitar Lucille.

Lucille Sojourner led me out of the Zone, a space containing both a day area and ten cubicles, each of which housed six women, and through a set of swinging doors into the cafeteria. Not realizing that we were being watched from above, I foolishly thought that we were coming and going at will, that life at Parchman was like, say, hard-core summer camp or an Outward Bound experience without the amenity of a concluding celebration after which you were able to return home.

After righting two chairs set upside down on a folding table, we shook hands, and I told Lucille of my growing interest in quilting. Then she began to piece together her narrative. Although her story confirmed some of what I had known about quilting as an art and a tradition, it also opened my eyes to the perspective of a black southerner quilting behind bars.

I let Lucille Sojourner tell her story.

She had been quilting since 1980, when she was sentenced to life in prison. A quiet woman, Lucille had been approached by a white prisoner, a quilter, who got her started. At that time she had no means of support. Soon after she completed her first quilt, however, a big freeze hit northern Mississippi, and when another inmate offered to buy the cover to keep herself warm, Lucille sold it right from her bed.

Financially strapped, Lucille was emotionally depressed as well. Neither her brothers and sisters nor her own children visited her on the farm. Her husband was in one of the men's camps. Soon she began to contract to make quilts for several women from Jackson, who provided her with good material and paid her $150 a quilt. She told me she had recently made "an old nine-patch" for them. It was not even a fancy patterned top, but those Jackson women had sold it for $90. Ecstatic, she could send that money to her sisters, who were caring for her seven children. When I spoke to her, she was piecing a churn dash crib quilt in muted Laura Ashley tones of brick and blue for one of the counselors in the psychiatric unit. When Lucille Sojourner modestly offered Round the World as her favorite pattern, given the quilter's name, I was not surprised.

Parchman is a violent place. Lucille told me of one of her "friend girls" who, as a result of gossip, had gotten severely beaten. She had lost the freestanding quilting frame the Jackson women had bought her when two inmates grabbed the frame, destroyed it, and used the legs as clubs. As a result, she had switched to a lap frame and begun quilting all day every day, taking time out only for trips to the bathroom. Wisely, as it turned out, she did not eat prison food: the week before I visited, seventy men in one of the camps had gotten food poisoning, and one of them had died. Lucille told me that she got canned goods at the canteen, figuring she could survive on those and candy bars until she came up for parole. Constantly working—to make the time pass—she could piece a top in a week and quilt it in three days.

About thirty other women in the unit quilted, and Lucille spoke admiringly of a woman who worked more complicated patterns, like the lily of the valley and the double wedding ring. Yet she displayed real pride in her own skill. Some of the prison's quilters used a sewing machine to piece their tops, but she found that sometimes their seams didn't hold. Thus, she preferred, as she said, "to sew on my hands." And then she showed me her bruised fingers, swearing that they were better and had been much worse.

"Why do it?" I asked.

"It gives me constellation," she responded unhesitatingly, meaning consolation, I thought.

She continued, telling of the guard who had asked her to quilt an already pieced cover for free, since she was a convict with time on her hands. Clearly insulted by the guard's assumption that her time was of no value, Lucille noted that she was studying for her Graduation Equivalency Diploma.

This meeting with Lucille Sojourner forced me to revise my entire understanding of Alice Walker's short story, and to examine my own position in the new narrative featuring the Yankee English professor's encounter with the convicted murderess. If Walker's Maggie, the stay-at-home sister of the story, was the type of meek, hardworking devoted daughter, Lucille (never mind the crime that had put her in Parchman) was the antitype, sewing for her place in the world, for her sanity. And if Dee/Wangero, was the type of culturally hip daughter who desired tangible evidence of her heritage while rejecting her family, I was the antitype.

Both Dee and I had been named for family matriarchs: she had been named after her grandmother, and I, in the tradition of assimilated American Jews, was given a Hebrew name, *Chaya*—Life—after my maternal great-grandmother. Our name changes reveal us to be cultural cross-dressers: Dee renamed herself Wangero, and I go by the English *Cheryl*. Lucille, too, had been renamed: she was #46496. Although Lucille was the only one of us to be literally incarcerated, from Mrs. Johnson's perspective, Dee was as truly imprisoned by some institutional structure that had stripped her of her familial identity. And although I was privileged by education and race, I nonetheless felt a curious kinship with Lucille and Maggie and Dee and her other self, Wangero. In the foreign Delta culture, I felt constrained, if not in many senses imprisoned, by my past; in being named, both Lucille and I had been given "life," as it were. But like Dee/Wangero, I was alienated from my personal history, wanting it to confer identity, yet rejecting it at the same time. My double bind hit home in the small synagogue in my Delta town during a Rosh Hashana service, to which I had gone, I reasoned, to please my mother. Here the High Holy Days liturgy, sung in transliterated Hebrew, in major modes by the members of the First Baptist Church choir, only heightened my alienation.

In Walker's story, Dee has ironically been given a sort of work-release in order to return home to appropriate the family quilts, which contain pieces of people's lives: scraps from a wedding dress and a Civil War uniform, for example. Dee/Wangero wants to hang them like museum pieces on her wall, a motive that declares with additional irony that this newly liberated, dashiki-wearing black woman is both a slave to trends in interior design and a woman bent on larceny, an imprisonable offense. Seeing her reentry into the dull life of her mother and sister as a diversion from her fashionable pursuit of her black heritage, Dee/Wangero plots to take what she wants and retreat once again from her past into a world that does not validate her familial history, into a social set whose project is to write a new narrative of African American power. Mrs. Johnson and Maggie, then, are the ones who, in Dee/Wangero's fiction, are imprisoned in their rural lives and in their ignorance, just like the students whom I had made it my business to enlighten.

In "Everyday Use," plain Maggie, who has remained at home with Mrs. Johnson, who is the focus of strength in the story, is, we remember, scarred, a description that gained a metaphoric import it had never had before my trip to camp 25, when I examined Lucille Sojourner's fingers. In fact, the whole notion of "everyday use" was transformed by my own sojourn at Parchman Farm. Originally, I had understood that, like the woman to whom Lucille made her first sale, Maggie would put the quilts to everyday use—she would use them to keep herself and her mother warm, to preserve their bodies as well as their souls—and in that fashion perpetuate the family's heritage in a way that displaying the quilts in a museum could never accomplish. She would use them *freely*, as a woman who gains strength from the narrative of her past, which she embodies. From the quilts, Maggie would derive, as Lucille would say, "constellation." Most interpretations of Walker's short story follow this line of reasoning, reading Maggie as the good sister, and Dee/Wangero as the evil sister in the flashy clothes. But Dee/Wangero does not want to destroy the quilts. True, she wants to remove them from everyday use, but her motive is, after all, preservation of personal family history in the context of larger cultural history, and preservation, as many recent feminist readers understand, of a valid text(ile) of women's tradition.

I am similarly engaged in making my own way through both family tradition and male and female literary traditions, taking what I want, for example, the copy of *Anna Karenina* that my grandmother brought with her on the boat from her Anatevka-like village (even though I can't read a word of Russian) and her volumes of the works of Sholem Aleichem (even though I can't read a word of Yiddish). Many critics have faulted Dee/Wangero for trying to "preserve" her past in the sterile, academic hanging out of the family linen as though it is the formal blazon that people like me make it out to be in our scholarship. I used to fault her, too.

But after my meeting with Lucille, who so reminds me of Maggie, though her only visible scars are on her fingertips, I felt a strong kinship with Dee/Wangero, who, had she been in my shoes, would have been called upon every Passover Seder to read the part of the Wicked Son, who does not believe. Like Dee/Wangero, I am trying to revise the old through the lenses of the new. But whereas Walker presents no evidence that Dee/Wangero questions her own motivations, I do: call it Jewish guilt; a habit of self-reflexively examining my assumptions borne of graduate courses in literature and theory; or a rhetorical strategy to fend off an imagined reader's criticism. Why did I ask to meet Lucille Sojourner in the first place? To talk with her about quilting and do serious scholarship, or to commission a quilt for my bed? An even more fundamental question, however, is why am I so interested in quilting? I neither quilt myself, nor do I collect quilts (although I have a few); no members of my family, immediate or extended, quilt. The tradition is foreign to my family. Is it, then, that to give me some identity—cultural, professional, ultimately personal—I have wrapped myself in the critical quilt of literary theory and feminist criticism that created the academic interest in quilting in the first place? If Lucille, Maggie, and Dee/Wangero are each imprisoned in ways both literal and metaphoric, am I a prisoner not only of literary trends but also of capitalist production and consumption, the system that, according to Michel Foucault, necessitated the existence of prisons in the first place? Admittedly, I did end up paying Lucille to make me a quilt of my own.

It has been over six years since I interviewed Lucille. Although I wrote to her several times, sending her at one point a photocopy of "Everyday Use," I never heard from her. Perhaps she was offended by my offer of the story, thinking that I was condescending to enlighten her. I hadn't thought I was, but my naive motive, that it might "brighten her day," might have been condescension after all. A few years ago, Parchman Farm closed camp 25, and the women inmates were moved to Jackson, where, for what it's worth, the chief proponent of "sense of place," Eudora Welty (whose mother was a West Virginian) lives.

I wonder if Lucille was ever granted parole. I wouldn't be surprised: she was an ideal prisoner, never causing trouble, doing little other than plying her needle. In abstract terms, terms admittedly lacking any immediate meaning for a prisoner, in her quilting she established her own *parole* from the general *langue* of art and humanity. The cover she quilted for me, patched in primary colors and backed in the bright red of Isis, the goddess of creativity, is that narrative that now gives me parole, passing down to me, as it were, like Maggie's quilts, her stories for everyday use. Even as I write this last sentence, however, I recognize that its allusions derive from scholarship and from a culture not originally my own; that this paper, if quiltlike in its narrative, is hardly for everyday use. Rather, it is a narrative designed to be metaphorically hung, to establish my identity as scholar, teacher, writer, feminist, to be used as a blazon.

Because I did not begin this essay with the requisite prefatory litany of past adventures in criticism, buying into the paranoia that the academy seems to foster by equating scholarship and objectivity with the ability to run a CD-ROM search of an MLA bibliography, I risk being called unprofessional and/or less than rigorous. I will take the risk, though, because, as Jane Tompkins writes in her wonderfully radical essay "Me and My Shadow," "This one time I've taken off the straitjacket, and it feels so good."[1]

I take Tompkins's "feels so good" to mean "feels honest and liberating," the kind of good one feels after accomplishing a difficult, perhaps even treacherous, task. Formulating the narrative of my sojourn at Parchman Farm feels so good to me because it—and its implied subtext, Alice Walker's "Everyday Use"—taught me that reading, writing, and teaching with real conviction necessitate personal engagement with the text. The Parchman experience has

1. "Me and My Shadow," 1092.

become, conversely, my personal subtext underlying Walker's narrative, a subtext that has allowed me to reread Dee/Wangero, not as some monstrous devourer of cultural treasures, but rather as a deeply conflicted young woman searching for her self in two different marginalized cultures, wanting familial memories for intellectual warmth yet able to treat them only as impersonal commodities for display. That, in turn, has given me a better sense of the teacher's responsibilities. Before visiting Parchman, meeting Lucille Sojourner, and re-envisioning "Everyday Use," I thought it my duty to teach my students about their own lives and history, about their oppression and racism. Now I see that my position was false from the outset. Like Dee/Wangero, I wanted not so much to teach as to insist on their according me, albeit tacitly, an access to their past since I couldn't cope with my own: I wanted a quilt. And since I didn't have one, I'd pay for one.

From the vantage point of a crop duster, the serpentine irrigation trenches seem to carve the rich Delta bottomland into purposeful ancient patterns or those made by aliens—or hoaxers. I don't think this modern alien left any mark at all on the Bolivar County topography: my stay was too short. The landscape certainly left its mark on me, though. All that flatness, that horizontal experience, prepared me, in a way, for West Virginia. Living in Mississippi taught me that reading across the horizon of a narrative is not enough. One must bring those vertical layers of personal texts to bear on meaning; one must not only read but also, in a sense, live a text to arrive at the broader view available from the mountaintops.

◆ "A History Reduc'd into Patches" ◆
Patchwork and the Woman Novelist
Audrey Bilger

I think I ought to say something in Favour of Patch-Work, the better to recommend it to my Female Readers, as well in their Discourse, as their Needle-Work.

Jane Barker, *A Patch-Work Screen for the Ladies;*
Or, *Love and Vertue*

In England, during the early decades of the eighteenth century, two innovative modes of expression caught the popular imagination, one in literature and the other in needlework. The literary innovation was, of course, the novel, a genre that has remained dominant to this day. Less remarked upon, but no less important in its own field, was the rise of patchwork. As forms that deal with pieces of everyday life, patchwork and the novel share a common texture of tradition and controversy.

Quilts, the site of most modern patchwork, had been widely popular during the late seventeenth century because of their use of the colorful Indian textiles that were then flowing freely into England. At the start of the eighteenth century, when a series of laws was passed to restrict the importation of foreign fabrics, quilts and other household items (such as clothing and furniture) began to display remnants of the banned fabrics as patchwork.[1] A method of connecting scraps of material into patterned pieces, patchwork showcased the ingenuity and inventiveness of its early practitioners.

Patchwork's rise to popularity would have little to do with the emergence of the novel if it were not for another early eighteenth-century development—the rise of the woman writer: "The skilled and subtle craft of the eighteenth-century needleworkers was much like that of contemporary novelists; women were moving into a territory that had previously been dominated by men and reshaping it to suit their own tastes. The development of both needlework and

1. For a concise summary of the history of patchwork in England, see Jonathan Holstein's *The Pieced Quilt: An American Design Tradition*, 13–24.

the novel owed much to domestic necessity and to the special female perspective of the emerging artists."[2] Only a needleworker would have noted the resemblance between the patchwork technique of joining miscellaneous fabric pieces and the novel's ability to shape details from everyday life into a meaningful pattern. To a writer like Jane Barker, the connection was obvious: both patchwork and the novel impose a design upon disparate elements, achieving unity amid diversity. Barker remarks upon the novelty of patchwork at the outset of *A Patch-Work Screen for the Ladies* (1723): "I do not remember any thing recorded relating to Patch-Work, since the Patriarch Joseph (whose Garment was of sundry Colours) by which means it has not been common in All ages."[3] In *A Patch-Work Screen*, Barker employs patchwork as a metaphor for the novel and thereby enlists what came to be called "women's work" as an acceptable model for female authorship.

A Patch-Work Screen appeared at a time when the sharpening division between art and craft began to imply a corresponding division between "serious" and "frivolous" works. In their study of domestic art, Rozsika Parker and Griselda Pollock explain how needlework and other crafts lost their artistic status as they first became associated, and then identified, with femininity. Up to the Renaissance, most professional needleworkers were men, and there were no rigid divisions "between art made with paint or stone and art media made with thread or fabric." As the advent of international trade led to an increase in the demand for embroidery, however, more female amateurs found a market for their creations, and gradually men abandoned the practice as it came to be seen as women's work. By the eighteenth century, women's relation to needlework was so firmly established that, according to Parker and Pollock, "to rebel against needlework was . . . to rebel against femininity."[4] Thus, when Jane Barker wrote *A Patch-Work Screen for the Ladies*, sewing was considered not only a proper feminine activity, but a definitive one.

Needlework's location in the domestic sphere made it an acceptable female occupation—in fact the only one for middle-class women, as those who sought recognition in more public fields discovered to their chagrin. Writing, especially, was regarded as a dubious pursuit for women; a woman writer was likely to be attacked for abandoning the needle, as Anne Bradstreet made clear when she registered her annoyance with "each carping tongue / Who says my hand a needle better fits" than "a poet's pen."[5] The placing of needlework in opposition to writing reflected the social division between domestic and public

2. Cecilia Macheski, "Penelope's Daughters: Images of Needlework in Eighteenth-Century Literature," 85.

3. *A Patch-Work Screen for the Ladies; Or, Love and Vertue,* v. Hereafter citations will appear parenthetically in the text.

4. *Old Mistresses: Women, Art and Ideology,* 16, 66.

5. "The Prologue," in *The Norton Anthology of Literature by Women,* ed. Sandra Gilbert and Susan Gubar, 62.

spheres, a division that ensured discrimination and inequality by establishing separate spheres of labor for women and men. Women were caught in a double bind exacerbated by the fact that women's work in the home was little valued: if they entered the field of letters, their work would be dismissed as unfeminine; if they plied their needles at home, their work would be disregarded as merely feminine.

Throughout her writing career (1688–1726), Jane Barker attempted to reconcile domestic and public vocations for women. She resisted the tendency then growing in society to trivialize the work that women did in their homes and, instead, strove to demonstrate that writing need not be at odds with cooking and needlework. By relating needlework to women's writing, Barker treated them as equally serious pursuits.

In order to understand more fully the guiding metaphor of *A Patch-Work Screen for the Ladies*, we must first identify the obstacles Barker overcame in her writing. After some background on early eighteenth-century views of women, we will look at an essay on needlework by a male writer, an essay to which Barker responds almost directly in her book. Once we have located Barker in relation to this opponent of women's writing (and ostensible proponent of women's needlework), we will be in a better position to recognize the design of Barker's *Patch-Work Screen*.

Although women poets, playwrights, and novelists had successfully entered the field of letters by the end of the seventeenth century, there continued to be strong resistance to their demands for equal treatment as beings capable of rational thought and creative intelligence. In 1709, for example, Richard Steele identified contemporary women who appear in public as "Shining Wits, Politicians, Virtuosae, Free-Thinkers, and Disputants" only to condemn them for being too "conspicuous." The well-known playwright and founder of the *Tatler*, the leading periodical of the day, favored the woman who strove to be "the best Housewife."[6]

The *Tatler*'s opinions both reflected and influenced early eighteenth-century attitudes toward women. In deference to a growing female readership, Steele apologizes in a later article before saying that women ought to limit themselves to domestic pursuits, but his remarks are nonetheless injurious: "I am sure, I do not mean it as an Injury to Woman, when I say there is a Sort of Sex in Souls. . . . The Soul of a Man and that of a Woman are made very unlike, according to the Employments for which they are designed." His claim that the difference between male and female souls does not imply male superiority had the same rationality in the eighteenth century as did the "separate but equal" racial doctrine in the United States during the twentieth century. The belief that women are "designed" for domestic activities rather than public ones is an implicit devaluation of women that sets the stage for one more

6. *Tatler*, no. 42.

explicit. Steele goes on to distinguish between women's work in the home and men's pursuits: "To manage well a great Family, is as worthy an Instance of Capacity, as to execute a great Employment." A woman's work might be compared to a "great Employment," but clearly, he believes that it is not the same thing. In Steele's view, women's proper tools are "Scissors, Needles, and Samplers," rather than "Quadrants, Books, [and] Manuscripts."[7]

Steele's prescriptions would have been unnecessary if women had been sticking to the employments for which they were "designed." His assertions about sex and souls indicate a degree of uncertainty about women's capacities. Since, as he admits, women were beginning to establish themselves as competent writers and even philosophers, Steele cannot deny that women are capable of taking on public roles, so he employs gender stereotyping to argue that it is *unnatural* for them to do so.

Like the *Tatler*, the *Spectator* promoted separate spheres of activity for its male and female audiences, and one *Spectator* essay continued the tradition of encouraging sexual segregation by validating the needle and casting aspersions on the pen. In a 1713 *Spectator* essay by Thomas Tickell, "Mr. Spectator" receives a letter from a woman begging him "to recommend the long-neglected art of needle-work" to her frivolous nieces and help keep them from "gadding abroad." Of her own relation to the art, the woman asserts, "I have plied my Needle these fifty Years, and by my good Will would never have it out of my Hand." Her hope is that because "Mr. Spectator" has "a great deal of the virtue of the last age" in him, he will be able to help "reform the present." The earnestness of her tone reinforces the moral message of the essay's epigraph from Virgil: "—mean time at home / The good wife plies the various loom." In this epigraph as in the essay, needlework distinguishes the "good wife," whose work takes place "at home," from her husband, who goes about his public employment.

The *Spectator* essay seeks to designate appropriate activities for women within the home, partly in order to keep them under control. Since middle-class men prided themselves on their ability to maintain leisured women, some precautions had to be taken lest leisure breed bad habits. The activities women might take up if they did not do needlework included gossip, adultery, and politics: "It [needlework] takes them off from Scandal, the usual Attendant of Tea-Tables. . . . While they are forming their Birds and Beasts, their Neighbours will be allowed to be the Fathers of their own Children; and Whig and Tory will be but seldom mentioned, where the great dispute is, whether Blue or Red is the more proper Colour." For this essayist, needlework is the best means of keeping women in line. Even a woman who has no talent with the needle and can "perform her part herein but very awkwardly" is instructed to persevere: "I must . . . insist upon her working, if it be only to keep her out of

7. Ibid., no. 172, no. 63.

harm's way." According to the essay, there are no alternative occupations for women (except, perhaps, as readers of the *Spectator*).

In order to encourage young women to leave off "gadding abroad" and return to needlework, Tickell proposes an incentive plan consisting of the following "laws":

> 1. That no young Virgin whatsoever be allowed to receive the Addresses of her first Lover, but in a Suit of her own Embroidering.
> 2. That before every fresh humble Servant, she be obliged to appear with a new Stomacher at the least.
> 3. That no one be actually married until she hath the Child-Bed Pillows, &c. ready stitched, as likewise the mantle for the Boy quite finished.[8]

Under this system, marriage would be the carrot and needlework the stick. The specific projects matter less than the woman's industriousness: she must labor for male attention.

To illustrate the approved brand of women's work, Tickell holds up the "chaste Penelope" as a model for his countrymen. He applauds Penelope's adherence to the custom of weaving a shroud for Ulysses's next of kin before accepting any suitors to replace her missing husband. Moreover, he praises Penelope for the constancy that impelled her to unravel at night what she had woven during the day. For Tickell, Penelope is the ideal woman worker, one who resigns herself to endless, repetitive tasks. Thus, the *Spectator* essay, though it ostensibly aims to redeem women from frivolity by sending them back to their needles, actually condemns women to meaningless labor they must faithfully perform to garner male approval.

This duplicity comes out even when Tickell seems to commend women's work. Although "Mr. Spectator" declares that needlework is "the most proper way wherein a Lady can show a fine Genius," he describes the activity in mock-heroic terms, which serve only to trivialize it:

> What a delightful Entertainment must it be to the Fair Sex, whom their native Modesty and the Tenderness of Men towards them, exempts from publick Business, to pass their Hours in imitating Fruits and Flowers, and transplanting all the beauties of nature into their own Dress, or raising a new Creation in their Closets and Apartments! How pleasing is the Amusement of walking among the Shades and Groves planted by themselves, in surveying Heroes slain by their Needle, or little Cupids which they have brought into the World without Pain![9]

In this passage, women's leisure is so complete that even their embroidery comes naturally and "without pain." The distance between men's "publick

---

8. *Spectator,* no. 606.

9. In *Gender and Genius: Towards a Feminist Aesthetics,* 85, Christine Battersby points out that this is the only mention of female genius in the *Spectator.*

business" and the "delightful entertainment" women find in their needlework is one the *Spectator* simultaneously indulges and seeks to reinforce. Significantly, the essayist maintains his distance from women's creations by suggesting that they alone delight in their projects. But this delight would at best be muted, since their handiwork seems to have neither cost any labor nor given them a serious audience.

Tickell's ostensible panegyric to needlework includes a denunciation of women writers. He lists what women "may" do with their needles in order to stress what they may *not* do with their pens:

> I cannot forbear wishing that several Writers of that Sex had chosen to apply themselves rather to Tapestry than Rhime. Your pastoral Poetesses may vent their Fancy in rural Landscapes, and place despairing Shepherds under silken Willows, or drown them in a Stream of Mohair. The heroic Writers may work up Battles as successfully, and inflame them with Gold or stain them with Crimson. Even those who have only a turn to a Song, or an Epigram, may put many valuable stitches into a Purse, and crowd a thousand graces into a pair of Garters.

To discourage women writers, he draws unflattering comparisons of their work—first to romantic clichés and then to domestic craftsmanship—which reveal a distaste for the female imagination in general. From his point of view, neither female writing nor needlework carries much weight. Although he acknowledges later in the essay that the needle-wielding woman can contribute to family economy and that her creations may at least be useful, his mockery seeks to deny women both originality and meaningful employment. In essence, this representative essay on two significant female activities is an exercise in the defamation of women's character.

Jane Barker disagrees completely with the *Spectator*'s position on women's work, and in *A Patch-Work Screen for the Ladies,* she responds to every point the essay makes. Taking patchwork as a metaphor for novel writing, Barker defends women's needlework and their writing from the *Spectator*'s trivialization. Most importantly, she opposes the patriarchal view that women must work for men by proposing that communities of women challenge male hegemony and celebrate female accomplishments.

Unlike the *Spectator,* Barker condemns unnecessary female labor. She applauds the women of her day for rejecting elaborate embroidery in favor of patchwork, a technique that can incorporate elements from everyday life: "I am glad to find the Ladies of This Age, wiser than those of the Former; when the working of Point and curious Embroidery, was so troublesome, that they cou'd not take Snuff in Repose, for fear of soiling their Work: But in Patch-Work there is no Harm done; a smear'd Finger does but add a Spot to a Patch, or a Shade to a Light-Colour" (viii). Barker attacks ornate embroidery because it constrains women's activities: the woman whose work cannot be soiled also cannot partake in the life around her. In contrast to the female

Spectator correspondent who boasts of constantly having her needle in hand, Barker makes it a point of honor for a woman to know when to put her needle down. But, although she questions the wisdom of her foremothers, she does not belittle them or their creations. Instead, Barker invokes a female tradition of needlework and claims solidarity with past wielders of the needle, whose "troublesome" tasks denied them any "repose."

As a form of needlework that can accommodate the spot made by "a smear'd Finger," Barker's patchwork is more realistic than embroidery. Her comparison of embroidery and patchwork reflects a generic distinction between romance and the novel: whereas the "higher" genres, like elaborate embroidery, deal with lofty themes and fantastic events, the novel, like patchwork, takes its cues from daily life. Thus, in the passage I cite as an epigraph, when Barker recommends patchwork to her readers both in their "discourse" and their "Needle-work," she is advocating her preferred genre, the novel, as an appropriate field of female endeavor. By the end of the eighteenth century, female writers would be more fully cognizant of what Barker suggests through her patchwork metaphor: that the novel, which concerns itself with life's ordinary details, is a favorable genre for women.

Barker defends women against the *Spectator*'s charge that they are prone to disputes and scandal by comparing their discourse to patchwork. Regardless of what men might think of women's tea-tables, Barker treats them as sites where political disputes lead to harmony rather than discord. She suggests that women enjoy patchwork because it mirrors their ability to unify diverse perspectives:

> Whenever one sees a set of Ladies together, their Sentiments are as differently mix'd as the Patches in their Work: To wit, Whigs and Tories, High-Church and Low-Church, Jacobites and Williamites, and many more Distinctions, which they divide and sub-divide, 'till at last they make the Dis-union meet in a harmonious Tea-Table Entertainment. This puts me in mind of what I have heard some Philosophers assert, about the Clashing of Atoms, which at last united to compose the glorious Fabrick of the UNIVERSE. (v-vi)

Barker prefers the discovering, recognizing, and incorporating of differences that go on at the tea-table to the bickering and fighting that lead to political instability and war. Rather than an emblem of a separate and homogenous female sphere, the tea-table is a microcosm of the universe; attending to the example it sets might bring about universal harmony.

Although Barker notes the conventional division between masculine and feminine spheres, she indicates that the patchwork metaphor applies to men as well as to women: "Forgive me, kind Reader, for carrying the Metaphor too high; by which means I am out of my Sphere, and so can say nothing of the Male Patch-Workers; for my high Flight in Favour of the Ladies made a mere Icarus out of me, melted my Wings, and tumbled me Headlong down, I know not where" (vi). That she regards herself as a female advocate is evident from her willingness to risk a "high Flight in Favour of the Ladies"; by mentioning "Male Patch-Workers" she manages to imply that men could benefit from women's example.

Having established the superiority of patchwork as a form of needlework and a harmonizing style of discourse, Barker posits a classical "mother" for women writers in Arachne, the archetypal weaver. Barker's allusion to Arachne signals a crucial "patch" in the *Patch-Work Screen:* the development of a model of literary maternity that frees women from unfair competition with males. Unlike Penelope (the *Spectator*'s model needleworker), who weaves and reweaves a shroud for one man in order to preserve her chastity for another, Arachne attracts a female audience and competes with another skilled female weaver. Before examining the relation between Arachne's tale and *A Patch-Work Screen,* however, some familiarity with the book and its interpretation of literary history is necessary.

A Patch-Work Screen for the Ladies, according to its title page, is "a Collection of Instructive Novels. Related After a Manner intirely New . . . By Mrs. Jane Barker." Writing long before the novel became a defined genre, Barker nonetheless attests to the popularity of early specimens: "Histories at Large are so Fashionable in this Age; viz. Robinson Crusoe, and Moll Flanders; Colonel Jack, and Sally Salisbury; with many other Heroes and Heroines." What makes Barker's own contribution distinctive is its rejection of the "history" that charts a linear course; hers is a "History reduc'd into Patches" (iv). She employs the metaphor of "patch-work" both to describe the literary work at hand and to inaugurate a "Manner intirely New." In so doing, Barker invites her female audience to join a community of women writers whose texts may together form part of the larger patchwork of literary and cultural history.

Along with *Love Intrigues* (1713) and *The Lining for the Patch-Work Screen* (1726), *A Patch-Work Screen for the Ladies* (1723) forms part of a semiautobiographical trilogy. Each book traces a stage in the heroine's growth as a writer. In *Love Intrigues,* Galesia loses her fickle lover and decides to lead a life of virginity in the company of the Muses; in *A Patch-Work Screen,* Galesia comes of age as a writer; and in *The Lining for the Patch-Work Screen,* an elderly Galesia looks back upon her career. As the segment which is most concerned with female authorship, *A Patch-Work Screen* details Galesia's struggle to overcome the many obstacles that she must confront as a woman writer in the eighteenth century. Since Barker's subtitle refers specifically to the "instructive" quality of the work, we may infer that Galesia's lessons are meant to teach the reader something as well. As it turns out, *A Patch-Work Screen* offers its "ladies" a sewing class, replacing textiles with texts, that tells the truth about female experience and schools the reader in the importance of female solidarity.

The introduction opens with the heroine in a stagecoach among fellow travelers who pass the time by telling stories. As in *The Canterbury Tales,* the passengers take turns, and there are both male and female storytellers. In *A Patch-Work Screen,* however, the order of succession is based on gender: the first three tales are told by men, the last two by women. And gender affects the quality of the tales: whereas the men tell stories that have been passed down with proverbs attached, the women begin from their own experience and relate events that occurred in places where they have lived.

At one stop, everyone but the heroine gets out. She continues on, but before the stage coach has proceeded very far, it crashes, sending Galesia into a river. Her heartiness during the trials that follow and the vivid details that the author includes in describing them reflect Barker's commitment to realism over romance. Galesia survives a fall, wet clothing, and a night's sleep in a room containing blankets that "smelt like a Pancake fry'd in Grease" and "a brown Chamber-pot, furr'd as thick as a Crown Piece." The narrator draws attention to Galesia's strength: "notwithstanding all these Hardships, she got no Cold, Cough, or Lameness; but arose well-refresh'd."

After Galesia leaves the alehouse where she spent the night, she meets a woman who offers her shelter. At this point begins the series of relationships and tale tellings to which the title, "patch-work screen," refers. The Lady—as she is called throughout the work—takes Galesia to her estate, where she and her husband live as partners. Partnership is but one of the many social ties this couple maintains. In particular, they boast a family history of patronage to women workers, as indicated by the narrator's description of the interior of their house: "glorious Appartments, adorn'd with rich Furniture of all Sorts; some were the Work of hers and her Husband's Ancestors, who delighted to imploy poor Gentlewomen, thereby to keep them from Distress, and evil Company, 'till Time and Friends could dispose Things for their better Settlement." One room contains furniture of the Lady's own making, "which was PATCH-WORK, most curiously compos'd of rich Silks, and Silver and Gold Brocades." All the patchwork in the room has been completed "excepting a SCREEN, which the Lady and her Maids were going about."

Once Galesia accepts the invitation to stay and help make the patchwork screen, "the Lady forthwith sent for [Galesia's] Things, hoping therein to find some Bits of one thing or other, that might be useful to place in the SCREEN." What she finds in Galesia's belongings surprises her:

> When the Trunks and Boxes came, and were opened, alas! they found nothing but Pieces of *Romances, Poems, Love-Letters,* and the like: At which the good Lady smil'd, saying, She would not have her Fancy balk'd, and therefore resolved to have these ranged and mixed in due Order, and thereof compose a SCREEN.
> And thus it came to pass, that the following SCREEN was compos'd. (n.p.)

Accordingly, the text of *A Patch-Work Screen* is divided into four "leaves," which contain Galesia's writings. The story of Galesia and the Lady working on the screen frames the disparate pieces—poems, tales, letters, recipes—and these are, in turn, framed by Galesia's life story, which emerges from the scraps like the pattern on a patchworked textile.

In its broadest sense, *A Patch-Work Screen* offers a hopeful vision of women's gradual entry and acceptance into the field of letters. The material contained in the introduction may be interpreted as an allegory of literary history. In the coach, men and women occupy the same space, but men dominate the story-telling at first, giving way to the women only after they have had their say. After the two women tell their tales, the coach party breaks up, and Galesia spends a brief period in isolation, a parallel to the events of Barker's own time, when the early women writers were falling out of favor (Aphra Behn being only the most notorious example).[10] From the point at which Galesia finds refuge in the Lady's house, literary history takes a turn for the better. Galesia and the Lady work in the company of other women, but they share a house with the Lady's husband and additional guests. Their patchwork, which represents the flexible medium of the novel, brings contemporary women's experience into a literature that had been limited by its forefathers.

A Patch-Work Screen for the Ladies is optimistic about women's chances for success in literary pursuits and domestic arts, but Barker recognizes that a significant social change must be enacted if women are to write without fear and do patchwork with the requisite sense of accomplishment. Barker believes that women should reject male models of literary production—which tend to promote male authorship and experience—and embrace a new model that will do justice to their specific female experience. For Barker, male literary production derives from an aggressive model of competition that is antagonistic to the integration of values, stories, and gender of *A Patch-Work Screen*.

The archetypal story of male literary competition, as represented by *A Patch-Work Screen*, is the myth of Icarus and Daedalus. When Icarus attempted to fly above Daedalus, the creator of labyrinths and wings, he failed and fell to his death; yet his boldness secured his fame. One critic explains the significance of the Icarus myth as an expression of rebellion, a crucial element of creativity: "The desire to fly—the desire to rise above the crowd, intellectually or socially, and to be admired for doing so—is but one mode of expression taken by individual rebellion, the revolt of the son against his father."[11] Because of this myth, and for obvious social reasons, Galesia's fear of falling is a recurring motif. Galesia, and every female author for the next two centuries, had to tread softly on volatile terrain. To be a woman writer was rebellious enough; women had to be cautious of incurring male resentment and acquiring a bad reputation.

10. Dale Spender discusses the fate of the early women writers in *Mothers of the Novel*. Jane Spencer covers this ground in more detail in *The Rise of the Woman Novelist*.
11. Maurice Schroder, *Icarus: The Image of the Artist in French Romanticism*, 55–56.

The young Galesia learns from her mother that women should not follow the example of Icarus:

> That I ought not to pass my Time in idle Dreams on *Parnassus,* and foolish
> Romantick Flights with *Icarus;* whose waxen Wings fail'd him so as to let him fall
> into the Sea; which indeed purchas'd him a Name, but became the perpetual
> Record of his Folly: And such a Name, such a Record, I should be glad, said she,
> you would avoid, by becoming a good Mistress of a Family; and imploy your
> Parts in being an obedient Wife, a discreet Governess of your Children and
> Servants; a friendly Assistant to your Neighbours, Friends, and Acquaintance:
> This being the Business for which you came into the World. (79–80)

According to her mother, gender is the primary obstacle to Galesia's succeed-ing at a writing career. "Romantick Flights" and falls are one thing for a man but quite another for a woman. Instead of making a name for herself, Galesia should be directing her talents to family responsibilities, the "Business" to which women are born and raised.

If Galesia had found only male literary models to guide her, she might have been more willing to follow her mother's advice. But in the early stages of her poetic career, she discovered the works of Katherine Philips, the leading female poet of Barker's youth. In describing her efforts to match Philips's poetry, Galesia introduces a mythological figure to replace Icarus, and thus recasts the story of literary competition in female terms:

> I began to emulate her Wit, and aspir'd to imitate her Writings; in doing of
> which, I think, I deserv'd *Arachne*'s Fate . . . Her noble Genius being inimitable;
> especially in Praise of Country-Life, and Contempt of human Greatness; all
> which I swallow'd as Draughts of rich Cordial, to enliven the Understanding.
> Her Poetry I found so interwoven with Vertue and Honour, that each Line was
> like a Ladder to climb, not only to *Parnassus,* but to Heaven: which I (poor Puzzle
> as I was!) had the Boldness to try to imitate, 'till I was dropp'd into a Labyrinth of
> Poetry, which has ever since interlac'd all the Actions of my Life. (3)

In this passage, Barker uses needlework terminology ("interwoven," "inter-lac'd") and alludes to "Arachne's fate" in order to point to the need for a female tradition. Instead of falling to her death, like Icarus, or into disfavor, like Aphra Behn, Galesia discovers that poetry can be stitched into the fabric of her life. Because Galesia's literary foremother, Katherine Philips, combined genius with female virtue, the young poet can follow her example and set her sights on Parnassus (and even beyond), without fearing the consequences of an unfortunate fall.

Galesia's career revises the myth of Arachne and Athene, which on the surface resembles that of Icarus and Daedalus. Both tales describe a younger person's attempt to surpass the accomplishments of a role model who is an inventor and a creator. But while Icarus fails spectacularly because he lets ambition carry him beyond his level of skill, Arachne's skill is undisputed, even by her rival. Moreover, unlike the father/son struggle between Daedalus and Icarus, the story of Arachne and Athene takes place not just between but among women: whereas the young man measures himself against his rival solely for the sake of competition, the two women create artifacts for the benefit of an audience.

Arachne, allegedly Athene's pupil, attracts a female audience of nymphs and village women who love to watch her weave and embroider. It is in front of these women that Arachne boasts she can weave more perfectly than the goddess Athene. In response to Arachne's challenge, Athene comes to her disguised as an old woman, telling her that the goddess would forgive her if she apologized humbly. When Arachne refuses, the two women enter into a fierce competition to see who can make the most perfect tapestry. For her subject, Athene depicts scenes in which the gods triumph over mortals and punish them for their pride. Arachne also takes up this theme, but her perspective is that of the human victim: her theme is rape, and she weaves picture after picture of the crimes committed by male gods against mortal women. When Arachne completes her tapestry, according to Ovid, "neither Pallas nor even Jealousy personified could find any flaw in the work."[12] In spite of the work's perfection, though, Athene tears it to shreds and strikes Arachne with her shuttle, causing the younger woman such shame that Arachne attempts to hang herself. Out of pity, Athene saves her rival from death and changes Arachne into a spider, punishing her (and her descendants) for her pride.

In claiming Arachne as the archetypal woman writer, Barker chooses both a fellow "spinster" and an artist who chronicled men's abuse of women. Like Arachne's tapestry, Barker's patchwork text contains cautionary tales against wicked men. In this sense, *A Patch-Work Screen for the Ladies* rescues the scraps from Arachne's shredded work and pieces them back together again. One "patch" tells of a man who goes to early church services so that he can pick out the most innocent young girl, trick her into a false marriage, and debauch her. Another describes the plight of a woman who gets taken in by a married man's talk of "platonick love," only to end up pregnant and abandoned. Yet sometimes Barker revises her treatment of the theme to favor poetic justice. In one patch, a rake who promised to reform if Galesia would marry him decides instead to commit robbery and finds himself on the gallows.[13]

---

12. *Metamorphoses*, 137.

13. With plots as sensational as this, it is amazing that a twentieth-century critic could dismiss *A Patch-Work Screen* as a "sober didactic" piece (Jerry Beasley, "Politics and Moral Idealism: The Achievement of Some Early Women Novelists," 229). Barker's purpose may be didactic, but her lessons do not necessarily correspond to eighteenth-century standards of femininity. As Patricia Meyer Spacks rightfully notes, Barker's teaching tactic involves "presenting socially acceptable opinions and undercutting them by fictional action" (*Imagining a Self: Autobiography and Novel in Eighteenth-Century England*, 68). Galesia repeatedly

Barker incorporates Arachne's themes into a framework that will accommodate women's triumphs as well as their betrayals. In her revision of Arachne's story, the heroine benefits from her association with a powerful woman. Galesia's writings are taken up by the Lady, who helps transform them into socially acceptable female works. In addition to serving as a patron, the Lady provides a healthy environment for the woman writer's development. Recalling her earlier experience in society, Galesia laments the difficult position of the learned woman: "A Learned Woman . . . [is] at best but like a Forc'd-Plant, that never has its due or proper Relish, but is wither'd by the first Blast that Envy or Tribulation blows over her Endeavours. Whereas every Thing, in its proper Place and Season, is graceful, beneficial, and pleasant" (11). If envy withers the isolated learned woman, this passage suggests, a place within a community of women might nourish her. Barker's female poetics thus includes an even more substantial revision of the Arachne myth; instead of isolating and demeaning Galesia, Barker has her latter-day Arachne embrace a female tradition and community. In the Lady's company Galesia finds a site for female creativity.

Barker's *Patch-Work Screen* hinges on women's cooperation rather than on their rivalry. As Nina Auerbach points out, disenfranchised women need communities of their own: "A community of women is a rebuke to the conventional ideal of a solitary woman living for and through men, attaining citizenship in the community of adulthood through masculine approval alone. The communities of women which have haunted our literary imagination from the beginning are emblems of female self-sufficiency which create their own corporate reality, evoking both wishes and fears."[14] In such groups, "many perspectives are possible because communities of women have no one official banner to wave" (13). Thus, in Barker's tale of female cooperation, the Lady and Galesia work together with other "maids" on a common project, the patchwork screen. Their textile text celebrates diversity, containing miscellaneous scraps from female life in a format that is multiple rather than monolithic (four leaves unite to form the screen). The fact that Barker's community of women engages in sewing would have made it all the more acceptable to her readers: "Sewing allowed women to sit together without feeling they were neglecting their families, wasting time or betraying their husbands by maintaining independent social bonds."[15]

Within the house, the group of women can work in their patchwork room, but they can also enjoy refreshments and share meals with men. The recipes that get sewn into the screen, like the metaphor of patchwork itself, establish a

---

attempts to reconcile herself to the traditional feminine role, but at every turn new evidence of male treachery crops up to discount the notion that women will be rewarded for submissive behavior.

14. *Communities of Women: An Idea in Fiction*, 5.

15. Rozsika Parker, *The Subversive Stitch: Embroidery and the Making of the Feminine*, 14–15.

continuity between domestic life and women's writing that fortifies both. When Galesia tells the Lady that "Books and Learning" are "useless, or rather pernicious . . . to our Sex," she faults them for causing "Stoical Dulness or humersome Stupidity" and for interfering with women's ability to relish "the Diversions or Imbellishments of our Sex and Station; which render us agreeable to the World, and the World to us" (79). Here, Galesia does not repudiate the learned woman; instead, she rejects the either/or equation that writers like Steele and Tickell applied to women, suggesting that women need not choose between the "Needle and the Distaff" or the "Pen and Standish" (8). Recipes for "The Czar's Punch," "Welsh Flummery," and "French Soup"—recorded in rhyme— pay tribute to women's housework by making it the stuff of poetry. Galesia's recipe poems expand the realm of poetry to include women's daily tasks.

By the end of *A Patch-Work Screen for the Ladies*, Galesia has exchanged her former "fantastic Companions the Muses" for the real company of women seamstresses, but without forsaking her writing. And by displaying her works to advantage and establishing them in a socially responsible network, the patchwork screen shields Galesia from the blasts that could blight a solitary female author. The patchwork text fulfills the same function for Barker. At the end of the preface, Barker advises her readers to "be sure to buy these Patches up quickly, if you intend to know the Secret" (viii), thereby alerting them to the possibility of a hidden message. Although Barker may not have had one specific "secret" in mind, the lessons concerning female solidarity are coded in needlework terms that would have been more comprehensible to women readers than to men. As Cecilia Macheski remarks, "Only if we remember that needlework was a shared experience between women of all classes and ages in the eighteenth century will we understand how natural it is to find it used as imagery in novels and poetry."[16]

The women's work on the patchwork screen concludes with a gesture toward the female community of novel-readers: "Hereupon the Lady looking over the Work, and finding there was enough to make Four Folds of a *Screen*, she said, she would have it made up, and fram'd, to see how it would look before they proceeded any farther" (131). The novel itself is the "made up" screen, which depends for its continuance upon female approval. Like Arachne, Barker brings her work before a tribunal of women; but unlike her mythologi- cal ancestor, Barker remembers to ask for their assistance in making her accomplishment a success. Her final work—*The Lining for the Patch-Work Screen*—indicates that she found a receptive audience.

Barker's call for female solidarity would be echoed at the end of the eigh- teenth century by one of her more famous literary descendants: "Let us not desert one another; we are an injured body."[17] Perhaps if the readers of *A*

16. "Penelope's Daughters," 86.
17. Jane Austen, *Northanger Abbey*, 37.

Patch-Work Screen had learned its lessons, women novelists like Jane Austen and George Eliot would have had more company in their climb to literary success. When, in *The Mill on the Floss* (1860), young Maggie Tulliver refuses to work on her patchwork, she implicitly rejects her connection to the wider community of women workers: "Oh Mother . . . I don't *want* to do my patchwork . . . I don't want to do anything for my aunt Glegg,—I don't like her." For Maggie, patchwork represents the futility of women's work in general: "It's foolish work, . . . tearing things to pieces to sew 'em together again."[18] Ironically, Maggie will have to struggle to patch together the conflicting pieces of her life; furthermore, she will learn that female solidarity is almost the only thing she can count on.

A Patch-Work Screen may be the fullest elaboration of needlework as a metaphor for women's writing; it is certainly one of the earliest examples of a female, if not feminist, aesthetics. According to Christine Battersby, "A feminist aesthetics is one that exposes the prejudice that represents the female as lacking, seeks to show how we can escape it . . . and then goes on to trace matrilineal traditions of cultural achievement."[19] Clearly, Barker wants to help perpetuate a female tradition of writing. Her choice of metaphors indicates a desire to revise the cultural myths that seek to deny women genius.

"There is no antique more expressive of our foremothers than patchwork," writes one historian of quilts and their makers.[20] That patchwork rose to popularity in England during the same period that gave us both the novel and the woman writer only adds to its metaphorical resonance. As Jane Spencer notes, "Galesia's story of her writing career is . . . set in a framework which justifies it by relating it to feminine accomplishments."[21] Even more importantly, however, Galesia's story shows that female accomplishments need to be rescued from their reputation for frivolity and that women's work, whether it take place in the home or in public, must not be discounted. Jane Barker seized upon the common flexibility of patchwork and the emerging novel, and, in defence of both her gender and her genre, she created a remarkable book that valorizes "pieces" and the art of uniting them.

18. George Eliot, *The Mill on the Floss*, 12–13.
19. *Gender and Genius*, 10.
20. Ruth Finley, *Old Patchwork Quilts and the Women Who Made Them*, 19.
21. *Rise of the Woman Novelist*, 68.

◆ Reading Lessons ◆
Anne L. Bower

The quilt on the bed at my grandmother's home was pretty—a fancy blanket formed of oddly shaped contrasting fabrics. I never thought to ask who had made it and when. It wasn't Art or something to think about; it was a bedcover. Sculpture, painting, plays, novels—those were Art. Sewing was just something women had always done.

So that old quilt (sold I suppose when the house and its contents were auctioned off back in 1951), with its luxuriant samples of bright silks and dark velvets, its silken embroidery stitches decoratively holding piece to piece, its tacking threads tied in neat bows to hold the patchwork top to the fabric backing, was lost to me. I don't really mourn the lost object. I mourn the long years I spent in ignorance of what that quilt could have told me. Unable to read that textile manuscript, I lived for years without a full sense of women's art, women's voices, women's traditions, and women's strength—my art, my voice, my tradition, my strength. It took thirty years to discover and recover them, time spent in high school, college, marriage and child rearing, farming, sales jobs, secretarial work, varied kinds of public administration. Not until midlife and graduate school, aided by teachers and texts and exhibits, did I gain access to my full cultural inheritance.

Unfortunately, many others have shared this form of textural/textual illiteracy. In "Common Threads," the last chapter of *Sister's Choice: Tradition and Change in American Women's Writing,* Elaine Showalter points out that only a few nineteenth-century artists and commentators recognized quilts' power to record, scrapbook-fashion, a woman's "life cycle from birth to death" or read patchwork for its representation of psychological and material states. Showalter's work, in conjunction with Elaine Hedges's essay "'The Needle or the Pen': The Literary Rediscovery of Women's Textile Work," documents evolving awareness of quilts as material and literary objects in the nineteenth and twentieth centuries. Not until the 1970s, following the Whitney Museum's landmark exhibit "Abstract Design in American Quilts," did feminist scholars and authors fully discover quilts' readerly and writerly qualities. Today, patch-

Quotations from Joyce Carol Oates, "Celestial Timepiece." From *Celestial Timepiece: Poems by Joyce Carol Oates,* Ill. Paula George (Dallas: Pressworks, 1980). Reprinted by permission of the publisher.

work quilts, along with many other previously ignored texts, are being re-valued. And while it is still the case that for too many people a quilt is just a quilt—pretty squares stitched together, an attractive yet "blank" page—many have learned to read in these objects what Jonathan Holstein, curating a recent quilt show, summed up as "the extraordinary vision, inventiveness and aesthetic achievement of America's quiltmakers."[1] Enabled to read, we move forward to create our own works with a new sense of possibilities.

This essay brings together six poems, published between 1976 and 1988, that have served as my primers. In these texts I first discovered the extraordinary energies activated by writers connecting to the products and processes of their quilting foremothers. I suspect that my belatedness in this form of literacy is not uncommon. In spite of widespread use of quilting metaphors in poetry and prose, students, graduate students, university instructors, and many scholars and critics *still* have minimal exposure to the full resonance of quilt references within literary texts.

Joyce Carol Oates's "Celestial Timepiece," Marge Piercy's "Looking at Quilts," Kathleen Spivack's "The moments-of-past-happiness quilt," Robin Morgan's "Piecing," Sandra McPherson's "Eve," and Marilyn Waniek's "The Century Quilt," use quilting tropes to provide lessons in literacy, not only teaching us to read quilts, but also extending our reading capabilities to encompass the variety of other print and non-print texts women have produced (from letters to lives) and helping us discover strategies by which to derive fullest understandings from these texts.[2] Looked at from an instructional point of view, each of the poems contributes special inspiration, strategies, and/or insights for the novice quilt reader.

A poet like Oates motivates the quilt-illiterate by enthusiastically proclaiming the quilt-texts' readability, demonstrating how these previously ignored texts record and document important information about individuals and events, about the past and the present. In this same vein, Waniek's poem asserts that claiming and reading a quilt can deepen positive ties to the past and strengthen one's belief in the future. However, some poets, like McPher-

1. "Common Threads," in *Sister's Choice: Tradition and Change in American Women's Writing*, 151, 155–57; "'The Needle or the Pen': The Literary Rediscovery of Women's Textile Work"; "Curator's Statement: Abstract Design in American Quilts," 5. In regard to the Whitney show, we need to note that just as it enabled insights for feminist scholars, feminist scholarship of the sixties surely nourished and inspired the show itself.

2. Relative to the continuing recovery of women's texts, I found interesting an article in the spring 1991 (volume 14) issue of the *Journal of American Culture*, "An Antebellum Woman's Scrapbook as Autobiographical Composition," in which Patricia Buckler and C. Kay Leeper "read" a pre–Civil War scrapbook as a woman's autobiographical text. A few scholars, myself included, are also now looking at yet another "non-literary" kind of text— the community cookbooks produced by many women in charitable organizations. I see these cookbooks as having readerly, narrative qualities so that they become forms of communal autobiography.

son and Spivack, warn the reader that quilt-texts may be impossible to decode or may require special strategies. Some of these poet-teachers show readers quilts as constructed objects, helping novices to perceive the components of the quilts and analyze their methods of construction so that we can better understand the organization and content of what we read. In this regard, I find Morgan's poem extremely helpful, although all my "primer poems" touch on one or more aspects of this issue. When the poets investigate language itself, particularly focusing our attention as readers on the feminist act of naming and renaming and the possibility of creating special forms to reflect women's experience, we move into a third area—a kind of quilt linguistics, if you will. I have drawn special instruction in this area from the quilt poems of Piercy, McPherson, and Oates.

My focus on these six poems as educational material derives from a need to repair a deficient past, to instruct myself so that I can claim my heritage. Even as the poets offer others new ways of "reading," they satisfy personal needs through adopting the particular figurative language of quilts. In aligning their own poetic texts in this special way, Marilyn Waniek, Joyce Carol Oates, Marge Piercy, and Robin Morgan claim for their work and themselves the durability, beauty, functionality, and warmth of the quilts. However, the quilting metaphor can also be used deconstructively. Kathleen Spivack and Sandra McPherson (and to some extent Robin Morgan) rip the quilt off the bed and the body, daring us to read the naked forms within our metaphors; they can undo the quilters' careful seams, disclaiming the comfort of past communities, domesticity, and the illusion of a neatly patterned happiness.

Motivational Lessons

Joyce Carol Oates's poem "Celestial Timepiece" values particular quilts for their power to document woman's past, a past otherwise lost, and recognizes that many viewer/readers do not understand the quilts.[3] She realizes that for many of us a quilt will only appear as a "Babel of textures"; if we were quilt-literate why would she even need to ask *"Can you read it? Do you understand?"* (ll. 45, 48). As teacher, Oates proceeds to explain that these objects do the work of "recording square by wondrous square / the years soon lost—1784, 1806, 1848— . . . Recording 1871, 1796" (ll. 11–12, 18). If we can learn to read the squares, presumably we can regain our history. Oates imagines that one woman, in the role of instructor, can take another's hand and pull it across the fabric squares, to provide instruction in reading: "Your fingers read it like Braille" (l. 50). Although we may have been blind to the meanings of these quilts as texts, we can now learn to see them more fully.

The messages encoded in the quilts Oates describes are historical and spiritual. In the fabrics, she finds the history of women who waited while men

3. Joyce Carol Oates, "Celestial Timepiece," 24–25.

went off to war, while economic cycles ebbed and flowed, while husbands/ soldiers died in body and/or spirit. These men were "Conquerors" or thought of themselves as such, whether victorious or vanquished; their work was recorded in maps, but "The men's maps are beginning at last to tear" (ll. 16, 35). That which history texts have presented to us—wars, maps, battles, soldiers, and horses, is only part of history. That which history texts have ignored—those women at home, struggling to maintain children, farms, gardens, relationships, businesses even—the other half of the story, is mapped in the quilts.[4]

For Oates the quilts chart something as or more important than the terrain and strategy of soldiers' maps. The sewn items chart "The resurrection of the body" (l. 28) through reused clothing and linens that once belonged to particular individuals. "Not all the quilts you love are beautiful" (l. 38). Even those that are "ugly" or "ungainly" testify to the past, to a reading of lives that tells more than any map. "Not all the quilts you love are sane" (l. 42). Eccentricity, a broken pattern—these are part of history too. The quilts become a literature of "History, their days, the quick deft fingers, / their lives recorded in cloth" (ll. 51–52).

Women's stories have often been silenced or subsumed, but Oates joins other feminist artists, scientists, historians, and teachers who are engaged in retrieving the past. "Celestial Timepiece" reminds its readers that the women of past times left us texts of

> coarse wool, fine wool,
> satin, lace, burlap, cotton, silk, brocade, hemp,
> and fussy dolls' pleats!
>
> (ll. 45–47)

It promises that we present-day readers *can* learn to read such texts, gaining thereby not only a sense of the past, but a sense of the spiritual hope of those women who slowly recorded, created, recycled materials to make these testaments, even when surrounded by death and destruction. "The resurrection of the body, then, in the quilt's squares!" (l. 28).

While "Celestial Timepiece" prompts us to read quilts to learn of (and from)

---

4. While Oates celebrates the strength of quilts to survive through time, other poets remark as well on their transience. For example, in "Things," a work that juxtaposes "Things: simply lasting, then / failing to last . . ." Jane Kenyon stresses the mutability of quilts with an image of a mouse pulling batting from a century-old quilt to use in building a nest.

In the same year that Oates published "Celestial Timepiece," she incorporated quilt names and quilting into her novel, *Bellefleur*, where Aunt Matilde, unconventional and selfruling, lives alone in a cabin at the family's "camp." Quilting becomes synonymous with following one's own path, creating one's own way. See the "Celestial Timepiece" section of *Bellefleur* (New York: Dutton, 1980), 327–29.

women's experience of the past, Marilyn Waniek's "The Century Quilt" provides a more personal and individualized kind of motivation by detailing the persona's reading process.[5] Neither the maker nor inheritor of a quilt, the speaker in the poem somehow comes to own a quilt that symbolizes for her the rich medley of her past. As the persona reads her "found" quilt, she stitches together disparate elements of her own mixed racial and regional heritage. Waniek's poem serves to inspire those of us in search of a lost personal heritage.

Waniek contextualizes the quilt that her poem describes by reminding us that in its most basic existence, a patchwork quilt, like any blanket, is simply a means to keep out the cold. However, "The Century Quilt" unfolds to concentrate upon other functions, particularly the magic and solace of a special quilt. Through the poet's associations with the colors and visual design of the quilt, we see that it becomes representative of a set of values important to her. If we can read a quilt, we can read part of our own cultural history.

The poem's persona had hoped to inherit her grandmother's special Indian blanket, but it went to her sister instead. Although cut off from this inheritance, she "found a quilt / I'd like to die under" (ll. 13–14). This one is a covering that will not only warm her but seems to have some of the same magic as the grandmother's blanket; it too can inspire dreams, and, because of its particular color choices, together with a design drawn from local flora, it can effectively symbolize her heritage. Based on her description of the quilt's pattern, I see it as made up of nine-piece blocks. Each block (or patch) consists of two white squares combined with "Six Van Dyke brown squares," and one "the yellowbrown of Mama's cheeks" (ll. 15, 17). A number of such blocks sewn together make up the quilt.

These repeated squares of brown, white, and yellow represent the skin colors of the persona's family. Meema, her beloved grandmother, had "yellow" skin: she was of mixed white and Native American background. The white skin of the persona's great-great-grandfather contrasts with her father's "burnt umber" coloring. Her mother is a woman of "ochre gentleness," whose skin is also termed "yellowbrown" (ll. 39, 40, 17). The colors of the squares then, pieced together, symbolize the blend of cultures from which the persona springs. That this quilt is one she could be happy to "die under" or, more immediately, one she's sure will bring "good dreams / for a hundred years" (ll. 21–22) is a way of saying that the melding of cultures from which she comes contents her. Seeing her mixed heritage as an orderly, coherent, connected, attractive design allows her to accept the past—"my childhood of miracles"— and to have dreams of a positive future, including a second child, "as yet unconceived" (ll. 38, 43). For me, the "found" quilt represents the given of her mixed background; her loving description of the object, with its special geome-

5. "The Century Quilt," 37–38.

try and coloring, indicates her active acceptance of her racial and ethnic inheritance.

The persona of "The Century Quilt" can also read a regional heritage in her quilt. The poem explains that each square bears a sweet gum leaf; whether embroidered or appliquéd, the voice does not say. Sweet gum is a native American tree with star-shaped leaves, growing in a region that encompasses southern New York, Connecticut, and Ohio south to central Florida and eastern Texas.[6] The visual symbolism here—a star natural not religious, a tree native not imported, a tree particular to a region, not one found throughout the United States, also seems to yield magical force for the quilt's owner. The "fingers" of these sweet gum leaves she imagines will "caress [her] into the silence" (ll. 19–20) of wonderful dreams.

In spite of the assurance offered new quilt readers by Oates and Waniek, we do well to realize that some lexical elements will not yield their significance easily, and some may be indecipherable. Such difficulties inform Kathleen Spivack's poem "The moments-of-past-happiness quilt."[7] In representing the scarcity and fragility of "moments-of-past-happiness," Spivack negates conventional notions of contented stitchers socially creating pretty patterns. Rare and isolated bits of happiness make up her imagined and intangible quilt. In this quilt, presumably a "friendship" quilt in which contributors signed their squares, one of the quilters' signatures is illegible, "too difficult to read" (l. 41). Did that woman deliberately blur her name, or are we inadequate to the decoding task? The persona finds the indistinguishable signature "rather like your own" (l. 42), her use of "your" pulling the reader into the poem. This reference to the reader's signature draws into consideration both the act of naming and the act of owning (text, property, another, the self). The reader can position her own experiences beside those of the women "quilters" in the poem. Do the texts we leave behind us obfuscate or clarify our histories? Will others be able to read our texts? This poem asks us to question our own signatures, our own texts.

If we see Spivack's imagined and impossible "moments-of-past-happiness quilt" as a metaphor for her own poem, then we should not read her work (read women's poetry in general?) for comfort, warmth, reassurance, or to see a beautiful, regular design, or in the expectation of finding celebration and brightness. When most of us think of patchwork quilts, it is those positive images we first receive. This poet asks us to read differently, keeping ourselves open to the individuality of each text, avoiding stereotypes, responding fully to the variety of women's texts—funny or serious, brash or meticulous, bright or dark, substantial or fragile.

Our poet-teachers move us back and forth among texts of ink and paper,

6. George A. Petrides, *A Field Guide to Trees and Shrubs*, 236, 133.
7. "The moments-of-past-happiness quilt," 223–24.

texts of fabric, and the implied texts of daily events. If we can read women's quilts, we can read other women's texts too. Sandra McPherson takes us a step further, for she asks us to remove cloth coverings from our beds and bodies and read the bodies themselves. In "Eve," the woman's body is a quilt of her own making, her skin colors, scars, years, and blood vessels available for reading once the clothes of propriety are stripped away.

Lessons in Construction, Design, Organization, and Choice

Poems that play with metaphors of quilting are often, then, about learning to read and the act of reading. But these poems also can focus on the components and construction of texts we read, whether those texts are women's lives or artifacts. What materials compose the text? What is the source of the text's design? Has the maker of the text simply accepted a pattern established by society, or is she able to interject something new, something creative? A poem that concentrates on these aspects of quilts, poems, and lives is Robin Morgan's "Piecing."[8] Quilters and poets and women striving to reshape their lives all suffer, Morgan shows, because their own subjectivity, their agency, their power to make choices, is ignored. As the voice of the poem puts it, although others may admire some part of the work produced, they seldom "notice the order, which is / the one thing you control" (ll. 53–54).

The epigraph to "Piecing," a quote from an anonymous woman quilter, draws attention to the all-too-common experience of having inadequate opportunities for structuring our lives and work. This woman's life has been one of making do: "You have to do the best you can with what you got." For this speaker, the beauty of piecing is in ordering the patchwork snippets: "You can put them in any order you like. . . . Piecing is orderly." For the anonymous woman quilter, life itself did not seem to offer choices; only in needlework could she exert her desires, her sense of organization, her designs. "Piecing" works both within and against the quilt metaphor to extend the concept of order and design beyond quilts, beyond art, into the realm of daily life.

Morgan uses the quilt metaphor to play with seeing both herself and her poetry as pieced together, finding in her evolving self and her work that strength grows from the power to create the design. This seemingly autobiographical poem, with its alliance of the piecing done in poems and quilt-making and one's own life makes me think of Carolyn Heilbrun's idea that there are various ways to "write a woman's life." A woman may write her own life in autobiography or fiction or some other genre; someone else may write it as biography; or "the woman may write her own life in advance of living it, unconsciously, and without recognizing or naming the process."[9] All of those operations seem present in "Piecing."

8. "Piecing," 3–5.
9. *Writing a Woman's Life*, 11.

The poem asserts that, within the economy of her life and work, the speaker uses and reuses the materials at hand. An "honest spending of the self" (l. 3) recycles her most essential ideas and images. She connects the life and the writing: she is a poet brave enough to create "the same poem over and over, not merely / rearranged, revised, reworded, but one poem" (ll. 11–12), always new, no matter how many times it is lived or written. Morgan sees a personal coherence in the artist's work and life: when one writes from the self, that self will always color the work so that there is a consistency of style, theme, and shape. The trope of quilting effectively underscores similar qualities in the piecing and patterning of a woman's life or writing. We know that just as our psychological needs force emotional repetition, just as aesthetic and intellectual interests yield artistic repetition, individual quilters have their styles and trademarks too: favorite stitches, patterns, and materials, particular ways of contrasting fabrics, distinctive embroideries, ways of appliquéing parts of the design, and so on.[10]

Morgan sets up equivalencies between scraps of the persona's life and the scraps that compose a quilt. The textures, colors, patterns, and weights of different fabrics describe past events: "This sturdy / canvas shred of humor"; a "fragment of pearl velvet, / a particular snowstorm"; "A segment of bleached muslin still crisp with indifference" (ll. 17–18, 18–19, 24). Then, with scrapbag in hand, so to speak, Morgan shifts to the question of ordering the pieces. While she does admit that the work of constructing (a quilt, a life, a poem) can be communal, imagining many individuals together "talking quietly while we worked / each with her unique stitch inward to the same shared center" (ll. 41–42), Morgan acknowledges that the communal approach only works some of the time.[11] Here Morgan questions the importance and idealization of community that have been central to American feminist scholars and artists.

As the speaker in Morgan's poem educates us about textual/ textural construction, she draws our attention to the role of critics and fellow artists. The poet/quilter persona is visited by people all too ready to comment on the work at hand. She finds that they "rarely notice the order, which is / the one thing you control" (ll. 53–54); their comments are frequently destructive—they

10. An exhibit of African American quiltmaking organized by the San Francisco Craft & Folk Art Museum focused on improvisation as a dominant feature. Viewing the show at Washington's Renwick Gallery (in December 1991), I was impressed with the highly individualized manipulation or combination of standard designs and by color and pattern use I want to call syncopated in some instances, rebellious in others.

11. One might think about writers' groups as "poetry bees" or "fiction bees." Having belonged to one such, I see many parallels between quilting and poetry gatherings. In our poetry group, we each worked on a separate poem (like the individually pieced blocks of the quilt) and then discussed them in the group. I imagine discussions as a kind of ephemeral stitching that pulls the various poems (and people) together. A number of writers' groups do end up publishing their collective work; one could think of those books then as quilts.

"slash rents across the section just perfected" (l. 51) or merely admire some particular piece of material. A few make contributions, offering a scrap that can still be incorporated. Our friends can be like this as they comment on our lives; our colleagues and critics can add to or destroy the texts and art we are trying to make. We, as readers, are thus cautioned against ignoring a text's careful design.

Morgan's final verse brings our eyes to that which we least often consider as a constructed text: the self. A pieced or stitched together self, while capable of alteration or repair is also in danger of being "all the more severely worn / into translucency" (ll. 72–73). When we realize that we have made ourselves, when we are able to read our self-construction, it leads to taking responsibility for our actions and opening ourselves up to criticism. The freedom we have to design and shape our lives brings with it the risk that others will hurt, misunderstand, ignore what we have stitched together. We will be "severely worn" (I do like that pun). Others may "wear" us—putting us on for warmth and comfort, but they will also "wear" us—use us up.

Piercy's "Looking at Quilts"[12] also contains sections that dwell on the materials available to women and their ways of structuring those materials into an "Art without frames" (l. 4). Made of "winter woolens, linens, blankets . . . / precious / scraps" (ll. 33–35) the quilts synthesize disparate experiences into a "worked jigsaw / of the memories of braided lives" (ll. 33–34) full of "intelligence" and "graphic wit" (l. 17). The quilts left behind by so many women demonstrate to the poem's speaker that these stitchers could not only perform what was expected, but could, amidst all the busy tasks, grasp "time" and make "new." Piercy's actual phrasing is "together, alone, / she seized her time and made new" (ll. 49–50). Seize here brings me to the notion of "seize the day" and all those *carpe diem* poems created by male voices, seducing or trying to seduce imagined women into sexual activity. The cooking, planting, sewing, child-tending women Piercy's poem praises were seized by dailiness; they could not abandon their domestic tasks for passionate adventures of body or mind. Yet Piercy finds the designs they chose for their quilts and their execution of the designs move beyond the ordinary. In fact, this art makes the ordinary special. The poet notices that "the love of the ordinary *blazes* out" (l. 9), and she perceives that "design *masters* the essence of what sprawled / in the afternoon" (ll. 15–16, italics added).

In contrast to the forceful and positive views of structure and design posited by Morgan and Piercy, Kathleen Spivack's 1987 "The moments-of-past-happiness quilt" interjects an almost cynical comment. She does not sing of the enduring spirit of women to structure the chaos of their lives, rescue the past, piece together comfort that stays with us, record history. While there may be some poems that we can read and use to guide our lives or comfort us,

12. "Looking at Quilts," 86–87.

other poems by women have a different goal, fleetingly, sparingly, insightfully showing us the difficulties of finding or designing beauty or happiness. In Spivack's vision, moments of happiness are all too rare. Especially for women, they seem hard to find and ephemeral. Many moments of happiness had to be gathered from many women to make one illusory quilt, and it is not the warming, useful quilt or the well-designed, even temporarily lasting quilt imagined by other poets. Instead "It won't wash. / It won't wear" (ll. 59–60). Contrary to others' ideas about quilts' durability "it does not last" (l. 65). So the poet advises us to store it away. Even to look at it abrades and fades it. Her last warning is that we not put it on a bed. This is *not* celebratory.

Sandra McPherson's "Eve"[13] moves in a different direction to undo or deconstruct the idea of order and structure. Whereas Spivack presents the notion of order as an illusion, McPherson depicts Eve replacing existing patriarchal notions of order with a gynocentric framework. No longer trusting the language and social patterns established by her "Father," Eve looks to her own body as the basis for designs more truthful to her own woman's experience. But for McPherson, a great deal of what can be structured or restructured is also played out within the act of naming, within language—a topic I'll turn to shortly.

Like Spivack's poem, McPherson's rejects many of the positive associations with quilts and quilting, along with sewing and clothes. McPherson's Eve is sick of clothing and prefers to "say nakedness / is our drab uniform" (ll. 4–5). The clothes that she rejects are ones she has learned to name as she learns to sew: the ones "Father has allowed" (l. 8) her to name. Here Eve has some Adamic power to name the items with which she covers her nakedness. And even though she reserves the right to temporarily enjoy "a full skirt, ruffles, necklace, watch and rings" (l. 12) as the costume in which (shades or shadows of Lady Chatterley's lover), she'll "rub a gardener's naked back" (l. 13), she will still prefer the outfit of her own pale skin.[14]

At first the nakedness seems an emptying, a neutral presentation of the self. But then the persona begins to see her skin as full of rich qualities: "purple, pale, okra-blossom bone-clothing, / the body scribbled on by a carried child" (ll. 23–24). Like Spivack, McPherson is undoing the fabric that covers—"to bare the thread, / to pattern what is raw-edged" (ll. 27–28).

Just as many quilts are structured from recycled clothing, so McPherson

13. "Eve," 31–33.

14. Mention of a gardener, and the use of the name Eve, call up, of course, the Garden of Eden, although it is not really the poem's setting. Nineteenth-century quilters used many, many garden patterns. Elaine Hedges points out that pioneer women especially were urged by "western promotional literature and fiction and the imperatives of the cult of domesticity" to make the wilderness into an Edenic paradise (see her "Hearts and Hands: The Influence of Women and Quilts on American Society," 64). But the gardening engaged in by the Eve of McPherson's poem is about *self*-cultivation.

turns at the midpoint of this poem and recycles her attention from images of clothes to those of quilts. The surface of Eve's body is now pieced together, "stitched for no one else, / with these patchworker's bloodstains" (ll. 30–31) so that she is both maker and made (male and female, Adam and Eve). In the Old Testament myth, Adam was wounded to make Eve, but McPherson reinvents the myth by having Eve claim her own blood, her own ancestry, her own wounding, while she tears and resews her essential material to recreate herself: "every quilt / wears its finger blood" (ll. 31–32). The speaker even celebrates such traces, for it "is not failure, to be harmed this way, / thimbles, bodices, all cast off" (ll. 34–35).

In *Stealing the Language*, Alicia Ostriker points out that "when women write to praise the body rather than to attack or joke about it, their most significant technique is revisionist metaphor."[15] In her effort to see the female body with the power and originality of the first born (Adam), rather than as that of a male manqué, McPherson partakes of such a metaphorical reworking. The poem rejects the idea of helpmeet made from and for man and the idea of femininity founded on being defined and desired by a man, subject to a language, politics, and domesticity that serve man. Eve seeks her strength not primarily in relationship to men but to self and daughter. She refuses to be "a glass woman" and wants to be "more than a fabric one" (l. 41). She will not take her place in the Bible; instead, she generates her own holy book: "The bible-leaves of the labia" (l. 42). Revisioning Eve (not the biblical Eve exactly but the idea of Eve), McPherson revisions the quilt metaphor too, blending it with metaphors of clothing, allowing her self-referential quilt/self maker to drop humility; this Eve is not ashamed of her nakedness. This Eve admires her own "workmanship" (l. 44). The quilt metaphor here concentrates on how a text might be restructured; the quilt-poem is an uncovering, not a covering.

Lessons in Quilt Language and Names

As our literacy broadens to include an understanding of structure and design in quilt texts, we also learn about language and naming in new ways. In my "primer" poems, I find what Ostriker designates as central to all contemporary women's poetry: "the quest for autonomous self-definition" and the related effort "to name ourselves."[16] In the ways they investigate the names of traditional quilt patterns and in their naming of the quilters' actions and motives, these poets restore language and selfhood to women. Poems using quilt metaphors reveal a fascination with the control and specificity that names relay.

Naming is certainly a key issue for McPherson's "Eve." She wants the power of naming for herself; she rejects names (and therefore patterns) that already exist. She is "Naming the quilt patterns" (l. 44) and, when told by

15. *Stealing the Language: The Emergence of Women's Poetry in America*, 108.
16. Ibid., 59.

"Father" to "be ashamed and name the clothes" (l. 45), she defiantly performs an intercultural striptease, divesting herself of head-covering, outer garment, face-covering, underclothes, and patriarchal language all at once: "I name. Wimple, haik, yashmak. Panties, slip, bra" (l. 46). Word selection for this last line is obviously partly based on sound, but the words' derivations also encompass a number of different cultures. As the dictionary reminds me, wimple is a Middle English word for a head covering; *yashmak* is Arabic for the veil worn by Moslem women to cover the face in public; *haik* is another Arabic word, signifying the large draped outer garment of cotton, silk, or wool that covers head and body; bra comes from the French *brassière;* panties is the diminutive of *pantaloon,* from the Italian; and slip is Middle English derived from Low German. Through the naming of clothes used to cover or bind the female body, the poem's persona linguistically establishes community with women of many cultures.[17]

Where McPherson's persona engages in uncovering and repiecing the body and self through naming, the speaker in Piercy's "Looking at Quilts" uses names to underscore the quantity and quality of women's labor. This speaker particularly notes utility: quilts can hold seeds, for instance, or cover a table, a bed, or a person. These functions are clearly tied to traditional feminine tasks of nurturing, feeding, warming, and holding. However, Piercy's vocabulary of words for the work done in quiltmaking stresses control and industry. Words like "design," "masters," "render," "means," "worked," and "issue" honor quilt sewing as a creative and difficult effort. These particular words place quilting within the world of hard work, rejecting earlier attitudes that quiltmaking was a necessary, attractive, easy, and relatively insignificant routine for the homemaker.

"Looking at Quilts" contains an extensive middle section devoted to the subject of naming. Since a poem works most directly with words, it seems "natural" that a poet would be fascinated by the most overtly lexical aspect of quilts. Piercy's interest in names is central to her own connection to the quilters. As she names various quilts, Piercy's persona is listing the range of activities and preoccupations of the quiltmakers; she is also highlighting the women's power to choose not only a pattern, but also a name, thereby drawing attention to their particular occupations, interests, and artfulness. Quilt historians aver that the choice of pattern and fabric plus the choice of name indicate "not only a personal but a public narrative as well: women used their quilts to register their responses to, and also their participation in, the major social, economic and political developments of their times."[18]

17. For feminists of various schools, language, and in particular, naming, has long been an issue. Cheryl Torsney introduced me to Ursula K. Le Guin's 1985 short story that investigates an aspect of this quandry. "She Unnames Them" is an inciteful, humorous, brief exploration of one Eve's desire not to *rename* but to *unname* living things, in order to free us from the limitations of labels and categories.

18. Hedges, "Hearts and Hands," 11.

Religion, nature, the frontier, historic events, and countries of origin are commonly cited sources for quilt names. Dennis Duke and Deborah Harding also list trades, courting, household utensils, love and courtship, square dances, and politics. Many of the quilts itemized in Piercy's poem take their artistic motifs from nature: Ohio Sunflower, Snail's Track, and Star of the West, to reproduce just a few. This last name could also refer to the westward movement of pioneer families, as does Rocky Road to Kansas, another pattern Piercy catalogs. Job's Troubles and the Tree of Life designs fall into the religious category, while the Double Irish Chain looks back to a national heritage. Piercy probably includes Hearts and Gizzards to refer to the kind of culinary economy so necessary on most homesteads. Fool's Puzzle, Puss in Boots, and Robbing Peter to Pay Paul all are illustrative of the "intelligence" and "wit" Piercy enjoys in the names of quilts. The Drunkard's Path, with curved edges demanding extra piecing skill, could reflect, within its name, the difficulties of many a wife with a drinking husband or other relative.[19]

Oates, like Piercy, incorporates actual pattern names. Many of the names she includes bespeak a spiritual or philosophical stance, such as Serendipity, Wonder-Working Providence, Celestial Timepiece, and Dance of Death. These titles seldom appear in standard illustrated quilting texts. To select an unusual or even idiosyncratic name is to assert oneself in this act against the standard practice, even if the pattern itself duplicates or is close to a design used by others. Oates's pleasure in this kind of naming practice stresses the quiltmakers' desire to present an individualized point of view or vision.

Beyond Lessons: Theoretical/Critical Acts

Waniek's explication of her "found" quilt is a reader-response type of reaction to her quilt-as-text, its colors and pattern realized more by what she brings to that reading than by what she knows of the text's history or of its makers' world. We find more historical readings in the poems by Piercy and Oates, with emphasis on names and dates of the exhibited quilts they are "reading." Morgan's poem is a fiercely feminist response to quilts and quilting, as are Spivack's and McPherson's. All three poets use the quilt metaphor to

19. For general information on names see Dennis Duke and Deborah Harding, *America's Glorious Quilts*, 67–68. "In their traditional names and sometimes in their construction, nineteenth-century quilts reflect what women saw around them and what was important in their lives" (Hedges, "Hearts and Hands," 64). John Rice Irwin points out that Snail Trail (or Track) and Monkey Wrench are basically the same design; a woman whose focus was on the garden might think of it as Snail Track; one who worked with hammer, wrench, nails, and saws, might think of it as Monkey Wrench. See Irwin's *A People and Their Quilts*, 201. Hedges explains that Drunkard's Path was a commonly used pattern during the height of the temperance movement and that frequently such quilts were pieced in blue and white, the colors of the Women's Christian Temperance Union ("Hearts and Hands," 84); see also Duke and Harding, *America's Glorious Quilts*, 16.

read women's lives anew, directing their interpretations toward women's past and present experiences of living in a fragmented and fragmenting world. Spivack's "The moments-of-past-happiness quilt" is also a deconstructive reading, playfully undoing the reality of a material quilt, while McPherson's "Eve" partakes of deconstructive and myth criticism, being a revisioning of language and images from past texts.

We are no longer novice readers. Now we may find ourselves tempted to measure and judge texts against each other. In these days of the "expanding canon," many of us seek bases from which to discuss our ways of valuing texts previously forgotten or not deemed worthy of the august title—"Literature." But the six poets whose work I have been discussing do not operate in a competitive economy that demands we say yes to one quilt-text and no to another. Rather, through the content and form of their poems, they use the quilting metaphor to question the evaluative issue of perfection and imperfection—in texts of all kinds.

The last verse of Piercy's "Looking at Quilts" hypothesizes that a quilt could be "the only perfect artifact a woman / would ever see" (ll. 45–46). Perfection according to whose standard? Hers as viewer or the quiltmakers'? (This is of course a problem we have with novels and poems and nonfiction writing too: whose standards should measure achievement?) "There was a common belief, adhered to by many, that to make a quilt too fancy and too perfect would be to tempt God. The Bible clearly points out our imperfections; to insure that everyone knew [s]he was imperfect, quilters sometimes deliberately created a flaw."[20] Whenever we are "looking at" the past, our own assumptions create perfections and imperfections that may not be true to those who lived in the past. Since she creates no hierarchies among the quilts she observes, we can finally assume that Piercy opens herself to multiple definitions of perfection.

The speaker in Morgan's "Piecing" knows that her piecework life, her piecework poem, will never be perfect, even though pieces of the work may temporarily be "perfected" (l. 51). After all, the speaker asserts, "nobody really hazards piecework in the expectation / that someday all these fragments might inevitably fit" (ll. 63–64) and stay put. For Morgan, evidently, a text or artwork is *not* about perfection. Her persona works to capture the imperfection that seems a most critical feature of the world. This imperfection must be accepted.

Poets can explore the question of perfection through their use of form as well. As an example of this formal approach, consider Oates's structuring of "Celestial Timepiece." This poem has its own perfection. It looks orderly. Although the eight stanzas are of different lengths, all the verses are separated by a standard, single white space. Three stanzas about men and their strategies of maps, fighting, and violent death are interspersed with five about

20. Irwin, *A People and Their Quilts*, 50.

women, quiltmaking, and quilt reading. Roughly, one could say, Oates alternates sections on quilts and their female makers with sections about men and battles.

One of the verses about the men (lines 15–19), however, also contains material about women's work. The poem then is not "neat" or dedicated completely to a set pattern. Perhaps this disruption is like the traditional quiltmaker's deliberate flaw, an admission that perfect control, perfect symmetry, is not our most important goal. Or is it, rather, a technique used to demonstrate the pull of individual creativity against a known pattern? Elaine Showalter explains that many viewers tend to overemphasize the rule of pattern in quilts: "Piecing was not simply a repetitive and unoriginal recombining of design elements, but a creative manipulation of conventions."[21]

Spivack's "The moments-of-past-happiness quilt" combines formal and content elements to destroy the notion of some set definition of perfection in art. In a move I see as humorous she opens a poem that is long and thin in shape with the words "This square." Since the squares of the quilt she describes are imaginary, "This square" is doubly nonexistent. "The moments-of-past-happiness quilt" is a conceptual work of art, more about what cannot exist than what can. I guess the only perfection Spivack admits is the constancy of imperfection.

Beyond Lessons: Creative Acts

When we learn to read, we can also learn to write. These six poets, experts already at writing, affirm both their own and our need to read the lost texts of women so that their (and our) own writing is strengthened. The writing may be a poem, or, by extension, a quilt, a garden, a building, a body, a way of life. These poems say to me that we need poems and other constructions as strong and beautiful as patchwork quilts. By borrowing quilt metaphors, these poets substantiate their work, adding, height, width, color, texture, and thickness to their poems.[22] A poem, that small thin thing: black scratches on a fragile piece of paper. The quilt makes the poem substantial, weighty. The reader, making connections between the poet's words and quilts, finds herself selecting scraps of her own to add to the text. (My memory of sleeping under a crazy quilt at my grandmother's house, a quilt I could not read, is such a scrap.)

While the parallels between quilting and poetry writing and constructing a life are more implied than stated in the poems by Oates, Piercy, and Waniek,

21. "Piecing," 227–28.

22. In her outline of a quilt's construction, in "Piecing and Writing," Elaine Showalter leaves out the layer of batting. She describes a typical quilt as having a top layer, composed of patchwork blocks (each pieced together according to some pattern) and "a heavy backing" (223). I am quibbling with this excellent essay because, although quilts can be made without a layer of air-trapping material to yield warmth, that padding has often been an essential element. Protection from the cold is central here.

in "Piecing," Robin Morgan explicitly aligns the three activities, seeing all of them as kinds of art. For Morgan the poem and the quilt and the life are all patchworks.[23] In each one the critical value is "the pleasure of rescuing some particle / into meaning" (ll. 68–69). Of course this meaning is fluid and shifting. One only holds it "For a while" (l. 69). The artist—poet or quilter or individual striving to assert her own desires—works "the same theme over and over" (l. 47) with subtle changes, sometimes using a known pattern, but at more challenging moments, discovering a new design as the work progresses. Rescuing "some particle" and discovering patterns and letting others see what you have made, you become vulnerable, you "risk being / all the more severely worn" (ll. 71–72). For Morgan, Waniek, Oates, and Piercy different elements of the quilt offer metaphors to be retrieved, interpreted, applied to the work of present and past women artists in mostly positive ways. But Sandra McPherson and Kathleen Spivack take the metaphor apart. Their poems are not artifacts: Spivack's quilt is an illusion; McPherson's, the woman's body itself. Still, the poet-quilter, whether she "constructs" or "deconstructs" her text, says to me: "Here—warm yourself in poems. Take from my work lessons in reading, so that your past is uncovered and recovered, your present more understandable, your future enlarged."

23. Another work that focuses on the patchwork construction of text is Barbara Guest's six-part "Quilts," 116–18. By combining six poems, each of which explores quilts and quilting differently, Guest manages an opulent response to the quilt trope, from its sheltering, protective, and even armoring aspects to its idealization of patterning and piecing, its relationship to natural forms, its textual qualities, and its shifting geography of places and bodies.

◆ Sisters' Choices ◆
Quilting Aesthetics in Contemporary African American Women's Fiction

Margot Anne Kelley

Taking a piece of cloth and using it for something other than defining social status and gender is not an aesthetic talent. It is a step to social deliverance.
Radka Donnell, *Quilts as Women's Art: A Quilt Poetics*

. . . when women make cloth, they have time to think . . .
Ntozake Shange, *Sassafras, Cypress, and Indigo*

In "African-American Women's Quilting: A Framework for Conceptualizing and Teaching African-American Women's History," Elsa Barkley Brown explains that quilts provide an excellent analytic framework for courses by enabling students to "center in another experience, validate it, and judge it by its own standards."[1] Books like Patricia Bell-Scott's *Double Stitch: Black Women Write about Mothers and Daughters* reinforce the aptness of her model. This anthology of essays, poems, fiction, and personal narratives is organized into six sections: "Threading the Needle: Beginnings," "Piecing Blocks: Identities," "Stitching Memories: Herstories," "Fraying Edges: Tensions," "Binding the Quilt: Generations," and "Loosening the Threads: Separations." The implication that quilting is integral to African American women's experiences recurs in many recent literary works, including Alice Walker's *The Color Purple*, Gloria Naylor's *Mama Day*, and Toni Morrison's *Beloved*. The quilting images in these works help to place them in a continuum of black women's creative efforts and to clarify the most significant features of that continuum. Perhaps surprisingly, an understanding of the African American quilting aesthetic and its function in these writings can also help critics to situate them in relation to the novels conventionally labeled "postmodern." Like many postmodern writers, these black women novelists are interrogating the prevailing assumptions about the

---

1. "African-American Women's Quilting: A Framework for Conceptualizing and Teaching African-American Women's History," 10.

subject, external reality, and representation. Through their quilting meta-phors, however, they venture a step further, suggesting alternative modes of perception and creation and offering new understandings of the relation of art to social life.

In her essay "Aesthetic Inheritances: History Worked by Hands," bell hooks celebrates her grandmother, noting in the "very first statement . . . about Baba" that she "was a dedicated quiltmaker" and *then* that her name was Sarah Hooks Oldham. hooks points out early in the discussion of Baba's quilts and quiltmaking practices that "the work of black women quiltmakers needs special feminist commentary which considers the impact of race, sex, and class." That need is exacerbated by the situation created "when art museums highlight the artistic achievement of American quiltmakers. . . . [O]ften representation at such shows suggests that white women were the only group truly dedicated to the art of quiltmaking. This is not so. Yet quilts by black women are portrayed as exceptions; usually there is only one. The card identifying the maker reads 'anonymous black woman.'"[2] Happily, traveling exhibits like "Who'd A Thought It: Improvisation in African-American Quiltmaking," a show organized by the San Francisco Craft & Folk Art Museum in 1988, are correcting the inaccurate impression that hooks decries.[3] At the same time, such shows enable those who cannot rummage through a grandmother's attic or sewing room to view African American quilts of the nineteenth and twentieth centuries and to understand them in relation to African textiles. This juxtaposition of quilts and West African cloths accentuates the aesthetic commonalities between the two materials, while also underscoring specific cultural significances of quilting itself.

Like some standard-traditional quilts,[4] African American (or "Afro-tradi-tional") quilts are composed of the scraps of material used in other projects, fabric from outgrown clothing, and pieces given to the quilter by friends and relatives. For the quilter, the diverse fabric sources create histories that are often significant; hooks explains that in her grandmother's case, each quilt had a "story [that] was rooted in the quilt's history" and that

2. *Yearning: Race, Gender, and Cultural Politics*, 116, 118, 115.

3. In "Aesthetic Principles in Afro-American Quilts," Maude Southwell Wahlman and John Scully mention two other exhibits: one that they organized at the Yale Art and Architecture Gallery in 1979 and another, entitled "Something to Keep You Warm," that was organized by Roland Freeman and toured the United States. Elaine Showalter refers briefly to "highly successful museum exhibits [of black women's quilts] in Dallas, San Francisco, New York, Mississippi, and Washington, D.C." in *Sister's Choice: Tradition and Change in American Women's Writing*, 163.

4. In *Who'd A Thought It: Improvisation in African-American Quiltmaking*, Eli Leon distin-guishes between the many quilting practices that originated in different parts of Europe and those from Africa—collectively referring to the former as standard-traditional, and to the latter as Afro-traditional. I find this distinction useful for my discussion.

Baba would show her quilts and tell their stories, giving the history . . . of chosen fabrics to individual lives. Although she never completed it, she began to piece a quilt of little stars from scraps of cotton dresses worn by her daughters. Together we would examine this work and she would tell me about the particulars, about what my mother and her sisters were doing when they wore a particular dress. . . . To her mind these quilts were maps charting the course of our lives. They were history as life lived.

This quilt connects the lives of grandmother, mother, and daughter, providing an opportunity for storytelling and a place to record domestic particulars, to artistically rework women's experiences. Moreover, since quilts are one of the very few sites in which African American women's creative impulses have been preserved (until recently), such a family heirloom "symbolically identif[ies] a tradition of black female artistry . . . [and] challenges the notion that creative black women are rare exceptions." Indeed, hooks goes on to assert that through quilts like those made by Baba "we are deeply, passionately connected to black women whose sense of aesthetics, whose commitment to ongoing creative work, inspires and sustains."[5]

The "sense of aesthetics" functioning in these quilts has been investigated by a number of scholars interested in both the differences between standard-traditional quilt patterns and Afro-traditional patterns, on the one hand, and the similarities of the latter to West African textiles, on the other. Briefly summarizing these inquiries in their article "Aesthetic Principles in Afro-American Quilts," Maude Southwell Wahlman and John Scully point out that connections have been made between appliqué quilts (like Harriet Powers's famous Bible quilts) and Fon wallhangings, between strip quilts and Ashanti and Ewe woven textiles from Ghana, and between the wide loom weavings of women in both the United States and Africa. The correspondences take into account not only large-scale similarities, but also some more particular shared aesthetic preferences distinct from those manifest in standard-traditional quilts. Wahlman and Scully enumerate five such qualities: in both West African textiles and African American traditional quilts, strips are used "to construct and to organize quilt top design space"; there is a partiality toward "large scale designs," as well as one for "strong, highly contrasting colors"; and color and design work together to produce both "off-beat patterns" and "multiple rhythms." To this list, we should add that both cloth-makers and quiltmakers evince a preference for—indeed a reliance on—improvisation. Quoting folklorist John Michael Vlach in the exhibition catalogue for "Who'd A Thought It," quilt collector Eli Leon observes that improvisation is "the basis of Afro-American creativity" and that "there is a use of formal design motifs but not a submission to them. There is a playful

5. *Yearning*, 120–21.

assertion of creativity and innovation over the redundancies of disciplined order."[6]

The strips and "strings" (very narrow strips) in African American quilts are usually long and rather narrow, running the length of the quilt and often alternating with patched blocks. Sometimes horizontal strips are added, creating a grid effect. In either case, the strips function both to structure the quilt top and "as a time-saving device"—enabling the quilter to make a large quilt with a bit less patching or to repair an existing quilt top. Whereas the background color of many standard-traditional quilts is a neutral shade that is not incorporated into the overall design,[7] "the color of the strips in a quilt is also a major element in the visual experience of the quilt. When the colors of the strips are different from the colors in the rows of blocks or designs, two distinct movements can be seen: one along the strips and the other within the designs." Wahlman, Scully, and others maintain that this preference for stripping entire quilts (rather than just the borders) "reflects a textile aesthetic which has been passed down for generations among Afro-American women who were descendants of Africans." In West Africa, men weave narrow strips of cloth on portable looms and then sew them together, a technique that allows great variety in the final product: "strips can be aligned so as to create regular, plaidlike patterns, checker-board designs, diamond patterns, or open-ended and asymmetrical arrangements."[8] "Women's Weave," the cloth made by women on large, stationary looms, often reproduces these patterns—suggesting that they are not so much an inadvertent by-product of sewing the pieces together as they are a distinct preference. To reinforce their claim that African American quilt stripping can be associated with West African textile "stripping," Wahlman and Scully asked Pecolia Warner, a quilter who has been the subject of several folklore articles, "what was the ideal width for a strip. And she said 'the width of my hand,' and laid her hand over a strip in one of her quilts. When presented with a single strip of West African narrow loom cloth, she immediately placed her hand over it, and found to her delight that it was the right width, the width of her hand."[9]

Afro-traditional quilts are also distinctive in their use of large-scale designs. While tiny, even stitches and myriad, precisely aligned patches are the hallmark of most high-caliber standard-traditional quilts, many African American quilters employ large, often abstract designs. In the earliest days of the Freedom Quilting Bee in Alabama, this design preference contributed to the group's success. Francis Xavier Walter, a priest involved in the civil rights movement, bought quilts from women in Gee's Bend and its environs, sent

6. Wahlman and Scully, "Aesthetic," 80–82, 86; Leon, *Who'd A Thought It*, 22.

7. Amish shadows quilts are one important exception to this generalization.

8. Wahlman and Scully, "Aesthetic," 83.

9. Ibid, 86.

them to New York to be auctioned, and gave the money to the women to support themselves and to reinvest in quilting—thus beginning one of the most successful, longest enduring quilting collectives in the nation. Among the quilts getting high bids at an early auction was "a quilt that was yellow and aqua. It was an amazing abstract design, as though the quiltmaker had taken almost a segment of one block and blown it up to full size." Tom Screven, one of the organizers of the auctions, surmised that this large design "came from a shortage of materials, or maybe they were making [the quilts] quickly to get them to the city [in time for the auction]." While not recognizing the links between this aesthetic preference and the African traditions from which it was derived, many purchasers at the auction liked and purchased the quilts because they "were so original" and "they looked like op art."[10]

Making these large designs all the more striking is a frequent reliance on strong, highly contrasting colors. In the first batch of Freedom Quilting Bee quilts were "two-toned quilts, not just in black-and-white, but blue-, red-, yellow-, even brown-and-white." Another volunteer who helped with the Bee in its early stages asserted that she could

> tell a Freedom Quilting Bee quilt from an Appalachian quilt as quickly as the snap of a finger because of the color strength in the Freedom quilt. The technical term is "high chroma," the use of primary colors at their most intense contrast. The quilts had a dynamism resulting from their combination of geometry and brilliance in juxtaposition of primary colors. What struck me when I first saw them was that as patchwork quilts so many of them were black-white, red-white, dark blue-white. Such opposition gave them a wonderful, almost Mondrian design.

Robert Farris Thompson suggests that such juxtaposition of strong colors might be looked at in terms of "something other than decorative intent." He notes that the "Bakongo believe that breaks in pattern, for instance terraced shifts from white to red to black, can symbolize passing through two worlds, the quest for the superior insights and power of the ancestors. I stop to consider how many of the finest quilters in Black America are devout church-goers, believers in the spirit. Then I regard the shimmering shifts of form and size and color spread out upon their children's beds. And I wonder." Whether the intent is spiritual or simply decorative, a further consequence of color pairing is a simultaneous emphasis on "both the color and the relationship [between colors]," a concurrent awareness of parts and wholes.[11]

A different but equally eye-catching effect is achieved when quilters interject colors in a random way, seeming to break whatever patterns they have estab-

10. Nancy Callahan, *The Freedom Quilting Bee*, 27.

11. Callahan, *Freedom*, 15–17, 53; Robert Farris Thompson, "From the First to the Final Thunder: African-American Quilts, Monuments of Cultural Assertion," 21; Wahlman and Scully, "Aesthetic," 88.

lished. Callahan describes such quilts as "less-than-perfect . . . marred . . . [by] their well intended, hit-or-miss color schemes—showpieces themselves in their crude, almost eerie approach. As one early buyer said of the quilt whose patches were all one color except for the red block at one end, 'If Picasso can do it, I guess they can, too.'" From a different aesthetic orientation, such an infusion of color can be understood as a way to demonstrate that the quilter has mastered the pattern and then deliberately broken free of it, emphasizing the importance of chance and accident to African American quilting. While seemingly random insets may be necessitated by the quilter running out of one fabric, as viewers usually presume, Wahlman and Scully explain that "the sporadic use of the same material in several squares when this material could have been used uniformly [suggests that] Afro-American quilters develop variation rather than regularity." Leon argues that such manipulations reflect the paradigm of "flexible classicism" that shapes traditional African art: "There are definite forms to which the artists are bound and within which they work . . . [but] great scope exists for individual expression. Improvisation is always encouraged, however contained within the traditional bounds." The misperception that Callahan records is quite understandable, though, since "structural variation in the reproduction of a quilt block, except in the most elementary cases, is an African American phenomenon unfamiliar in the standard tradition."[12]

Color is coupled with design to produce both offbeat patterns and multiple rhythms. The dominant light and dark accents in the columns or rows of a quilt can be likened to the beats in music. Wahlman and Scully explain that "when the accents in one row match the accents in another row, the design is 'on the beat.' But when the accents in one row do not match up with the accents in another row, then we have what can be termed 'off-beat' designs." These are often bemoaned by standard-traditional quilters, who prefer more symmetric, balanced, "on the beat" designs. In fact Blanche and Helen Young, in their *The Lone Star Quilt Handbook,* advise novice quilters that "in the Lone Star quilt, the fabrics should blend, or flow, from one diamond to the next, graduating from light to dark. Avoid alternating lights and darks; sudden changes in color intensity will give the Star a choppy, or checkerboard, look." Offbeat patterns may seem choppy, because their asymmetry destabilizes the pattern and propels the viewer into a tension between focusing on the individual colors and concentrating on the pattern. Or, as in the red-block quilt mentioned in the Callahan quote above, an irregularity in the design may prompt a reconsideration of the whole design.[13]

Callahan describes one of the early Freedom quilts that sold for a high bid

12. Callahan, *Freedom,* 17–18 (one wonders, given the importance of African art to Picasso's work, if perhaps *he* could do it for precisely the reasons that *they* could); Wahlman and Scully, "Aesthetic," 89, 90; Leon, *Who'd A Thought It,* 43–44, 26.

13. Wahlman and Scully, "Aesthetic," 90; Blanche Young and Helen Young, *The Lone Star Quilt Handbook,* 7.

as "a coral and blue rendering whose pattern could be perceived as two designs," a likely indication that this piece was made by someone with a passion for the medium. Wahlman and Scully point out that while "off-beat patterning occurs in many Afro-American quilts made by women who quilt occasionally for family and friends . . . multiple rhythms usually occur in quilts made by women who 'love' to quilt." One can easily imagine the colors in a two-tone quilt shifting before the eye as one color is regarded first as ground, then as figure. However, improvisational quilts often also manifest both off-beat patterns and multiple rhythms. The presence of these gestalt qualities is surprising when one realizes that "many quilts are the result of last minute aesthetic choices. Often quilters do not plan their quilts, but piece together scraps as they come out of a box or bag. Yet all will say that the patches must 'hit each other right' or 'show off the design well.'" The quilter often does not precisely measure her pieces, either, which means she must make frequent adjustments to the overall design to compensate for differences in size and shape. Eli Leon argues that the improvisational abilities that enable the quilters to work in this way result from their ability to work from "models in their minds," a way of approaching design that some quilters also attributed to their mothers and grandmothers. Connecting this approach to that used by the Kuba people of Kongo for making embroidered raffia cloth, Leon quotes art historian and anthropologist Monni Adams: "In textile design the Africans of the Kasai-Sankaru region do not project a composition as an integrated repetition of elements . . . Kuba women use neither sample patterns nor sketches on the cloth; they are working from models in their minds." The effect of these improvisations in both quilts and textiles "is to double, triple, and fragment patterns and rhythms so that one can see multiple accents which disrupt and suspend any regular flow of movement with color or form. . . . One or more patterns fade or fragment without completion."[14]

In short, then, the aesthetic governing African American traditional quilting is profoundly different from that implicit in standard-traditional quilting. This aesthetic is less and less often being displayed by members of groups like the Freedom Quilting Bee, as "the pressures of commercialization force[ ] the Bee to discontinue production of several whimsical but labor intensive patterns" and their mainstay accounts (notably Sears, for which they produce pillow shams) demand uniformity.[15] Nevertheless, quilt images in noteworthy African American fiction keep the principles of this aesthetic alive and enable us to ponder the correspondences between them and those evident in much post-modern literature.

Perhaps the most metaphorically resonant quality of quiltmaking is a trait

14. Callahan, *Freedom*, 27; Wahlman and Scully, "Aesthetic," 90, 91; Leon, *Who'd A Thought It*, 30, 26; Wahlman and Scully, "Aesthetic," 91.

15. Callahan, *Freedom*, 115.

shared by European and African American traditions—the promise of creating unity among disparate elements, of establishing connections in the midst of fragmentation. Quite often, this connectivity applies across time as well as space, uniting the women of different generations, who join the pieces of fabric as much as the scraps of material themselves. bell hooks maintains this in her commemoration of her grandmother, as does Radka Donnell in *Quilts as Women's Art: A Quilt Poetics*. There, she asserts that "a great many quilts have been made . . . to forge links between daughters, mothers, and mothers' mothers. . . . I want to acknowledge that the strongest single force connecting a quiltmaker to quilts is a woman's connection to other women, and above all her connection to her mother."[16] The fiction writers considered here employ quilting images to emphasize the importance of woman-woman relationships to their work. While Gloria Naylor and Toni Morrison do so by concentrating on intergenerational connections, Alice Walker uses quilts as sites for establishing relationships among peers.

In Naylor's *Mama Day*, Mama Day/Miranda and her sister Abigail create a double wedding ring quilt for Cocoa, Abigail's granddaughter, as a wedding gift. Mama Day grouses lovingly about having to sew the complicated design: "From edges to center, the patterns had to twine around each other. It would serve her right if it took till next year, and it probably would."[17] When Abigail points out that Cocoa "did finally say she'd settle for a simple pattern," Mama Day is no less critical, and she reminds Abigail that the quilt will "be passed on to my great-grandnieces and nephews when it's time for them to marry. And since I won't be around to defend myself, I don't want them thinking I was a lazy old somebody who couldn't make a decent double-ring quilt" (136). Mama Day is aware that she is sewing herself into the quilt, creating an heirloom that will preserve a part of herself when she is no longer "around," much as she is sewing in the rest of the family through the pieces of fabric she uses: "A bit of her daddy's Sunday shirt is matched with Abigail's lace slip, the collar from Hope's graduation dress, the palm of Grace's baptismal gloves. . . . Her needle fastens the satin trim of Peace's receiving blanket to Cocoa's baby jumper to a pocket from her own gardening apron" (137). Mama Day wants to incorporate a piece of "Mother's gingham shirtwaist" as "it would go right nice into the curve between these two little patches of apricot toweling," even though she knows "Abigail would have a fit" (137). Working with the fragile, old cloth, Mama Day's clairvoyant connections to both its wearer and the recipient of the quilt are heightened; she realizes that the piece joins her own unhappy mother to "another woman who could not find peace" but that "it was too late to take it out of the quilt, and it didn't matter no way." She knew before asking that the answer to her rhetorical questions "Could she take

---

16. *Women's Art*, 85.
17. *Mama Day*, 135. Hereafter citations will appear parenthetically in the text.

herself out? Could she take out Abigail? Could she take 'em all out and start
again?" (138) would be "no." Naylor uses the quilt to reinforce the reader's
awareness of the interconnections of the women across space and time, and to
underscore the potency of these links. Indeed, as Linda Wagner-Martin has
put it, "The mystery, the complicity, the interrelation of women's lives and
friendships are here imaged in the quilt . . . reminding [Naylor's] readers that
women's lives, and their patterns of experience, are the focus of *Mama Day*."[18]

Explicit in regarding the quilt as a manifestation of familial relationships,
Naylor articulates through Mama Day the kinds of connections that Toni
Morrison implies in *Beloved*. When Baby Suggs gives up on living, she goes to
bed in the keeping room and just stays there. Involved in her own turmoil,
daughter-in-law Sethe only understands that in that room Baby is "starved for
color. There wasn't any except for two orange squares in a quilt that made the
absence shout. . . . [In the bland room,] the dominating feature, the quilt over
an iron cot, was made up of scraps of blue serge, black, brown, and gray
wool—the full range of the dark and the muted that thrift and modesty
allowed. In that sober field, two patches of orange looked wild—like life in the
raw."[19] This quilt becomes a site for making connections among the many
women in 124. Like Baby Suggs, the next woman in the narrative to exist in
the liminal space between life and death craves the orange of the quilt. At the
same time that this parallelism suggests a connection between Baby and
Beloved, the quilt itself helps foster a bond between Beloved and Denver: "It
took three days for Beloved to notice the orange patches in the darkness of the
quilt. Denver was pleased because it kept her patient awake longer. She
seemed totally taken with those faded scraps of orange, even made the effort to
lean on her elbow and stroke them. An effort that quickly exhausted her, so
Denver rearranged the quilt so its cheeriest part was in the sick girl's sight line"
(54). Such patience is new to Denver, who strives to keep happy this girl whom
she is certain is her sister's ghost.

Beloved's interest in the orange squares is more than just a delight in bright
colors, though, for she says that the "yellow flowers in the place before the
crouching . . . are on the quilt now where we sleep" (214). "The place" is
Africa, and "crouching" refers to Africans being crowded into a slave ship's
hold. This conflation of the bright flowers and the bright patches connects
Beloved to Sethe (whom Beloved thinks picked the flowers), to Sethe's own
mother (who actually was brought to America on a slave ship) and, more
generally, to all slave-women. In "Nameless Ghosts: Possession and Dispossession in *Beloved*," Deborah Horvitz maintains that Beloved "represents the spirit
of all the women dragged onto slave ships in Africa and also all Black women
in America trying to trace their ancestry back to the mother on the ship

18. "Quilting in Gloria Naylor's *Mama Day*," 7.
19. *Beloved*, 38. Hereafter citations will appear parenthetically in the text.

attached to them."[20] Creating this complicated transatlantic chain of women is one of Morrison's aims; she is trying to present the stories and histories of African American women that have not "been passed on." Beloved's "reading" of the quilt is one of the most specific instantiations of this effort.

Although Beloved and Sethe rework the quilt, adding bright, lively fabrics, the new colors do not change the quilt's literal and symbolic significance, simultaneously connecting them to one another and marking the place where members of this family of women choose between life and death. At the close of the novel, Paul D finds a third woman on the life-death brink beneath the bedcovering. Sethe rests in the keeping room "under a quilt of merry colors" in a repose that makes Paul "nervous" (271). He realizes "what he is reminded of and he shouts at her, 'Don't you die on me! This is Baby Suggs' bed! Is that what you planning?'" (271–72). Although Sethe's literal ghost, Beloved, has disappeared, Paul D will not let Sethe "give up the ghost," and helps her decide instead to live. As representatives of three generations in this family, Baby Suggs, Sethe, and Beloved touch one another through the quilt with the orange squares, reminding the reader that quilts are not just symbolic, but are inevitably linked to the body—to birth (and rebirth) and death, as well as to the living in between.

For Alice Walker in *The Color Purple*, figurative rebirth occurs through the connections made among women who quilt together. Celie has told her stepson Harpo to beat Sofia for not "minding." Sofia confronts Celie in a rage and throws the curtains that Celie has made for her. After talking through the ways that each woman deals with the suffering implicit to her cultural position, the two reconcile by "mak[ing] quilt pieces out of these messed up curtains."[21] Their action recalls one of Radka Donnell's verses, "rage submits to the homing / power of cloth." This power, as Donnell goes on to say "rock[s] each one / of us back into consciousness, / to self-recognition and rest."[22]

The relationship which is most critical to Celie's rebirth, that with Shug, also begins with the two making blocks for a quilt. As unremarkable as her quilting is, Shug's attempts to stitch mark the beginning of her warmth toward Celie, a change in attitude that Celie is quick to sense:

> Me and Mr.— both look up at her. Both move to help her sit down. She don't look at him. She pull up a chair next to me.
>
>   She pick up a random piece of cloth out the basket. Hold it up to the light. Frown. How you sew this damn thing? she say.
>
>   I hand her the square I'm working on, start another one. She sew long crooked stitches, remind me of that little crooked tune she sing.

20. "Nameless Ghosts: Possession and Dispossession in *Beloved*," 157.
21. *The Color Purple*, 47. Hereafter citations will appear parenthetically in the text.
22. *Women's Art*, 26.

That real good, for first try, I say. That just fine and dandy. She look at me and snort. Everything I do is fine and dandy to you, Miss Celie, she say. (60)

As their relationship develops, Shug donates a yellow dress for the Sister's Choice quilt Celie is making, and later she enables Celie to establish financial independence through her sewing.

The quilts and quilting reflect a concern with women's relationships to one another central to much recent literature by African American women. Furthermore, the specific details provided about the quilts indicate that the writers share the "sense of aesthetics" that hooks affirms among black women artists. Understanding the function of quilting images prompts us to think about aesthetics more generally; and in regarding organization and structure from this new perspective, we can recognize the reconfigurations of the novel undertaken by each woman. Further guiding our re-perception is the novelists' inclusion of characters who consciously associate Afro-traditional quilting aesthetics with African textile aesthetics, as we find in *The Color Purple*.

Among the first things that Nettie reports to Celie about Africa is the fact that the Senegalese wear "brilliant blue robes with designs like fancy quilt patterns" (131). After arriving at the village where she is to work as a missionary, she writes to Celie that "the Olinka are known for their beautiful cotton fabrics which they handweave and dye with berries, clay, indigo, and treebark" (146) and, in another letter, explains that "the Olinka men make beautiful quilts which are full of animals and birds and people" (170). Nettie's descriptions of Olinka and Senegalese cloths recall both Fon appliqués and West African narrow strip textiles. She goes on to note that upon seeing these materials, the missionary Corrine "began to make a quilt that alternated one square of appliqued figures with one nine-patch block" (170). M. Teresa Tavormina has read Corrine's quilt keenly, noting that her combination of appliqué and blocks produced "an icon dense with history—personal, familial, artistic, national, racial, human—and with union and reunion. It brings together differences without denying them or subjugating them one to another—here a flowered square, there a checkered bird."[23] That Corrine's quilt also serves to reestablish trust between Nettie and Corrine adds still another facet to the already numerous signification functions in which it participates.

While it is difficult to be certain whether Celie's quilts are stripped like African cloth, or whether they have small or large designs,[24] Walker does indicate that both Celie and Corrine work in blocks (60, 170)—a technique routinely used in making strip quilts, albeit also in many other types. Morrison also intimates that Baby Suggs stripped her quilt when she writes that Sethe

23. "Dressing the Spirit: Clothworking and Language in *The Color Purple*," 227.

24. The one pattern she specifies, Sister's Choice, is a variation of the Ohio Star, and is used typically in sampler or block quilts that combine many small blocks. In it, Celie uses many tiny pieces of Shug's dress, an indication that she probably does keep that scale small.

and Beloved "tack[ ] scraps of cloth on Baby Suggs' old quilt" (241) for, as Wahlman and Scully argue, their potential for being easily refurbished or augmented in this manner is one of the appealing features of strip quilts.

Whatever the patterns used, the characters in these novels clearly share a preference for bright colors. Celie loves the yellow of Shug's old dress both because it is from Shug and because "the little yellow pieces, look like stars" (62). Sethe and Beloved add "carnival colors" to Baby Suggs's quilt, presumably leftover scraps from the "blue stripes and sassy prints" (272, 240) they purchase with all of Sethe's savings. And Mama Day and Abigail craft striking rings: "The overlapping circles start out as golds on the edge and melt into oranges, reds, blues, greens, and then back to golds for the middle of the quilt" (137). The circle into which Mama Day works her mother's gingham includes "apricot toweling" and "light red crepe" (138). These bright shades and the variety of fabrics are a dazzling alternative to those found in the traditional Double Wedding Rings, which were "often made from a kit, pieced of pastel floral prints on a white ground."[25]

Leon persuasively argues that the "vital force" of Afro-traditional Double Wedding Rings distinguishes them from the "fragile perfection" of their stand-ard-traditional counterparts. And in an essay entitled "Sea Island Black Quilters," Nan Tournier makes a parallel claim that is especially applicable to *Mama Day*. Tournier argues that the quilts made by African American women from the islands off the South Carolina shore "often display a highly individual interpretation of a traditional quilt design." She goes on to observe that these interpretations can be linked to African aesthetics, in large part because the islands have "large, stable communit[ies]," so that "there is little difficulty in retaining through the generations a creative philosophy which can subtly reflect the African cultural heritage" despite the islanders' proximity to the shore and to

---

25. Leon, *Who'd A Thought It*, 35. Eli Leon highlights the difference between the standard Double Wedding Ring and its African American counterpart through the following anecdote (Leon is showing his collection to five sisters, aged 62 to 75, who all quilt): "When I got ready to show the 'Double Wedding Ring,' I asked if everyone was familiar with the pattern. One of them wasn't sure, so I spread out a spellbinding example of a 1930s standard 'Double Wedding Ring,' the kind that was often made from a kit, pieced of pastel floral prints on a white ground. The quilt was in mint condition, lusciously crisp, exqui-sitely quilted, a pristine example of an archetype of Anglo-American femininity at a high point in standard American quiltmaking. The ladies loved it and a chorus of 'ain't that nice' in hushed, cooing tones circled the room. Seeing the quilt afresh, through their eyes, I felt the same reverence and, unexpectedly, some fearful anticipation about the reception the Hall 'Wedding Ring' would get. This was really a hard act to follow.

But I proceeded to bring out Emma Hall's worn and roughly crafted quilt and was thunderstruck by their reaction. These five stately women, a moment before so sweet and serene, started to hoot and stomp until the house shook. The room became a stadium; the fans gone wild. It was an exhilarating experience and it gave me some information I had been unwittingly seeking about cultural differences in standard- and Afro-traditional aes-thetic intention" (35–37). [Pictures accompany this account.]

Anglo-American culture. The heritage Tournier describes bears marked similarity to that attributed to Naylor's residents of Willow Springs, an island off the East Coast at the same latitude as the South Carolina–Georgia border; the island remains almost unchanged over time because it is claimed by neither state. Additionally, Mary Arnold Twining notes in her dissertation, "An Examination of African Retentions in the Folk Culture of the South Carolina and Georgia Sea Islands," that the quilters on these islands often combine diverse types of fabric in a single quilt: "They mix velvet, broadcloth, upholstery fabric, nylon, batiste, twills, woolens, rayon all in the same quilt." While this sort of assemblage likely originated as an economic rather than an aesthetic choice, Tournier and Twining both note that the stability of the community perpetuates and reinforces certain aesthetic preferences and cultural practices. We may suppose that economic necessity has been transmuted into aesthetic preference on the Sea Islands and in *Mama Day,* for Abigail and Miranda—who are not financially troubled—employ materials as diverse as those on Twining's list.[26]

While Naylor does name the quilt Abigail and Mama Day are making, and Walker mentions the Sister's Choice in particular, few of the quilts that appear in these three novels are named. Therefore, we must piece together from textual fragments whether or not these characters worked in offbeat patterns and employed multiple rhythms, as is characteristic of much Afro-traditional quilting. Celie, who loves to sew, quite probably did; making the Sister's Choice quilt, she asserts that she "work[s] in a piece" of Shug's yellow dress "every chance I get" (62). Celie's words suggest that rather than incorporating the material at regular intervals, as one would expect her to do, since she is employing a standard design, she is playing with the pattern to some degree. Analogously, Leon's descriptions of Afro-traditional Double Wedding Rings and Tournier's of Sea Island quilts, especially when we combine their insights with our knowledge of the color choices Mama Day describes, reinforce our supposition that Cocoa's wedding quilt is a "highly individualized variation" of the traditional design. And much as the red square in the Freedom quilt simultaneously calls attention to itself and to the pattern it disrupts, the orange squares in Baby Suggs's quilt create an impression of both order and interruption, a new pattern made explicitly part of an African aesthetic because it is employed to help forge a link between Beloved and the "sixty million and more" who did not survive the middle passage and whom Morrison acknowledges in the epigraph.

As many of the descriptions above have implied, the improvisation that is the hallmark of Afro-traditional quilting is also critical to these characters' quilting practices. While working on the Sister's Choice, Celie decides that "if

26. Leon, *Who'd A Thought It,* 37; Nan Tournier, "Sea Island Black Quilters," 41–42, 46; Mary Arnold Twining, "An Examination of African Retentions in the Folk Culture of the South Carolina and Georgia Sea Islands," 187.

the quilt turn out perfect, maybe I give it to her, if it not perfect, maybe I keep" (62), an attitude that indicates that she does not know precisely what it will look like when she finishes, even though she is nominally working from a pattern. This perspective recalls the "flexible classicism" Leon ascribed to African aesthetics. Furthermore, even when working from a "basket full of scraps on the floor" (60), Celie is able to generate striking designs, as did many of the quilters Wahlman and Scully describe. Mama Day and Abigail also work from scraps; in Abigail's living room, they sit "almost knee deep in bags of colored rags, sorted together by shades" (137). And like many of the African American quilters interviewed by folklorists, these two do not measure their scraps precisely; when trying to incorporate a bit of her mother's dress, for example, Mama Day "tries and tries again just for a sliver," which she must eventually baste to a bit of gingham before "she can shape the curve she needs" (137–38). Similarly, as both Baby Suggs's staid color choices and Sethe and Beloved's flamboyant ones suggest, these quilters worked with what they had, creating the most interesting designs possible with limited supplies.

By emphasizing the improvisational qualities and the principles of combination and connection inherent to quilting in their texts, Gloria Naylor, Toni Morrison, and Alice Walker suggest that these qualities are important to creative black women—that they are part of the aesthetic inheritance that hooks makes visible and seeks to perpetuate. Because they are contributing to this tradition through their narratives, we are prompted to look at the structure of the novels in a new way, to try to recognize how these principles contribute to a restructuring of this historically white, bourgeois, European form.

While the three novels are not identical to one another in structure, they all deviate quite clearly from the conventions of the classic realist text. All are "patchworked"; Walker's epistolary form may make this structuring most obvious, but the shift among several narrators and the manipulations of chronology in Naylor's and Morrison's texts achieve similar results. Discussing *The Color Purple*, Tavormina discusses the efficacy of quilts and epistolary forms in refocusing one's attention away from linear causality and a single perspective on experience, two attributes of the classic realist novel: "The art—Walker's art—is not only in the creation (or the transmission) of the two lives [Nettie's and Celie's], but also in the arrangement that juxtaposes and interlocks moments of revelation in Africa and America. . . . Letters, like quilts, transcend time's boundaries. . . . yet quilts and correspondence, besides transcending time, record its parts."[27] Naylor's use of the voices of Willow Springs, of Mama Day, of Cocoa, and of George after he has died to narrate meld a variety of perspectives while disrupting our customary ontological borders— both a place's "spirit" and a dead man's voice have the same ability to speak and evaluate as do the living individuals, an attribution of agency that is

27. "Dressing the Spirit," 226.

strikingly at odds with the conventions of most serious fiction written for adult readers. Similarly, Morrison has overtly defied the boundaries of space and time because she has constructed a ghost story; but Beloved is not the only character for whom the space-time continuum does not conform to our usual understanding of it. Sethe explains to Denver that "rememories" are like afterimages of past events and places, that

"If a house burns down, it's gone, but the place—the picture of it—stays, and not just in my rememory, but out there, in the world. . . ."

"Can other people see it?" asked Denver.

"Oh, yes. Oh yes, yes, yes. Someday you be walking down the road and you hear something or see something going on. So clear. And you think it's you thinking it up. A thought picture. But no. It's when you bump into a rememory that belongs to somebody else." (36)

Morrison remembers and (re)constructs through the arrangement of her text: she reaches forward and backward in time, selecting and highlighting details as they become important, clarifying information in ways that accentuate fundamental interrelationships among people and events and the processes of thinking and storytelling.

Although the unwieldy nature of the task prohibits me from demonstrating that *The Color Purple, Mama Day,* and *Beloved* display the literary equivalents to the multiple rhythms and offbeat patterns of Afro-traditional quilts, readers familiar with the three texts will readily recall the presence of these gestalt qualities. Similarly, such readers may regard the vibrant, highly individualized characters involved in permutations of primal situations as a writer's analog to the strong, highly contrasting color and design of the quilter's palette. While reaffirming the Afro-traditional quilting aesthetic of their matrilineage, Walker, Naylor, and Morrison also develop an aesthetic in these books that bears some unexpected similarities to that typically labeled "postmodern."

In many of the books that have received academic acclaim during the last four decades, we can discern a set of features now termed "postmodern." Some philosophical consensus exists concerning the meaning of this category, as Jane Flax notes in *Thinking Fragments.* There, she maintains that "postmodern stories about contemporary social transformations have at least one common organizing theme: There has been a breakdown in the metanarrative of Enlightenment . . . ideas that now seem problematic include such independent concepts as the dignity and worth of the 'monadic' (socially isolated and self-sufficient) individual and the interconnections between reason, knowledge, progress, freedom, and ethical action."[28] The conciseness and relative clarity of this definition notwithstanding, literary critics and theorists have yet to agree upon precisely what is meant by postmodernism, or when it began, or

---

28. *Thinking Fragments: Psychoanalysis, Feminism, and Postmodernism in the Contemporary West,* 7.

why it has become so pervasive. Most literary theorists, however, do maintain that postmodernism is not limited to specific examples of the elite arts and academic discourse but is a manifestation of the above-mentioned breakdown in the perceived efficacy of the Enlightenment metanarrative, that it involves a transformation within our cultural matrix. In his article "The Fine Art of Rap," Richard Shusterman emphasizes the ubiquity of postmodern aesthetic when he argues that hip-hop manifests many of the stylistic features that postmodernists use to question the assumptions implicit to earlier forms, including "recycling appropriation rather than unique originative creation, the eclectic mixing of styles, the enthusiastic embracing of the new technology and mass culture, the challenging of modernist notions of aesthetic autonomy and artistic purity, and an emphasis on the localized and temporal rather than the putatively universal and eternal."[29]

This incredulity toward metanarrative and the manners in which it is expressed remind us that the most significant preoccupations postmodern literary writers grapple with concern the subject, history, representation, and space/time—the parameters of "reality." The subject, which used to be understood as individuated, autonomous, and capable of exhibiting agency, is regarded by postmodernists alternatively as dead, fragmented, culturally constructed, or a bourgeois illusion—a point that Fredric Jameson emphasizes in his writings.[30] History, which was once perceived as a single, linear narrative, is understood as one construction among many. Representation, once considered a potentially unbiased depiction of some ontologically prior "reality," is now regarded as necessarily ideologically inflected and not necessarily prior to whatever "reality" it describes. And space and time, rather than being absolute, are being viewed with some uncertainty. While a list like this one can provide only a hasty overview of some of the concerns and techniques of postmodern writers, it does suggest a starting point for making connections between the quilting aesthetic and the postmodern one.

Through the quilting images, the African American women writers discussed above have been able to concertedly theorize a subject who is not the monadic self of the Enlightenment narrative, but who can nevertheless project a "rational, coherent, effective identity"—the traits most feminist critics find crucial to any new definitions of subjectivity.[31] This identity is explicitly constructed of fragments that make a strong whole; for example, by aligning her with the double wedding ring quilt that Mama Day and Abigail make, Naylor presents Cocoa as constructed from a little bit of Abigail, a little bit of Mama Day, a little bit of Cocoa's great-grandmother, and bits of others. Naylor does

29. "The Fine Art of Rap," 614.

30. See both *The Political Unconscious: Narrative as a Socially Symbolic Act* and "Postmodernism, or the Cultural Logic of Late Capitalism."

31. Patricia Waugh, *Feminine Fictions: Revisiting the Postmodern,* 6.

not suggest that Cocoa is simply the sum of her ancestors through a Naturalistic calculus. Instead she emphasizes that our inevitable constructedness also involves the promise of incorporating new parts that can further strengthen the self—as Cocoa learns after coming to terms with George's death, thereby gaining some of his fortitude.

An analogous patchworking of time also occurs in these narratives. Of the three writers, Morrison most overtly depicts history as constructed from a multiplicity of stories—many of which have been silenced and are only slowly reemerging—rather than as a linear narrative. While one rarely finds the slave's perspective on slavery in history textbooks, for example, that vantage would provide significant information about historical conditions. Yet, Morrison reminds us that history cannot simply be rewritten from the slave's vantage, since Stamp Paid's and Sethe's perspectives on being a slave, for example, are no more equivalent than are Mr. Garner's and schoolteacher's ideas about being a master. Consequently, she re-presents history through lots of narrative vantages—all of them obviously and inevitably partial. This process stresses the need to combine the fragments in order to have a viable whole, to stitch scraps together into a comforting cover.

Morrison's linking of revisionary history with alternative forms of representation closely parallels the postmodernist intermingling of history and representation. Linda Hutcheon discusses this intertwining, noting that "postmodern representational practices . . . refuse to stay neatly within accepted conventions and traditions . . . and [they] deploy hybrid forms and seemingly mutually contradictory strategies." She goes on to note that the complicated strategies (re)present "postmodern relativity and provisionality . . . [which are] perhaps the very conditions of historical knowledge. Historical knowledge may thus be seen today as unstable, contextual, relational, and provisional, but postmodernism argues that, in fact, it has always been so." Despite the doubts postmodern writers evince about the viability of accurately presenting history, many postmodern works are historiographic metafiction—a genre discussed at length by critics of postmodernism Patricia Waugh and Linda Hutcheon. For Morrison, the importance of re-presenting history lies in the artistic and literal remaking it enables. As she explained to Nellie McKay, she tries to tell "the same story again and again. I can change it," she added "if I contribute to it when I tell it. I can emphasize special things." In presenting black women's experiences, a new focus in novels, Morrison and the other novelists contribute both to the story and to our awareness of storytelling. They force us to think about the ways in which the stories we tell have, as Fredric Jameson argues, "reflect[ed] a fundamental dimension of our collective thinking and our collective fantasies about history and reality."[32] Such attention re-presents narrative

32. Linda Hutcheon, *The Politics of Postmodernism*, 37; Hutcheon, *Politics*, 67; Nellie McKay, "An Interview with Toni Morrison," 421; Jameson, *Political Unconscious*, 34.

itself and, like the more conspicuously experimental forms of postmodernism, opens it up to scrutiny.

Finally, as I suggested above, the disruptions of chronology (through flashbacks, letters, and rememory), and the unsettling of spatial parameters (through the juxtaposition of Nettie's Africa and Celie's United States or George's New York and Cocoa's ambiguously placed Willow Springs), like the conflation of past and present through the fabrics of an heirloom quilt, encourage the reader to rethink her or his understanding of space and time—both their significance and their relation to what we name "real." In talking about another of her books, *Meridian*, Alice Walker said that she "wanted to do something like a crazy quilt . . . something that works on the mind in different patterns. . . . A crazy-quilt story is one that can jump back and forth in time, work on many different levels, and one that can include myth. It is generally much more evocative of metaphor and symbolism than a novel that is chronological in structure, or one devoted, more or less, to rigorous realism."[33] Like Walker, Naylor and Morrison have also shaped stories that "work on the mind in different patterns."

The correspondences between postmodern practices and these quilting/ literary aesthetics are significant for their shared interest in rethinking the subject, in grappling with the subject's relation to space and time, and in finding socially appropriate and viable forms of representation. However, most critical discussions of postmodern texts note that the rethinking in these works involves much more questioning than answering. One of the most important distinctions we can make between postmodern texts and these African American women's works, therefore, is that the latter go one step beyond the former: many of the black women writers whose works are now gaining attention try to offer plausible, nonreactionary rescripting of the terms that postmodernism has undecided.

Just as their mothers employed various colors and sizes of fabric to piece a quilt top, these literary women rely on partial, local, and fragmented knowledge to make a narrative. The writers acknowledge that both the quilts and the narratives—as well as the beings who are their makers—are constructed. However, they regard the need to piece and seam not as a reason for despair but as an opportunity to rework the outmoded, whether it be in clothing, novel structures, or conceptions of the self. Similarly, while doubt about the efficacy of history or representation often paralyzes characters in postmodern narratives, the women in the three books I have discussed are liberated through the rescriptings. Shug's and Celie's refusals to conform entirely to someone else's patterns do not, in the long run, inhibit them from creating. Instead their improvising ability opens new alternatives, as does Walker's form. And while the ghosts of *Beloved*, magic/hoodoo of *Mama Day*, and serendipity of *The Color*

---

33. Claudia Tate, *Black Women Writers at Work*, 176.

Purple remain difficult for some readers to accept because the paranormal cannot be incorporated into their worldview, they do open new ontological possibilities for what we call reality. As Toni Morrison once explained, "Birds talk and butterflies cry" in her stories because such things are "not surprising or upsetting to [black people]. These things make the world larger for them."[34]

The writings of Alice Walker, Toni Morrison, and Gloria Naylor "make the world larger" and more vibrant for their readers by wrapping us in quilts of many colors. Through their images of quilts and their adaptations of the novel form, they simultaneously describe and participate in an alternative aesthetic tradition. This tradition, which can be traced back to Africa, is one that their foremothers perpetuated in the patching and stitching of threadbare, often roughly sewn bedcoverings that bear only a general resemblance to standard-traditional quilts, creating an alternative that "stands," as Houston A. Baker and Charlotte Pierce-Baker assert, "as a signal instance of a patterned whole-ness in the African diaspora."[35] And indeed both these African American writers and the women whom they remember with reverence seem to have discovered that quilts are an apparently innocent means by which "women could send a hidden message to other women," a message that, in this case, preserves and continues their aesthetic heritage.[36] Conscious of and valuing this heritage as both women and artists, these novelists incorporate images of quilts and quilting into their works. While arising from different cultural and material conditions, this inheritance enables the novelists to participate in the kind of radical questioning endemic to the postmodern era, and frees them to suggest some possible ways to resolve the queries that are so often now being raised.

Without insisting that either quilts or quilting aesthetics in narrative offer a solution to all of our literary and existential woes, I would argue that through their reliance on such an aesthetic, the novelists described in this essay have been able to remind us that the assembly of a lowly bedcovering can suggest valuable ways to reconceptualize our senses of self, community, lineage, and the connections between art and its social function. Such reconceptualizations seem to signify that the search for meaning in a postmodern world might well begin at home.

34. McKay, "Interview," 428.
35. "Patches: Quilts and Community in Alice Walker's 'Everyday Use,'" 706.
36. Marsha MacDowell, "Women, Quiltmaking, and Social Change in America," 72.

The Color Purple and the Poetics of Fragmentation

Judy Elsley

The first question to ask is therefore the following: how can women analyze their own exploitation, inscribe their own demands, within an order prescribed by the masculine? Is a women's politics possible within that order?

Luce Irigaray, *This Sex Which Is Not One*

In Yeats's "Crazy Jane Talks with the Bishop," the speaker is a wild old woman, a culturally marginal figure, who meets the epitome of respectability in the form of the Bishop. The Bishop responds predictably to Jane, despising her broken body and exhorting her to turn his way toward "a heavenly mansion." But social respectability means little to her. She answers his reproof in her strong, life-affirming voice, unintimidated by him or the patriarchal law he represents. Her reply refuses the epistemology of opposition, showing the Bishop that what seems opposed is, in fact, interdependent:

> "Fast and foul are near of kin,
> And fair needs foul," I cried . . .
> "For nothing can be sole or whole
> That has not been rent."[1]

To the Bishop and those he represents, her aphorisms seem like non sequiturs. Yet she makes sense in an untraditional way by asserting that wholeness is composed of that which it is not: fragments.

"Crazy" is just one of the labels patriarchal society attaches to women it doesn't understand, women who won't fit in, or who refuse to play the masculinist game. But Jane is not so crazy. She speaks a wild wisdom, which, while it does not coincide with linear reasoning, does show a profound understanding of a way of being for the many women who have spent their lives being marginalized by a culture that uses women for its own convenience. Nothing can be sole or whole that has not been rent.

1. W. B. Yeats, *Selected Poetry*, ed. A. Norman Jeffares, 161.

A woman makes the world her own by taking apart the patriarchal ways of being to create a space for herself. That space allows her to accept her own fragmentation, embrace those fragments, and thus validate herself. Recognizing rather than denying her pieces is often a woman's way to becoming "sole or whole" in a more feminocentric way.

Alice Walker's use of the quilt metaphor in *The Color Purple* illustrates just such a journey to self-empowerment in the person of Celie. Walker is herself a quilter who integrates textile and text naturally into her daily routine, a mixture of activities that suggests cohesive fragmentation: "My good days were spent teaching, writing a simple history book for use in black child-care centers in Jackson, recording black women's autobiographies, making a quilt (African fabrics, Mississippi string pattern), completing my second book, a novel—and trying to become pregnant."[2] In "Writing *The Color Purple*," Walker speaks specifically of the integration of writing and quilting in the creation of that novel. After searching for a place in which her characters were comfortable enough to speak, Walker says, "I bought some beautiful blue-and-red-and-purple fabric . . . and a quilt pattern my mama swore was easy, and I headed for the hills." As she waited for the characters and plot to take form in her mind, Walker "worked on my quilt," finding that it "began to grow. And, of course, everything was happening. Celie and Shug and Albert were getting to know each other, coming to trust my determination to serve their entry . . . into the world to the best of my ability, and what is more—and felt so wonderful—we began to love one another."[3] Quiltmaking, self-fashioning, and the construction of a woman's text are all part of the same process, not only in Walker's life, but also in her text.

Whether she uses old clothes or crisp new cottons, the quilter begins work on her patchwork quilt by cutting or ripping the fabric apart. Indeed, a patchwork quilt cannot come into existence without that tearing. This deconstructive act is, paradoxically, also one of the quilter's most creative acts—an act of courage, necessity, and faith. Tearing seems a singularly appropriate place for a woman to begin, whether with a quilt or with finding a way to autonomy, because being torn is so familiar an experience for women, as Walker suggests through her representation of Celie.

Celie begins her narrative by writing "I am," a locution she then negates by crossing it out, indicating her lack of confidence in her self.[4] We learn in the first few letters she writes that she has experienced life as a series of tearings. She has been torn from childhood by "Pa's" incestuous rapes, torn from the two children she bears by him, whom he takes from her, and torn from the one

---

2. "One Child of One's Own: A Meaningful Digression within the Work(s)," in *In Search of Our Mothers' Gardens*, 367.

3. "Writing *The Color Purple*," in *In Search of Our Mothers' Gardens*, 358.

4. *The Color Purple*, 11. Hereafter citations will appear parenthetically in the text.

person she loves, her sister, Nettie, through a marriage that she doesn't want. Her life is made up of sacrifices—to Pa's destructive desires, to Nettie's safety, and to Mr.—'s needs and brutality. Each time the sacrifice is the same: her self. Celie has been rent into pieces that are given away to others, mostly at the insistence of the men who dominate her.

In the simple process of writing her letters, however, Celie has unconsciously begun to work toward a sense of self-worth, for, as Hélène Cixous suggests, writing is a way to replace the misrepresentation of others with self-creation: "To write. An act which will . . . give her back her goods, her pleasures, her organs, her immense bodily territories which have been kept under seal." *The Color Purple* tells the story of Celie learning to speak the "marvelous text of herself that she must urgently learn to speak."[5]

Celie's journey to creating a text of herself entails transforming herself from commodity to person. She begins the novel as a useful object, an item of exchange between Pa and Mr.—. Pa gives Celie to Mr.— as very little more than a labor-saving device. "Men make commerce *of* them [women], but they do not enter into any exchanges *with* them."[6] No wonder Celie has no sense of herself. Her society has deliberately stripped her of that which would give her value, turning her into a human machine, a convenient workhorse—what Walker elsewhere, quoting Zora Neale Hurston, called "the mule of the world." Although Celie begins by striking out her "I am," by the end of the novel, she owns the store, literally and metaphorically. As a place where she can enter into exchange with men and women through buying and selling without becoming herself an item of exchange, the store represents self-possession. *The Color Purple* traces Celie's progress from commodity to person.

However, claiming her "I am" is more problematic than Celie can imagine: while, on the one hand, she must learn to claim the first-person pronoun as a sign of selfhood, on the other hand, there is a deep wisdom in her early refusal of that single whole. Given traditional Western constructions of personhood, if Celie were to ask the question "Who am I?" (which she never does), chances are that she would be searching for a fixed self, some sort of unchanging essence.

Identifying with a single "I" also means identifying oneself as "other." The belief in that single self, that essence, is a dangerous illusion for women seeking self-empowerment precisely because it conforms to a traditional male model. Jessica Benjamin lucidly explains why identity based on self/other is problematic:

> Both in theory and practice our culture knows only one form of individuality: the male stance of overdifferentiation, of splitting off and denying the tendencies toward sameness and reciprocal responsiveness. In this "false differentiation" the

5. "The Laugh of the Medusa," in *Critical Theory since 1965*, ed. Hazard Adams and Leroy Searle, 312. Hereafter citations will appear parenthetically in the text.

6. Luce Irigaray, *This Sex Which Is Not One*, 172. Hereafter citations will appear parenthetically in the text.

other subject remains an object, rather than emerging as a person in her/his right. This way of establishing and protecting individuality dovetails with the dualistic, objective posturing of Western rationality.[7]

The traditional "I" defines itself in the binary terms of self/other, which inevitably marginalize female into "other."

Since neither living in unconnected pieces nor adopting the single "I" makes a satisfactory way for a woman to live, Celie's means to a healthy sense of self does not come from either option, but from a route that lies between them, like a quilt, which is whole but also composed of fragments. Celie begins that process by rejecting separation from other women—she has experienced the ill effects of that all her life—in favor of connection with others, moving toward "the recognition that differentiation is not necessarily separateness, distance, and alienation from others, but a form of *connection* to others."[8] This constitutes a major shift in perception. When Celie begins to connect with other women, she also begins to connect the different fragments of herself. Self-definition through connection rather than separation is her way to salvation.

Celie's changing attitude toward her physical body illustrates this idea. Her early experience of her own sexuality parallels the fragmentation Irigaray describes as "shards, scattered remnants of a violated sexuality" (30), as Pa and Mr. — make their forced entries, and the babies she gives birth to are forced out. Only when she discovers masturbation, loving her own parts, with the help of Shug, does she begin to feel a sense of herself sexually. Celie claims her sexuality by making relationship both with herself and with another woman. Indeed, connection to self is integrally bound to connection with others. Irigaray explains what Celie discovers intuitively: "This sex which is not one," always in communication with itself, as a source of strength for a woman. By identifying the nature of woman's sexuality, Irigaray also suggests what self-hood means to women: "Woman 'touches herself' all the time, and moreover no one can forbid her to do so, for her genitals are formed of two lips in continuous contact. Thus, within herself, she is already two—but not divisible into one(s)—that caress each other" (24). Thus Celie's wholeness, paradoxically, is a matter not of embracing a single sense of self, but of embracing, touching, caressing the different parts of herself.

Who is she? Celie, like any other woman, can't be defined in a single word. It's not so much a case of making a whole out of the fragments as recognizing and validating the fragments. Irigaray, asked to define "woman," replies, "I believe I've already answered that there is no way I would 'answer' that question. The question 'what is . . . ?' is the question—the metaphysical question—to which the feminine does not allow itself to submit" (122). Cixous

7. "The Bonds of Love: Rational Violence and Erotic Domination," 46.
8. Patricia Waugh, *Feminine Fictions: Revisiting the Postmodern*, 11.

answers the same question by focusing on the mélange of pieces that constitutes a single woman, defying definition: "There is, at this time, no general woman, no one typical woman. . . . What strikes me is the infinite richness of their individual constitutions" (309). Celie's search for feminine identity is grounded in a diversity that prevents any simple, close-ended definition.

Composed of fragments that are connected to each other, sewn in layers that are in continual contact with each other, made by two women in communication with each other, the quilt Celie makes with Sofia out of "messed up curtains" acts as both the first step and the paradigmatic metaphor of Celie's process of claiming herself.[9] Radka Donnell-Vogt, a professional quilter, (whom Elaine Showalter describes as "the Kristeva of quilting, the Other Bulgarian"[10]) could have been describing Celie's quiltmaking rather than her own process when she said, "In their geometry lie undeciphered the record of women's struggle to affirm their anatomy against all cultural odds."[11]

Separated within herself, Celie is also separated from the women in her life. Bonding with another woman, whether Sofia, Shug, or Nettie, is essential to Celie's process of self-reclamation. Her history illustrates Luce Irigaray's theory in "Women on the Market," that because patriarchal society puts value on women only to the degree that they serve the purpose of commodities of exchange between men, women must be kept separate from each other in order for the system to work (170–91). This dynamic is worked out in the first incident in which quilting is mentioned in *The Color Purple*. Having failed in his efforts to control his powerful wife, Sofia, Harpo asks Celie for advice. She repeats the patriarchal attitude: "Beat her. I say" (43), thus participating in what Cixous calls men's "greatest crime against women": "Insidiously, violently, [men] have led [women] to hate women, to be their own enemies, to mobilize their immense strength against themselves" (310). When Sofia discovers Celie's betrayal, she storms over to her house to confront her. The

---

9. Most critics recognize this novel as a journey of self-discovery. Daniel Ross, for example (in "Celie in the Looking Glass: The Desire for Selfhood in *The Color Purple*," 69–84), argues that Celie's starting point in her journey takes place when, with the help of Shug, she looks at her genitals in the mirror for the first time. This is indeed an important step in her process, but not the first one. Quilting with Sofia is the beginning, not only because it happens earlier in the novel, but because the act of quilting those "messed up curtains" parallels so closely putting together her fragmented life.

Elaine Hedges makes a similar argument to mine in her essay "'The Needle or the Pen': The Literary Rediscovery of Women's Textile Work" 354–56. My essay was originally written as a chapter for my Ph.D. dissertation, completed in 1990. I was flattered to see that Elaine Hedges, whose work I have long admired, was approaching *The Color Purple* in a parallel way to me at approximately the same time, even though we were unaware of each other's work.

10. "Piecing and Writing," 226.

11. Interview with authors, *Lives and Works: Talks with Women Artists,* ed. Lynn F. Miller and Sally S. Swenson, 50.

scene is set in rupture and violence, that between Harpo and Sofia, that between the two women, and that within Celie herself as she thinks with shame of the advice she gave Harpo. There has to be a better way. Irigaray suggests that "it is essential for women among themselves to invent new modes of organization, new forms of struggle, new challenges. . . . [I]nstitutions, hierarchy, and authority—that is, the existing forms of politics—are men's affairs. Not ours" (166). Celie and Sofia discover just such a new mode of organization through making a quilt. Quiltmaking suits their task of putting their ruptured lives together, for quilting privileges "a distinctively woman's craft as *the* signal mode of confronting chaos through a skillful blending of patches."[12]

The honest communication that ensues, as Celie admits her guilt and asks Sofia's forgiveness, makes the setting for the two of them to begin their quiltmaking. As Donnell-Vogt says, "The quilt is first of all a speculum by which a woman looks into herself, and when she finds her unknown and disregarded beauty, she can find also the courage to prevail along with others for her share in the world."[13] Putting together the fragments of "messed up curtains," torn in a fight between Sofia and Harpo, the two women reconfigure their bond. Guilt is transformed into quilt as discarded fabric and rejected women are sewn into something whole and beautiful.

Celie uses fabric scraps. For many women the fragments are made of time and words. Adrienne Rich describes her own process, moving along the same road as Celie but using text rather than textile to reach her "I am":

> In the late fifties I was able to write, for the first time, directly about experiencing myself as a woman. The poem was jotted in fragments during children's naps, brief hours in a library, or at 3:00 a.m. after rising with a wakeful child. I despaired of doing any continuous work at this time. Yet I began to feel that my fragments and scraps had a common consciousness and a common theme, one which I would have been very unwilling to put on paper at an earlier time because I had been taught that poetry should be "universal," which meant, of course, nonfemale. Until than I had tried very much *not* to identify myself as a female poet.[14]

Rich lucidly describes the process Celie is about to begin. Her life is in fragments, given away to other people, and invalidated. As she acknowledges and accepts the fragments as part of her womanhood, she can begin to come to autonomy. She moves from the outside world's negative estimation of her to an inner confidence in who she is. As Rich says, "The enemy is always outside

12. Houston A. Baker, Jr., and Charlotte Pierce-Baker, "Patches: Quilts and Community in Alice Walker's "Everyday Use," 720.

13. *Lives and Works*, ed. Lynn F. Miller and Sally S. Swenson, 56.

14. "When We Dead Awaken: Writing as Re-Vision." *The Norton Anthology of Literature by Women*, ed. Sandra M. Gilbert and Susan Gubar, 2053.

the self, the struggle somewhere else."[15] The enemy outside, according to
Rich, is "the Man." Whether the Man terrorizes, as in Celie's case, or en-
courages, as with Rich, the effect is the same:

> My own luck was being born white and middle-class into a house full of books,
> with a father who encouraged me to read and write. So for about twenty years I
> wrote for a particular man, who criticized and praised me and made me feel I
> was indeed "special." The obverse side of this, of course, was that I tried for a
> long time to please him, or rather, not to displease him. And then of course, there
> were other men—writers, teachers—the Man, who was not a terror or a dream
> but a literary master in other ways less easy to acknowledge.[16]

Sewing is one way for women to begin the process of self-reclamation because
it represents, more than other activities traditionally associated with women, a
powerful and elemental symbol of connection. As Rich says in *Of Woman Born*,
"The conversion of raw fibers into thread was connected with the power over
life and death; the spider who spins thread out of her own body, Ariadne
providing the clue to the labyrinth, the figures of the Nates or Norns or old
spinning women who cut the thread of life or spin it further, are all associated
with this process."[17] Both Celie and Rich journey from accepting an identity
imposed from without, an enforced and uncomfortable single "I," to working
from the inside, stitching their fragments together in a pattern to suit themselves.

The quilt pattern Celie selects—"Sister's Choice"—gives name to her particular journey. By simultaneously asserting her right to choose as well as
affirming her community with other women, Celie takes the first step toward
living autonomously and integrally. "Sister's Choice" is a traditional pattern
documented in an exhaustive survey of patchwork patterns made by Hall and
Kretsinger in their 1935 classic, *The Romance of the Patchwork Quilt in America*.
They write of this pattern: "The simple contacts of everyday family life are
responsible for many of their quilt names."[18] The familial contact between
Sofia and Celie may be simple, but it has radical significance. They are
declaring their sisterhood not only through marriage, but also in terms of
gender. Their new bond relies not so much on the men in their lives as on their
recognition of each other as individual women. Their decision to work to-

15. Ibid., 2056
16. Ibid., 2048.
17. Rich, Adrienne, *Of Woman Born: Motherhood as Experience and Institution*, 101.
18. Celie's choice of quilt pattern has further ramifications. As its title suggests, she is
implicitly reaffirming her connection with her beloved sister, Nettie. Moreover, at the heart
Sister's Choice is a nine-square patch, which is the design Corrine chooses to make her
African quilt.
Later in the novel, Celie and Shug make a choice for each other as sexual sisters. Hence
the quilt pattern joins all the major female characters in the novel.

gether has political implications for they are, in effect, rejecting the social order that condemns them to commodity status. Instead, they turn the world of commodities on its head. "Commodities," writes Irigaray,

> can only enter into relationships under the watchful eyes of their "guardians." It is out of the question for them to go to "market" on their own, enjoy their own worth among themselves, speak to each other, desire each other, free from the control of seller-buyer-consumer subjects. And the interests of businessmen require that commodities relate to each other as rivals. (196)

Sofia and Celie break their commodity status by relating directly with each other, not as rivals, but as sisters. Celie's decision to make the quilt with Sofia is thus the turning point in her life because it represents the first step she takes toward her own empowerment via connection with other women.

Celie's and Sofia's quiltmaking enacts a process of healing, because they are no longer passive victims who are torn. In turning being torn into tearing, quiltmaking turns object into subject: active creation replaces passive victimization as the two women, their sisterhood reaffirmed, set about constructing a pattern of their choice out of the fragments of their lives. The same fragmentation that traps and oppresses Celie becomes her way to salvation.

Fragmentation underpins Celie's process of quiltmaking (and healing) at every stage in the process. Her fabric comes from curtains that function through their ability to separate; the curtains are torn in a fight between Sofia and Harpo, which makes a second layer of fragments. The fabric is further cut to make up the patchwork pattern, so that the quilt she makes is composed of at least three layers of both material and metaphorical fragments. The quilt Celie and Sofia make becomes a celebration of fragments, a recognition and reverence for pieces. The self she is creating, like the patchwork quilt she makes, is not so much an integrated whole as it is a vindication of fragments, a commemoration of multiplicity.

The process of making fragments creates a necessary space, one that allows for disruptive and destabilizing behavior, from which a woman can begin her task of self-creation. "No woman can assume herself because she has yet to create herself," says Myra Jehlen, and in the beginning of that process "all women must destroy in order to create."[19] Tearing fabric apart has the effect of creating space between the pieces. This place of liminality, this undefined space, becomes a place of creative freedom for the quilter, for it allows her to arrange her pieces of fabric and thus create her pattern "as a fragment, it [patchwork] is also rife with explosive potential of the yet-to-be-discovered. Like a woman, it is a liminal element between wholes."[20] Radka Donnell-Vogt

19. "Archimedes and the Paradox of Feminist Criticism," 593, 583.

20. Houston A. Baker, Jr., and Charlotte Pierce-Baker, "Patches: Quilts and Community in Alice Walker's 'Everyday Use,'" 706.

describes that liminal element in her own process of quiltmaking: "The double function of quilt-making, to help collect one's thoughts and provide an image of spatial integration that does not freeze one in one place as the observation of stationary paintings, was essential in giving me a base for exploring my situation as a woman and as an artist."[21] While Donnell-Vogt is more consciously articulate than Celie, both women are involved in the same business of freeing up space for themselves.

The space that Celie or any other quilter creates for herself has long been recognized and valued by feminist theoreticians. Sandra Gilbert uses the metaphor of the sibyl to express in a mythical way this same necessity for women to take the fragments of their lives, and, in the space they create, find a way to speak in order to re-create themselves. Taking her cue from Mary Shelley's *The Last Man,* Gilbert imagines the sibyl in "a female space," a cave. She is "a prophetess who inscribed her 'divine intuitions' on tender leaves and fragments of delicate bark." But "the Sibyl's leaves are now scattered, barely comprehensible,"[22] like Celie's letters, written in black vernacular, which are barely comprehensible to a white culture (or a black male culture) that refuses to acknowledge the perspective they bespeak. Quilting with words and fabric, Celie represents the sibyl's descendent, working within a space she has created for herself, "biting that tongue with her very own teeth to invent for herself a language to get inside of," with her letters and her fragments of messed up curtains (Cixous, 316).

In "The Laugh of the Medusa" Cixous describes the need for "everywoman" to make such a space for herself in order to create herself. She begins her paragraph fittingly by literally making a space for herself: "Let me insert here a parenthetical remark." Her main point is that woman has never had "her turn to speak—this being all the more serious and unpardonable in that writing is precisely the very possibility of change, the space that can serve as a springboard for subversive thought, the precursory movement of a transformation of social and cultural structures (311). Irigaray, like Cixous, points to the disruptive potential of a woman-created space:

> For the exploitation of women does not constitute a *limited* question, within politics, one which would concern only a "sector" of the population, or a "part" of the "body politic." When women want to escape from exploitation, they do not merely destroy a few "prejudices," they disrupt the entire order of dominant values, economic, social, moral, and sexual. They call into question all existing theory, all thought, all language, inasmuch as these are monopolized by men and men alone. They challenge the *very foundation of our social and cultural order,* whose organization has been prescribed by the patriarchal system. (165)

21. *Lives and Works,* ed. Lynn F. Miller and Sally S. Swenson, 49.
22. "Literary Paternity," in *Critical Theory since 1965,* ed. Hazard Adams and Leroy Searle, 494.

Certainly Celie and Sofia, laughing over their quilting, are creating a space that "can serve as a springboard for subversive thought," as we see in their conversation about killing Mr.—:

> Well, sometime Mr.— git on me pretty hard. I have to talk to Old Maker. But he my husband. I shrug my shoulders. This life soon be over, I say. Heaven last all ways.
> You ought to bash Mr.— head open, she say. Think about heaven later. (47)

As they sew they talk, plotting the overthrow of the men who dominate them, in a radical maneuver that makes space for themselves. To Celie, that space is undoubtedly a disruptive, destabilizing place that makes room for change. We recognize it as the "wild zone" Showalter writes of in "Feminist Criticism in the Wilderness."[23] Using Edwin Ardener's model of overlapping circles to show dominant and muted groups, Showalter labels that part of the circle that falls outside the interlocking circles "women's wild zone." It is outside the patriarchal order of things and, therefore, a place where women can move more freely.

Making the quilt reverses another kind of tearing familiar to women—that of interruption and discontinuity. Celie's life, like that of many women, is composed of fragments of time, mostly allotted by others and for others. Virginia Woolf wrote that "Jane Austen would slip her writing beneath a book if anyone came in, and Charlotte Bronte stopped in the middle of her work to pare the potatoes."[24] Adrienne Rich suggests that this is not merely a problem for nineteenth-century women: "I was writing very little, partly from fatigue of suppressed anger and loss of contact with my own being; partly from the discontinuity of female life with its attention to small chores, errands, work that others constantly undo, small children's constant needs."[25] Rich shows that being torn from one's writing and torn from oneself are extensions of one another. But as Tillie Olsen remarks in *Working It Out*, "Interruption becomes a habit even when the circumstances change."[26]

The discontinuity, the space between things, the constant interruption becomes a working cognition. We see this not only in Celie's patchwork quilt, which consists of discontinuous pieces of fabric, sewn together in the space created between other duties, but also in the kind of writing Celie does. Celie's chosen form of self-expression, letter writing, consists of short, discrete units of discontinuous prose, broken off and interrupted by the oppressive demands of her life. Yet Walker makes that discontinuity into a shapely narrative, composed out of the very stuff of interruption. Celie works with fragments in her text as well as in her textiles.

23. "Feminist Criticism," 262.
24. Barret, *Virginia Woolf on Women and Writing*, 69.
25. Rich, "Dead," 2052.
26. Interview by authors, in *Working It Out: Twenty-Three Women Talk about Their Lives and Work*, ed. Sara Ruddick and Pamela Daniels, 335.

Celie takes the materials that are available to her, bits and pieces of the everyday. As Teresa Tavormina notes, "The whole novel is crafted from these everyday materials, 'pieced' from patches of memory, from patches woven of different threads and from different wear, but brought together so as to make a whole meaning from Celie's and Nettie's seemingly separated lives."[27] Quilt-makers have traditionally found their working materials in the everyday scraps around them. Patricia Cooper and Norma Bradley Allen record New Mexico quilters who took pride in this economy of materials: "Then we have light weight blankets or electric blankets that we pull the electric parts out of for the inner lining. Things are so high now that we don't buy batting. One lady does the linings and sometimes she has to patch and piece to get big enough lining."[28] Geraldine Johnson gives a more extreme example of the blue Ridge Mountain women who "collected the thread to piece the quilts and sometimes to quilt them by unravelling worn-out socks or feed sacks, winding the thread on the spool and using it later in the quilt."[29]

As one who puts fragments together, Celie becomes what Lévi-Strauss designates a *bricoleur,* that is, a marginal figure who transforms the materials the world has rejected, turning "back to an already existent set made up of tools and materials, to consider or reconsider what it contains and, finally and above all, to engage in a sort of dialogue with it, and, before choosing between them, to index possible answers which the whole set can offer to his prob-lems."[30] But rather than confine her to a structuralist masculine model, we can see Celie as one who practices Miriam Schapiro's *femmage,* the feminine equiva-lent of *bricolage.* This "process of collecting and creatively assembling odd or seemingly disparate elements into a functional, integrated whole" is distin-guished from *bricolage* in that "femmage denotes an aesthetic of connection and relationships."[31] And indeed, appropriate relationships with herself and others is Celie's quest. The relationships between the material of creation itself, between maker and material, and between different makers that develop through quilt-making reflect the increasing connections Celie is generating with her world and those in it. By the end of the novel, she has successfully created her own re-lationships, though they lie outside social norms, of friendship with her ex-husband, her lover, her children, and most important, with herself.

As she empowers herself, Celie discovers that the patriarchal system no longer has the control she believed it had. This is perhaps clearest when Celie discovers that "Pa is not Pa," but a pretender to the position. Celie begins the novel believing in the Father, whether it is God, or Pa, or Mr.—, as the one

27. "Dressing the Spirit: Clothworking and Language in *The Color Purple,*" 225.

28. *The Quilters: Women and Domestic Art,* 114.

29. "More For Warmth than Looks: Quilts of the Blue Ridge Mountains," in *Pieced By Mother: Symposium Papers,* ed. Jeanette Lasansky, 51.

30. *The Savage Mind,* 18.

31. Kay Turner, "Mexican American Home Altars: Towards Their Interpretation," 7.

who *knows*, but she grows to realize that she herself is the agent of knowledge. Thus, she can refuse both the father's "no" and his knowing. Pa is revealed as not the father; Mr.— is abandoned in favor of a woman, Shug; and Ole Maker is replaced by Celie's sister, Nettie. Men who tear are supplanted by women who bond. The power of the quilt, then, in *The Color Purple* is its ability to transform a woman's life from disparate fragments to a self-fashioned cohesion of pieces.

Quilts also help women to join with each other. As we have seen, quilting bonds Sofia and Celie, inspiring Celie to adopt some of Sofia's fighting spirit for herself. In a parallel situation, another quilt joins two other women, Nettie and Corrine, in Africa. As with Celie and Sofia, a misunderstanding arises between Corrine and Nettie; this one occurs when the dying Corrine suspects Nettie of being the biological mother of her children. Nettie proves the truth by finding a quilt made of pieces of fabric Corrine was buying when she met Celie years before: "Do you remember buying this cloth? I asked, pointing to a flowered square. And what about this checkered bird? She traced the patterns with her finger, and slowly her eyes filled with tears. She was so much like Olivia! she said. I was afraid she'd want her back. So I forgot her as soon as I could" (171). This recognition not only brings Nettie and Celie closer together as joint mothers of the children, but reunites Celie with her babies by Corrine's acknowledgement that Celie is their mother. Nettie, writing about the Olinka mothers sewing together, could be commenting on all the women in the novel who are bonded through fabric: "It is in work that the women get to know and care about each other" (153).

Tavormina takes the idea of the nine-patch representing relationships one step further in this astute observation: "It is intriguing to speculate as to whether there is more than a chance parallel between the nine-patch (a very common quilt element) and the three principal marital arrangements in the novel, with their three-fold structures—Celie, Mr.—, Shug; Sofia, Harpo, Mary Agnes/Squeak; and Nettie, Samuel, Corrine."[32] Three pairs of "sisters," Celie and Shug, Sofia and Mary Agnes, Nettie and Corrine, make choices for and against the men in their lives in pairs that also re-pair with each other. The relationships between women can appropriately be described as "Sister's Choice" in the novel, none perhaps more amusingly than that of Sofia and Mary Agnes who, after their initial dislike of one another, pass Harpo back and forth as they choose better lives for themselves:

> Go on sing, say Sofia, I'll look after this one till you come back.
> You will? say Squeak.
> Yeah, say Sofia.
> And look after Harpo, too, say Squeak. Please ma'am. (185)

32. Tavormina, 230.

The narrator's benediction on these two sisters' choices brings the incident and the chapter to an end with "Amen."

The quilt Nettie shows Corrine becomes a vehicle to wider issues of connection than marital relations. The quilt encapsulates the past, "using the clothes the children had outgrown, and some of her old dresses" (170), and through the remaking of that history, also makes sense of the present, helping Corrine to be reconciled to Nettie, Samuel and her adopted children before she dies, and thus allowing for possibility of marriage between Nettie and Samuel in the future. Corrine's quilt, then, connects past, present, and future.

Celie has a similar experience of time connection when she works on a later quilt. As she sews, Celie has a vision of herself sitting between Albert and Shug, quilting, a dream that will come true by the end of the novel, but at the moment of her dreaming forms no more than an idea. Yet merely imagining such a reunion is revitalizing. As Celie says, "For the first time in my life, I feel just right" (61).

Quilting also connects two black cultures, as we see in Corrine's quilt, with its alternating blocks of African and American designs:

> Corrine's quilt is an icon dense with history—personal, familial, artistic, national, racial, human—and with union and reunion. It brings together differences without denying them or subjugating one to another—here a flowered square, there a checkered bird. Like the full set of both Celie's and Nettie's letters, it preserves, juxtaposes, and connects; it creates a meaningful, functional beauty out of a variety that admits both pain and happiness.[33]

Like Celie's quilts, Corrine's is a revision and rewriting of both personal and social history.

As a novel, *The Color Purple* represents a revision and rewriting of literary history. Walker reinterprets the authority implicit in the traditional canon as well as the controlling role of the author. By writing the novel as a series of letters, Walker participates in the major literary tradition of the epistolary novel and, in particular, subverts the first novel in that tradition, Richardson's *Clarissa,* a story of another woman who, much like Celie, is abducted and raped. There are some significant similarities and differences between these two novels. Clarissa's story concludes with a rape; Celie's begins with it. What for Clarissa is the end of her world, metaphorically and literally, is the beginning for Celie. Rape destroys Clarissa, but the same act of abuse catalyzes Celie into writing. Both Clarissa and Celie take up letter writing as a way to come to terms with a painful and chaotic world, because, as Terry Castle notes, letter writing is a way to inscribe oneself into meaning. However, Clarissa's letters are constantly obstructed, interpreted, and condemned by other characters. Terry Castle reads *Clarissa* as a tragedy precisely because her

33. Ibid., 227.

words bear no authority: "The excruciating situation *Clarissa* dramatizes is that a rhetorical system is *not* 'powerful' unless grounded in political power. Clarissa's 'story' everywhere lacks force. Hence it remains a fragmentary, futile utterance subject to the radical incursions of a more potent collective rhetoric—the patriarchal discourse of the Harlowes and Lovelace."[34] This would seem to echo Celie's situation. Her letters are addressed to those who cannot answer her, first God and then the supposedly dead Nettie. The letters drop into a void as damaging to their authority as the undermining criticism *Clarissa* receives. Any positive response, in the form of Nettie's replies, is suppressed by Mr.—. But Celie has support that Clarissa did not, that of other women. Shug helps her to claim her sister's letters and thus begin a correspondence that will strengthen her and the bond she feels with Nettie. Revising the fiction of the "fathers" of the English novel, *The Color Purple* stands as a black, feminocentric *Clarissa*, which ends not with the death but with the rebirth of its female protagonist.

Clarissa's voice is censored by her author, who organizes her life into seduction and death. Walker, however, subverts the author's traditional role as controller to create a more reciprocal relationship with her characters. She gives up her dominance in the role of author by acknowledging in the epigraph that some other power, "the spirit," was necessary for both the book and herself to be written. By ending the text with thanks to "everybody in this book for coming," she becomes the self-named medium rather than the controlling author. Walker recognizes that both she, as author, and Celie, as character, are the readers, writers, and, therefore, also the creators of their own lives.

Celie speaks, if haltingly, with her own voice. The novel validates a marginal form of English in Celie's black vernacular, at the same time validating Celie as a person. She speaks her own truth with her own vital language in a way that acts as an example of what Irigaray calls women's "style or writing": "This 'style,' or 'writing,' of women . . . does not privilege sight; instead, it takes each figure back to its source, which is among other things *tactile*. . . . It is always *fluid*, without neglecting the characteristics of fluids that are difficult to idealize: those rubbings between two infinitely near neighbors that create a dynamics" (79). Textmaking and quilting are not far apart. Irigaray's description of women's writing, with its emphasis on the tactile, and the connection of pieces as whole-and-still-pieces depicts quilt construction as well as Celie's form of expression.

Quiltmaking, then, acts as a paradigm for how Celie goes about reinscribing her life. What begins with quilting messed up curtains culminates in facing up to Mr.—. Celie takes all the pieces of information that haven't been acknowledged before and pulls them together into a whole that adds up to this (con)summation: "You a lowdown dog is what's wrong, I say. It's time to leave

---

34. *Clarissa's Ciphers: Meaning and Disruption in Richardson's "Clarissa,"* 25.

you and enter into the Creation" (181). Creation, of course, is also self-creation. When she examines her life, her fragments are parallel in worth to those cast-off curtains: "I'm pore, I'm black, I may be ugly and can't cook, a voice say to everything listening. But I'm here" (187). That last affirmation is the whole that those pieces are sewn into. Cixous sums up the process in "The Laugh of the Medusa": "If she [woman] is a whole, it's a whole composed of parts that are wholes, not simple partial objects but a moving, limitlessly changing ensemble, a cosmos tirelessly traversed by Eros, an immense astral space not organized around any one sun that's any more of a star than the others" (317). This flexible, ever-changing "whole" is always also pieces. When the patchwork quilt is complete, the pattern stands as a constant reminder that this whole is constituted of many fragments.

Although the novel is primarily concerned with Celie's individual move from fragmentation to wholeness, that change marks a shift in social relations. Unlike the traditional patriarchy, which puts a price on everything and wishes to own not only things but people, the quilt that Celie and Sofia make belongs to neither and to both of them. Jointly made, the process of making the quilt becomes more important than who eventually owns it. In an act of love, Celie gives the quilt to Sofia when she leaves Harpo, for, Celie comments, "I don't know what her sister place be like, but we been having right smart cold weather long in now. For all I know, she and the children have to sleep on the floor" (69). The quilt represents a new kind of commodity: not the greedy possession that maintains the autonomous "self," but the open-handed giving as one woman considers her sister's particular needs.

This renunciation of singular ownership is extended to family relations, in terms of how Albert, Celie, and Shug relate to each other at the end of the novel. They live as an undefined but loving family of three, having created the space that allows them to give and take love freely. A sign of Celie's success in that process of self-creation is her ability to incorporate Albert back into her life. Exclusion is a characteristic of the traditional male model of autonomy, a model that no longer works for Celie. Ironically, when the characters replace owning with sharing, they find that they own everything they want. Celie has a house, a store, the love of Albert and Shug, and eventually her children— significantly referred to as "our children"—as well (250). The habit of *femmage*, creating relations between fragments, has become a way of life for Celie by the end of the novel for it has been and continues to be her way to empowerment:

> Me and him and Shug sitting out on the porch after dinner. Talking. Not talking. Rocking and fanning flies. Shug mention she don't want to sing in public no more—well, maybe a night or two at Harpo's. Think maybe she retire. Albert say he want her to try on his new shirt. I talk about Henrietta. Sofia. My garden and the store. How things doing generally. So much in the habit of sewing something I stitch up a bunch of scraps, try to see what I can make. (249)

What she is making is her own life. Celie's struggle is more dramatic than most women's experience, but her journey is a familiar one. All of us in academia, especially those involved in feminist studies, are quiltmakers, making a space for ourselves in order to gather up our fragments into the construction of a pattern to our own liking. Cheryl Torsney elaborates:

> Multipatterned and multicolored, stitched by women and men from various racial and national cultures with various critical predispositions, the feminist critical practice forms a sort of critical quilt, an alternative to the critical methods of the past. Moreover, like a pieced quilt, feminist literary criticism is clearly meant for everyday use, in readings of all genres in all periods.[35]

Diversity and fragmentation become not a limitation but a trademark, a strength, a defining characteristic of feminist critical theory. Like Celie, we are getting in the habit of stitching up a bunch of scraps to see what we can make.

35. "The Critical Quilt: Alternative Authority in Feminist Criticism," 191.

Fabricating a Reading of
◆ Toni Morrison's *Beloved* as a ◆
Quilt of Memory and Identity

Cathy Peppers

[White middle class] Feminism's double bind is that it cannot speak "for" other women, nor can it speak "without" or "apart from" other women.
Elizabeth Meese, *(Ex)Tensions: Refiguring Feminist Criticism*

What is questionable [about the post-structuralist/postmodern project] is that it is a project that dismantles notions of authorship (Barthes), notions of tradition (Foucault) and notions of subjectivity (Lacan) during a period when blacks, feminists and other marginalized groups are asserting authorship, tradition and subjectivity.

Mae Henderson, "The State of Our Art"

For over a decade now, feminists of color have been challenging white feminists to dismantle racist assumptions that have caused them to elide differences between women in the construction of a fictional monolithic identity for woman. In the face of the "double bind" Meese describes above, recent theoretical work has focused on strategies that, instead of colonizing "the difference of the other woman," seek to negotiate similarities and differences between the traditions and goals of culturally specific feminisms. At the same time, academic feminisms have been polarized around the "theory versus practice" debate prompted by what Barbara Christian calls "the race for theory." Feminists generally have resisted wholesale allegiance to deconstructionist/post-structuralist (in general, postmodern) theories for the reason Mae Henderson describes above; feminists of color are additionally critical of the way these European-based theories talk a good game about heterogeneity, the decentered (white male) subject, and "otherness" while rarely considering texts by artists of color.

It is not my intention here to reduce what is, in reality, a complex matrix of differences to a simple series of "essentialist attacks" on the "tradition of the canon." Among black feminists, such critics as Hortense Spillers, Patricia Hill Collins, and Mae Henderson are selectively appropriating ideas from various postmodern theorists to be incorporated into their Afrocentric theories; meanwhile, other black feminists, such as June Jordan, feel that postmodern theories are "an abject worshipping of European fathers . . . elitist . . . [and] obviously anti-democratic and proud of it."[1] The "theory vs. practice" debates among white feminists are also myriad; Elizabeth Meese's *Crossing the Double Cross* and *(Ex)Tensions* offer useful (though partisan—she's "pro-deconstruction") analyses of the conflicts. My brief representation of these contested notions about the uses of "theory" is designed to be indicative rather than exhaustive; my intention is to establish some sense of the conflicted location from which I, as a white academic feminist, will construct a reading of Toni Morrison's *Beloved*.

On the one hand, I believe that no critical practice is completely uninformed by theory, and I have found it useful to appropriate specific ideas from postmodernist discourse to enhance my own readings of texts. In particular, confronted with a text like *Beloved*, which is Morrison's reconstruction of an historical newspaper account about an ex-slave woman who murdered her child, I see how her novel participates in what Craig Owens sees as a project of postmodernism: this narrative is a radical critique of the master narrative of slavery (pun intended). On the other hand, I am leery of resting with the claim that Morrison's novel simply "deconstructs" the "legitimacy function" of this master narrative, pointing to the "melancholia" and "dispiriting effects of our culture's loss of mastery."[2] Obviously, Morrison's disruption of the hegemonic white male narrative of slavery is not "dispiriting" to black (or white) women (or men). In addition, like Barbara Christian and bell hooks, I feel that the language so often used by postmodern criticism is a "language rooted in the very master narratives it claims to challenge. If radical, postmodernist thinking is to have a transformative impact, then a critical break with the notion of 'authority' as 'mastery over' must not simply be a rhetorical device."[3] Unfortunately, in *Yearning*, hooks does not seem to offer an alternative language that would allow a reader of *Beloved* to usefully appropriate Owens's discussion of "postmodern narrative" and "indeterminancy" of meaning.

But I am mindful of Morrison's own suggestion that the critic "develop [a] theory of literature that truly accommodates Afro-American literature: one that is based on its culture, its history, and the artistic strategies the works employ to negotiate the world it inhabits."[4] And, I would add, a truly non-colonizing critical approach will also notice ways in which the analysis of an

1. "The State of Our Art," 24.
2. "The Discourse of Others: Feminists and Postmodernism," 58.
3. bell hooks, *Yearning: Race, Gender, and Cultural Politics*, 25.
4. "Unspeakable Things Unspoken: The Afro-American Presence in American Literature," 11.

African American text, in turn, changes any "mainstream" theoretical notions brought into play. Rather than insist on my own critical "mastery" over this text, my desire is to "create a space for the gifts of respect and reciprocity,"[5] where my reading of the text can consider its relation to other black women's texts, and where the text, in turn, can inform my own feminist theoretical practice.

Beloved is Morrison's most nontraditionally structured novel to date:[6] the nonlinear, fragmented narrative, told in a plurality of voices, emphasizes that the "truth" may be different at every telling; the level of discourse shifts to include sermon, black vernacular, and "literary" diction; the formal elements of character and sentence structure are disrupted. But each of these textual features points not toward postmodernist indeterminancy (read: indifference) and anomie, but toward a depth of meaning(s) and a sense of communal identity. Rather than see *Beloved* as a pastiche of fragments which add up to nothing, I would like to transform the language of postmodern discourse to account for an alternative aesthetic which can recognize a sense of feminine authority and tradition. As Sandra Gilbert and Susan Gubar explain, "feminine authority" is not marked by the same Bloomian anxiety and desire to rebel against the fathers that marks masculine authority, and that, I think, marks the postmodern "sons'" insistence upon an "anti-aesthetic" in relation to their modernist "fathers." Gilbert and Gubar offer an alternative perspective on this "family romance" by noting that "feminine authority" can also draw on a "maternal" tradition.[7] Within the world of traditional women's work, the cultural work of the theoretical *bricoleur,* who fashions meaning from the fragments of discourse at hand, finds powerful embodiment in the figure of the quiltmaker. However, because I live in a time and place where mass-produced "heirloom" quilts, for sale via mail-order catalogs or at department stores, are part of the home fashion industry's technology for constructing a desire for "instant heritage" in a primarily white affluent market, I need to turn back to bell hooks to find a more historically and culturally relevant representation of the aesthetics of quiltmaking.

In "Aesthetic Inheritances," hooks describes quiltmaking as one of the primary aesthetic activities used by rural black women to "negotiate the world" they inhabited (in a manner similar to the tradition of rural white women);

5. *(Ex)Tensions,* 35.

6. This article was in the process of publication when Toni Morrison published *Jazz,* and time constraints do not allow me to engage in any comparison of the two works. However, since my intention here is to attempt to construct an alternative aesthetic discourse for discussing *Beloved,* I would add that, if *Beloved* is not more "nontraditionally structured" than *Jazz,* at least the more recent novel's title provides its own reading aesthetic.

7. *The Madwoman in the Attic: The Woman Writer and the Nineteenth-Century Literary Imagination,* chap. 2.

what she describes is quiltmaking as a technology for the embodiment of lived experience: "Although she did not make story quilts, Baba [hooks's grandmother] believed that each quilt had its own narrative—a story that began from the moment she considered making a particular quilt. . . . To her mind these quilts were maps charting the course of our lives. They were history as life lived."[8] Morrison's recreation of the history of slavery is a fabrication of the untold "herstory" of female slave experience; she gives aesthetic form to the historical experience of black women, which has only recently begun to be documented, as in bell hooks' *Ain't I a Woman*. And, as Hortense Spillers shows in "Mama's Baby," to construct an adequate representation of female slaves, the "grammar of racism" needs to be transformed to account for the uniquely gendered/ungendered black maternal body.[9] In this sense, the fact that Morrison focuses her telling of the effects of slavery on the bodies of her characters reflects the aesthetics of quiltmaking, which often uses scraps of fabrics imprinted by the bodies who wore the clothing, and seems more relevant to the novel than the postmodern aesthetic's talk of a rather disembodied "difference."

In my reading of Morrison's novel, I focus on how the recurring image of Baby Suggs's quilt represents the changing relationship between Sethe and Denver and the larger black community. Denver and Sethe wrap themselves in, fondle, and add scraps to the quilt when they conjure up memories with which to construct a history of/for Beloved, and the quilt reflects the changing constructions of their own identities. The presence of the quilt in the novel also situates *Beloved* within a black feminist tradition that offers a corrective to white feminist practice. Alice Walker's story "Everyday Use," which also uses a grandma's quilts as a symbol of the daughter's connection to memory and identity, establishes an explicit argument between the assimilated daughter Dee's desire to possess the quilts as material commodities and the traditional daughter Maggie's intention "to put them to everyday use." Dee's fussing about hanging the "priceless" quilts on the wall speaks to the feminist critic's desire to divorce the aesthetic object from cultural tradition and ensconce it in her own museum of theories about female identity; it is the gesture of the colonizer. While for Dee (or the insensitive feminist critic) the quilts would serve only to fulfill the desire for "instant heritage" described above, they represent to Maggie her lived connection to her "heritage."[10] The white feminist critic is reminded that a reading of black female identity forged through "traditional" white (female) separatism (from men) would betray a respectful reciprocity by seeking to reconstruct the identity of the "other" woman in the image of the "same."

As an image in *Beloved*, we see the quilt for the first time when Sethe goes

8. *Yearning*, 120–21.
9. "Mama's Baby, Papa's Maybe: An American Grammar Book."
10. "Everyday Use," 57, 59.

down to the "keeping room" the morning after Paul D's arrival. The room and the quilt both belonged to Baby Suggs, and it is to her space that Sethe goes whenever she needs to "talk-think," to get maternal advice and comfort in times of change or confusion. This description of the quilt focuses first on its drabness, which matches the complete lack of color in the room as a whole, "except for two orange squares in [the] quilt" which, in contrast to the "blue . . . black, brown and gray" field, "looked wild—like life in the raw."[11] These two orange scraps are associated with Baby Suggs's final quest for color, the only mental pursuit in which she can find happiness after the white men "came into her yard" and provoked Sethe's killing of her baby. Throughout the novel, vivid colors come to stand for liveliness and hope, which in this scene are the emotions Paul D has awakened in Sethe. Conversely, "the two orange squares . . . signaled [to Sethe] how barren 124 really was" (39), indicating the isolation of Sethe and Denver from the rest of the black community. Already, in this one scene, Morrison has constructed a complex web of associations around the quilt, and the significance of this symbol is enhanced with the arrival of Beloved.

While she is bedridden, Beloved "seemed totally taken with those faded scraps of orange" in the quilt (54), and it is her attachment to the quilt, in addition to its association with Baby Suggs, that ties it even more clearly to its relationship with memories and constructions of identity. As a catalyst for memory herself, Beloved prompts Denver (and later Sethe) to feed her insatiable hunger for stories of Sethe's life. In one such scene, Denver and Beloved are in bed, and "the dark quilt with two orange patches was there with them" as Denver begins to tell Beloved the only story she likes to tell—that of her own birth. Previously, Denver's selfishness has kept her telling of this memory focused on her own pleasure as "star"; this time, however, "through Beloved," the memory is transformed as Denver is able to feel "how it must have felt to her mother." As Denver's "monologue" becomes a "duet," the sharing of her pleasure in remembering with Beloved allows her to connect both emotionally and bodily with her mother's legacy of strength. The imagery of Denver's bodily engagement with her past (she gives the memory "blood" and "a heartbeat") is intertwined with quilt imagery ("scraps" of memory), so that Denver is both creating a new sense of herself and transforming the quilt (which "was smelling like grass and feeling like hands" [78]).

Just before the scene of Denver's telling breaks to an unmediated narration of the rest of her birth story, the consciousness of Denver, Beloved, and Sethe blur into "she"; the blurring of subjectivities among the three women will grow more pronounced as more scraps of memory are added to the story quilt they are creating. Morrison seems to insist that both "truth" and individual "iden-

---

11. Toni Morrison, *Beloved*, 38. Hereafter citations will appear parenthetically in the text.

tity" can only be established in relational terms. Just as the full pattern of a quilt can only be seen in the relationship between individual scraps, so too can the true story at the center of the novel be known only through the three versions written in the center of the text from Schoolteacher's, Paul D's, and Sethe's points of view.

Morrison's remark in a videotaped interview that "only artists can deal with [the story of] slavery" causes us to consider her "anthropological" intent in retelling a "true" story as anthropology with a difference:[12] the "objective" telling of Beloved's murder from Schoolteacher's point of view reads like the original newspaper article must in its objectification of the "crazy nigger woman and her pickaninnies" (148–53). Schoolteacher's story, which tells the "lesson" of what comes of "mishandling animals," might be seen as the bare backing for the quilt of Morrison's refabrication. Immediately after it, Paul D's confrontation with the event, as recounted in the article Stamp Paid shows him, is a tale of denial (154–58). But his "sweet conviction" that Sethe did not kill her child is shattered by Sethe's own method of telling. By "spinning" around the room and the subject, her telling insists that the "truth" of the event has nothing to do with the "black scratches" of the newspaper account, that the words "hadn't any more power than she had to explain," and therefore can neither be understood or denied on "rational" terms: "Sethe knew that the circle she was making around the room, him, the subject, would remain one. That she could never close in, pin it down for anybody who had to ask. If they didn't get it right off—she could never explain" (155, 161, 163).

Instead, Sethe's story must be understood in relation to her pride in "getting them [her children] all out [of slavery]," her "deep and wide love" for her children, which could only exist outside slavery, even in relation to the objects in her kitchen which also serve as scraps for memories (159–65). Unfortunately, Paul D cannot understand this "transformed grammar of slavery" as it is written on a woman's body. As a black man, he feels her "love is too thick" because embodied—"what she meant could cleave the bone" (164)—so he reduces her identity to that of an animal: "'What you did was wrong, Sethe. . . . You got two feet . . . not four'" (165). Paul D's harsh judgement of Sethe's action rips away the complex fabric of contexts and motivations that, from Sethe's and the novel's point of view, must be added to the bare plot of what happened in the woodshed if the event is to have any real meaning. When Paul D ignores all this, he reduces Sethe as Schoolteacher did, putting her "characteristics on the animal side of the paper."

The reading lesson we might take from these contrasting versions of Sethe's story might seem to be the familiar postmodern one: Sethe's "discourse of the Other" has clearly disrupted/deconstructed Schoolteacher's master narrative

---

12. *Toni Morrison.*

about the inherent animality of blacks, which supports the logic of slavery, as well as the alternative white abolitionist narrative constructed by Edward Bodwin, who used Sethe's "infanticide" to "build a further case for abolishing slavery" (260) when he freed her from jail. And, as a white feminist reader, I am tempted to say good riddance to Paul D, whose own narrative about surviving slavery—that it is better to burn like Sixo than to be reduced to something less than human—ends up being complicit with Schoolteacher's assessment of Sethe. But Morrison's novel is not only about deconstructing such master narratives and fragmenting Truth, is not about constructing an "anti-aesthetic." As the frontispiece (an image of a memorial stone), the dedication (to the "Sixty Million and more" victims of the African diaspora), and the haunting presence of Beloved herself all attest to, this is also a novel about "re-memory," about re-collecting the scattered scraps of Sethe's story and identity. From the perspective of Morrison's alternative aesthetic, the aesthetic of quiltmaking, we might view the function of this section as a session of seam ripping and cutting, which will be followed by a new piecing together of Sethe's identity.

As we saw earlier in the scene between Denver and Beloved, this novel's alternative pattern for individual identity will be a rewriting of the traditional Freudian "family romance." But while the construction of Sethe's identity will not be achieved by the usual Oedipal separation from the mother (which Freud assumed daughters must also undergo, although his primary model was the mother-son relationship), neither does the novel work toward the achievement of a poststructuralist version of decentered identity. Rather, with Paul D out of the house, the text constructs an almost utopian scene of pre-Oedipal mother-daughter symbiosis in the poetic "monologues" of Sethe, Denver, and Beloved, which follow shortly after the tellings of the "Misery."

As each character constructs her identity in shifting mother-daughter relations to each other, the language begins to set up a representation of what Jessica Benjamin calls "intersubjective desire," where "the interior of the body and the space between bodies form an elusive pattern, a plane whose edge is ever shifting," which can allow for both "recognition in and by the exciting other, and the holding that allows the self to experience desire as truly inner."[13] Each character begins her monologue by establishing her relation to Beloved—"Beloved, she my daughter"; "Beloved is my sister"; "I am Beloved and she is mine" (200, 205, 210)—primarily in terms of possessing the other that allows the self a new sense of presence, as when Sethe says, "Now I can look at things again because she's here to see them too" (201). Then, as Sethe begins to piece together her relationship to her own mother, which she will continue to do as she tells more stories to Beloved through the rest of the

13. "A Desire of One's Own: Psychoanalytic Feminism and Intersubjective Space," 94–96.

novel, the possession of (the) Beloved shifts to include possession by (the) Beloved: "and when I tell you you mine, I also mean I'm yours" (203). Rather than achieving an identity through a desire for individuation, the "she is mine" refrain in all three monologues emphasizes the intersubjective nature of their constructions of self; none can completely represent her identity without relation to (the) Beloved (other), and in Beloved's case, to Sethe—the (m)other.

This intersubjective desire, which psychoanalytic feminist theorists, such as Benjamin and Nancy Chodorow, claim is a desire to recreate an originary pre-Oedipal relation with the mother, is strong in Sethe's monologue, a bit weakened in Denver's (whose construction of self is also marked by a desire for the return of a father she never knew), and finds its fullest expression in Beloved's monologue, where the syntax itself is further wrenched away from prose into poetry: "I am not separate from her / there is no place where I stop / her face is my own and I want to be there in the place where her face is and to be looking at it too" (210). Beloved's language of desire pushes toward an identity of complete pre-Oedipal merging ("I want to join" [214]), even as it pushes the text toward the final section of these monologues, the "poem," where all three characters' voices of longing are stitched together.

This section begins with Beloved's association of the flowers being picked by the woman (a maternal figure now named as Sethe) with the patches of color in the quilt (214), and moves through two stanzas that appear to represent dialogues between Sethe and Beloved and Denver and Beloved. From there, the poem moves to a complete blurring of subjectivities in unassigned dialogue, representing a kind of song of what Nancy Chodorow would call "permeable ego boundaries" between mother and daughter(s):[14]

Beloved
You are my sister
You are my daughter
You are my face; you are me
I have found you again; you have come back to me
You are my Beloved
You are mine
You are mine
You are mine

. . . .
You are my face; I am you. Why did you leave me who am you?
. . . .
You are mine
You are mine
You are mine (216–7)

14. See Elizabeth Abel, "(E)Merging Identities: The Dynamics of Female Friendship in Contemporary Fiction by Women," 417.

Since Paul D is now out of the house, the three women are free to inhabit a seemingly utopian space of pre-Oedipal union, as is reflected in this chant of desire.

Yet here, again, the text resists any white feminist's imposition of separatist notions about "female" identity. Although the utopia constructed in this poem pleasurably disrupts subject-object boundaries, allowing "I" and "you" to slide into each other, there is no room here for any distinctions among the identities of the three women, nor for any consideration about the material realities of how they will maintain this utopia. In particular, such a pre-Oedipal symbiosis is achieved only at the cost of excluding both Denver's desire for her father and the presence of Paul D, as the novel reminds us by turning to a description of his isolated life of drunken paralysis after leaving Sethe's house. Similarly, the tendency of white feminist critics to privilege a nostalgic notion of pre-Oedipal symbiosis as the origin of female identity should be critiqued as separatist; as Alice Walker might note, this is the difference between (white) feminist and "womanist" ideas about "healthy" identity. To Walker, a "womanist" is a woman who is "committed to survival and wholeness of entire people, male *and* female. Not a separatist, except periodically, for health."[15] So, though the piecing together of Sethe, Denver, and Beloved's identities may begin in the isolation of a "separate sphere" where such women's work has traditionally been done, the finished quilt will not achieve its full aesthetic purpose until it is put to "everyday use," and the women are reconnected to their community. While Elizabeth Abel's application of pre-Oedipal symbiosis as a primarily female dynamic in her "(E)Merging Identities" is seductive, readers must also be aware of how her reading, for example, of the relationship between Nel and Sula in Morrison's *Sula*, constructs "female identity" out of context. To apply a theory of the origins of identity that rests on essentialist notions of "female," "mother," and "daughter" to a novel in which each of these constructions is marked physically and psychologically by the historical narrative of slavery would be like appreciating the surface beauty of a quilt without including a sense of the lived stories of the separate pieces of fabric.

Sethe, Denver, and Beloved have desired nothing more than to be alone with each other, and the merging of their memories has enabled them to strengthen their sense of meaningful identity; but by the beginning of part 3, the utopia of their isolation has become a dystopia. On the surface, Sethe dresses them in flashy clothes to reflect the new liveliness in the house; Sethe has lost her job and spends their "life savings" to "decorate themselves with ribbon and dress goods, which Sethe cut and sewed" into "bright clothes—with blue stripes and sassy prints . . . [and] yellow ribbon, shiny buttons and bits of black lace" (240). But the color is too much; they look like "carnival women," and the excess is reminiscent of Baby Suggs's axiom that "good is knowing when to stop" (87).

15. *In Search of Our Mothers' Gardens*, xi.

Though Sethe attempts to represent the hopefulness of their mother-daughter(s) union in the bright colors of the clothes she sews, the dresses, unlike Baby Suggs's quilt, are in no way connected to their lived histories, are paid for by money they cannot afford to spend, and in fact are fabricated as "decoration," which mocks the "everyday use" to which they are put.

Though Sethe and Beloved also work at "tacking scraps of cloth on Baby Suggs' old quilt" as they continue to tell each other their memories, "the mood changed," and most of their new relationship, which is marked by Beloved's accusations of abandonment and Sethe's abject apologizing and justifying, is expressed in Sethe's attempt to make it up to Beloved by giving her the best of the food, ribbons, and other tokens. Their relationship moves toward complete fulfillment of mother-daughter merging, separating them not only from the rest of the community, but also from the context of their histories embodied in the quilt, and even from Denver. As Beloved "becomes" Sethe— "talk[ing] the way she did, laugh[ing] her laugh and us[ing] her body the same way down to the walk," even in the end becoming pregnant and larger/the mother—Sethe begins to become more like Beloved/the daughter, shrinking from starvation and deferring to Beloved's desires, until "it was difficult for Denver to tell who was who" (241). Finally, their symbiotic possession of each other has left no room for individual identity. This is the lesson of Morrison's critique of privileging a fantasy of the pre-Oedipal mother-daughter bond: while the scraps on a quilt gain meaning in relation with each other, each scrap must still remain distinct.

Denver senses the destructiveness of Sethe's and Beloved's stifling "love that wore everybody out" when she is rejected from their intimacy; as she sees it, their relationship "worked with three—not two" (243). Two scraps of color on a quilt are not enough to erase barrenness; they only enhance it. In order to save them from starving and to continue the healing process of piecing together their identities, Denver must leave the isolated mother-daughter pair and reconnect with the larger community. The contrast between three and two seems to imply that three people may create a stable triangle on which to build relations to others. Certainly, as the narrative moves toward bringing the rest of the community into confrontation with the isolated pair, the number three is associated with the decisions and motives of the community. Morrison offers three possible reasons for the town's letting go of their grudge against the pride at 124 (249); the women who gossip about the situation at 124 fall into "three groups" of opinion (225); there are thirty women who converge on 124 at three in the afternoon for the exorcism of Beloved, and three reasons are offered for why some women don't come (257). While Sethe and Beloved are locked in a duality of either/or choices—revenge/forgiveness, domination/sacrifice, merging/separation—the community of plurality built to include the third terms of compromise, judgement, and action insists on the necessity of a wider field of relations.

By the end of the novel, the sorry, barren quilt with only two patches of orange has become a "quilt of merry colors" (271). The brightness of the quilt suggests that ambiguity has been stitched into it as well. While Sethe and Denver have been reintegrated into the community to participate in the larger pattern of life, they also, like the quilt itself, will continue to bear the traces of Beloved's presence. And Beloved, whose status is marked by her presence as a red light at the beginning of the novel and her absence, which Paul D must still work "to get through," at the end (270), whose identity confounds the dualities of ghost/flesh, daughter/mother, individual/a whole people (the "sixty million and more"), is the very function of ambiguity in this text, which closes with an epigrammatic prose poem on the necessity of forgetting/remembering.

As Sethe, whom Ella has formerly "junked" because she "lived as though she were alone" (256), is stitched back into relation with the (primarily female) community, the novel (and readers) must also move to include Paul D, adding a "fourth" term to the "triangle" described above. When Paul D corrects Sethe's question, "[Will you] count my feet?" by offering to "rub [her] feet," thereby rejecting his earlier objectification of her as an animal, I am reminded that the original scraps on the quilt were squares. Paul D "examines the quilt patched in carnival colors" in the final scene, and, as if in response to its invitation (however ambiguously coded), decides "he wants to put his story next to [Sethe's]." Remembering Sixo's description of his relationship with the Thirty-Mile Woman, Paul D realizes that Sethe will be able to "gather" the "pieces" of his fragmented sense of self, and "give them back . . . in all the right order." In turn, when he emphasizes the value of Sethe's identity as her own "best thing," the fragmentation of the novel resolves itself into a healing pattern that began with a house possessed and ends with Sethe's possession of self (272–3). The "truth" of the "Misery" and the histories of the characters' lives have been filled in to a rich perspective.

Like a quilt, *Beloved*'s narration is a patchwork of scraps of memory that contains the remnants of lived, bodily experience. Like a quilt, the scraps of memory are stitched together by recurring voices, images, and phrases, so that the aesthetic effect of the whole is greater than the sum of its parts. Like a quilt, this text is designed to be used, to bring comfort; as a metaphor for the novel as a whole, the quilt in *Beloved* stands for a "spiritual process . . . a form of meditation . . . a work which renew[s] the spirit."[16] As a reader, I have had to piece together the scraps of memory along with the characters. Although I do not feel as if I possess the full pattern in its entirety, I have participated in a text that, to paraphrase bell hooks, is not a "story quilt" (traditional narrative) but a quilt that tells a story. As with a quilt, I have had to fabricate my reading of this text with scraps from a variety of sources. I began my initial reading with one scrap, the image of the quilt, but the entire pattern of my reciprocal

16. hooks, *Yearning*, 116.

reading was not complete until I could stitch that scrap to a sturdy backing of theoretical practice.

What I have discovered is a renewed sense of the importance and power of the explanatory metaphor a reader chooses. There is not only an aesthetic but an ethic built into any examination of storytelling. Just as Paul D's temporary judgement of Sethe's action as animalistic causes him to become somewhat animalistic himself in his drunken life away from Sethe, so too must a reader be aware of the reciprocal effects of naming. While I cannot ignore my own history of being situated within academic postmodern and white feminist discourses, I can at least offer an alternative language for "postmodern" criticism, one that, derived from the "feminine" aesthetics of quiltmaking, is not allergic to notions of identity and heritage. At the same time, I have had to let this novel teach me how to critique essentialist notions about female identity by paying attention to culturally specific contexts in order to avoid an easy commodification of the "other woman's" identity. In this way, I have attempted to put the quilt that is *Beloved* to "everyday use," allowing its "reading lesson" to help me fabricate a sense of aesthetics in relation to contemporary debates within postmodern, black, and feminist theories.

◆ Butor's Scissor Marks ◆
Quilts and Origins in Mobile
Page R. Laws

Ce "Mobile" est composé un peu comme un "quilt."

Michel Butor, *Mobile*

American feminist writers and critics of the past two decades have appropriated the quilt as the privileged metaphor for a movement. So useful and pervasive is the quilting trope in literature (as in Alice Walker's *Meridian, The Color Purple* and "Everyday Use") and criticism (as in Elaine Showalter's "Piecing and Writing" found in *The Poetics of Gender*), that a feminist flag of the seventies and eighties would surely have fluttered with patches rather than those old patriarchal—apologies to Betsy Ross—stars and stripes. It is all the more noteworthy, therefore, to revisit the work of a French man, circa 1962, who wrapped himself and his still controversial book in the most cherished symbol of American feminism.

Michel Butor, along with Alain Robbe-Grillet, is, of course, the best known of the French *nouveau romanciers* who produced their genre–exposing/imploding novels during the 1950s. Challenging the ontological status of fiction, Butor's early works included *L'emploi du temps* (1956, a detective story revolving around a stained glass window *mise en abyme*); *La modification* (1957, written entirely in the second person); and *Degrés* (1960, about a school class studying the New World). *Mobile,* subtitled *Étude pour une représentation des États-Unis,* is Butor's most thorough (though not his only) treatment of the America theme, a venerable topic for traveling Europeans, dating back to Tocqueville. *Mobile* is based, in part, on Butor's own experience in the United States as a peripatetic visiting scholar. It bears little relation in form, however, to any other European America novels and is generally relegated to the even more

My sincere thanks to Robert Shaw, curator of the Shelburne Museum, Shelburne, Vermont, for tracking down a copy of *Pieced Work and Appliqué Quilts at Shelburne Museum,* the catalog Butor used. Thanks also to my research assistant Kris Long. Photographs reproduced in this essay are by Ken Burris and are used courtesy of the Shelburne Museum, Shelburne, Vermont.

avant garde phase of Butor's later career called the *nouveau nouveau roman* or Romanesque II.[1]

A truly thorough description of *Mobile* would fill this volume as it has dozens of critical articles and interviews written over the past thirty years.[2] Suffice it to say that *Mobile* is an enormously complex quiltlike book composed of old cloth and new. It takes the form of an imaginary journey (or many journeys) through the fifty states, which have been arranged in French alphabetical order.[3] The traveler(s) is anonymous, perhaps the reader himself or herself. The Erzählte Zeit is forty-eight hours, with night and day influencing what can and cannot be seen. Place names (Butor is especially interested in ones of European origin) are one key thread in the rhythmic ever-moving design. Interspersed with these names are lists of cars, with colors based on ice cream flavors; flora and birds, arranged into arrow-shaped ideogrammatic poems;[4] a sea poem, arranged in a wave pattern; plus the ongoing dreams of a southern white couple, obsessed with black sexuality and racial guilt. These are the main pieces of Butor's new cloth (his original written-for-*Mobile* material). Interspersed with these patches, however, are bits of old cloth (borrowed materials). They include citations from Thomas Jefferson's *Notes on the State of Virginia* "maliciously" selected, as Butor himself readily admits, to show Jefferson's racism.[5] They also include citations from Benjamin Franklin, Andrew Carnegie, William Penn, Indian historians, historians of the Salem witch trials, plus catalogs (Sears, Roebuck & Company) and promotional brochures. All these disparate items—and more—are stitched together by Butor according to self-imposed content/design rules that are far more strict than is immediately apparent. Butor has had to explain his rules in interviews that followed some

1. Michelle Rogers, "Interview avec Michel Butor," 511. Butor credits Jean Ricardou with the nouveau nouveau roman rubric. Butor leaves such labeling to the scholars: "Pour moi maintenant ce sont les professeurs qui s'occupent de cela." Ricardou is the author of "La Fiction Flamboyante," 210–28.

2. Other seminal critical essays on Butor include Roland Barthes's "Littérature et discontinu," 817–29; Georges Charbonnier's book *Entretiens avec Michel Butor* (1967); Georges Raillard's *Butor* (1968); Jean Roudaut's "Parenthèse sur la Place Occupée par l'Étude Intitulée '6 810 000 litres d'eau par seconde' parmi les autres Ouvrages de Michel Butor"; Léon Roudiez's "Gloses sur les premières pages de *Mobile* de Michel Butor," (1972); Roudiez's book *Michel Butor* (1965), and F. C. St. Aubyn's "Michel Butor's America" (1964). These and other essays, plus *Mobile* as a whole, are more fully discussed in "*Mobile:* A Quilt of Guilt," a chapter of my dissertation entitled *Mythic Images of America: Four Recent European Novels.* Slightly more recent books on Butor include Mary Lydon's *Perpetuum Mobile: A Study of the Novels and Aesthetics of Michel Butor* (1980) and Marianne Hirsch's *Beyond the Single Vision: Henry James, Michel Butor, Uwe Johnson* (1981).

3. See above and also F. C. St. Aubyn, "À propos de *Mobile*. Deuxième entretien avec Michel Butor," 427–28.

4. Seda A. Chavdarian, "Images of Chaos in Butor's *Mobile, 6 810 000 litres d'eau par seconde*, and *Où*," 50.

5. St. Aubyn, "Deuxième entretien," 436–37.

initial attacks on the work as unreadable. One set of these guidelines involved the homonymical place names. When Butor mentions one of this country's several towns named ARLINGTON, for example, he can then mention another ARLINGTON (*sic,* the place names are always in capitals) in a contiguous state. Once he mentions it in that second state, he can mention it in all states contiguous to that second state, and so on. Certain elements always appear in 10-point roman type, others always in 10-point italics, with or without quotation marks.[6] Certain elements always appear in the far left margin, certain ones indented to a second margin, certain ones at a third marginal stop, etc. The location of a place name relative to the state being currently visited can (with the aid of a map and great effort) be determined by which marginal stop has been used. Only the recto pages are numbered, encouraging the reader to see both verso and recto as a visual whole. Roland Barthes, an early defender of *Mobile,* best explained the total effect of all these visual cues when he said that the ideas in *Mobile* are not developed but "distributed."[7] Butor dedicates the volume not, as one might expect, to Calder, but instead to Jackson Pollack, a "distributer" of paint onto canvas.[8]

The analogy with the graphic arts is clear, as is Butor's kinship to composers of polyphonic music.[9] In interviews, Butor has mentioned other analogies: the book is inspired by aerial views of patchwork fields; it is like the dots that make up the image on a T.V. screen.[10] However, Butor's analogy with the quilt is by far the most helpful and privileged above all the others by being mentioned explicitly in the text of *Mobile* itself: "*Ce 'Mobile' est composé un peu comme un 'quilt'*" (29). Nowhere else in the book does Butor step out authorially and speak reflexively about the work itself. If this peculiar fact were not enough to convince one of the essential importance of the quilt metaphor to this French writer, the remaining three mentions of quilting within the text would. For the quilt (singular) is not only a true object *mise en abyme* by the author to pedagogically mirror a work so difficult to understand, but quilts (plural) are also an important content element. Butor has "borrowed" the description of three specific quilts he saw in a Shelburne, Vermont, museum from a catalog of the collection and interspersed said descriptions in the text itself. While many critics have made mention of the quilt metaphor in *Mobile* and alluded to the

6. Judith D. Suther, "Apology for *Mobile,*" 57.

7. Ibid., 58.

8. Ibid.; F. C. St. Aubyn, "Entretien avec Michel Butor."

9. Butor subtitled his book *6,810,000 litres d'eau par seconde* (1965) an "étude stéréophonique" to make the music analogy clear in that work. Few critics can speak of Butor's works without resorting to analogies of one kind or another, an activity encouraged by Butor's own remarks about the kinship of the various arts. For analogies with the visual arts, see especially Léon Roudiez's "Michel Butor: Text and Graphics" (1985). Butor's many works since *Mobile* have moved even further towards a fusion of art forms.

10. Raillard, *Butor,* 198.

quilt passages,[11] no one, to my knowledge, has yet discussed the origin of the borrowed passages or Butor's translation and selection process. Thanks to the discovery of the out-of-print 1957 Shelburne Museum catalog Butor must have used as his source, it is for the first time possible to study the method he used to "cut out" the passages in question. Butor has left, figuratively speaking, scissor marks on the old bolt of cloth (the original catalog) he used. What one sees by close study of said marks (that is, by studying the changes he made when translating the original material for inclusion in *Mobile*) is eminently revealing of the Butorian process. We see, in effect, the quilter in the earliest stages of his craft—selecting and cutting away patches from the old cloth.

It is interesting to note in advance that the old Shelburne catalog in question, *Pieced Work and Appliqué Quilts at Shelburne Museum*,[12] was written by a woman, Lilian Baker Carlisle, whose name is clearly given on the frontispiece. Butor never mentions Carlisle's name, leading one to assume that he places the catalog on a different plane of importance than the works of Jefferson, Carnegie, and Franklin. This is in some ways understandable and defensible while in other ways not. Carlisle is obviously not so famous as the gentlemen just mentioned, nor is she singled out as a woman for omission. (Butor borrows many other undocumented materials—some surely by men—without stating their authors.) While Butor's credit-giving procedures may leave something to be desired, this is, after all, not a scholarly work. Butor is not an out-and-out plagiarist in the cavalier tradition of, say, Bertolt Brecht cribbing from Kipling. Butor stands closer to Thomas Mann, silently borrowing from a Nietzsche biography in *Doktor Faustus*, but talking about it later as "montage." Butor's pronouncements on "collaborating" with previous authors toward his "Livre Futur"—a non-hierarchal Book of Books—have been public and clear.[13] No one expects each patch of a quilt to be brand new material; indeed the beauty of the art form lies in the recycling-of-memories idea. Before condemning Butor for sexism and/or plagiarism, it is perhaps best to see him in action, snipping and stitching away.

The first mention of a quilt in *Mobile* comes on page 29 in the chapter devoted to Connecticut. Butor has not yet started using the Shelburne catalog, but speaks—up until the direct authorial mention of *Mobile*—in the voice of an anonymous traveler: "Dans le village de Shelburne on a rebâti un certain nombre de maisons anciennes condamnées à la déstruction dans le Vermont,

11. Gamila Morcos, "*Mobile* de Butor: typographie et justification," 56–76. Morcos focuses on the quilt as an important object *mise en abyme* in *Mobile*, but Morcos also sees Freedomland as being roughly of the same importance. While I agree that Freedomland implicitly mirrors America as a whole (and therefore *Mobile*), I prefer to call Freedomland a microcosm of the U.S., saving the *mise en abyme* terminology for the quilt.

12. *Pieced Work and Appliqué Quilts at Shelburne Museum*.

13. For a discussion of Butor's "Livre Futur" vis à vis Mallarmé's concept of the Book, please see "*Mobile:* A Quilt of Guilt" above.

constituant ainsi un singulier musée. La partie la plus étonnante en est peut-être la collection de courtepointes, ou 'quilts', en mosaïque d'étoffes. Ce 'Mobile' est composé un peu comme un 'quilt'" (29).

The chief function of this passage is to establish the *mise en abyme* relationship between the Quilt and *Mobile.* Critic Gamila Morcos has pointed out that this pedagogical hint for the reader—"Think of this book as a quilt"—comes along at exactly the "moment clef."[14] We're far enough into the book to have some sense of what's going on and yet to be thoroughly baffled. Morcos cites the earlier French critic Lucien Dallenbach to explain the function of an object *mise en abyme:* "Cette réflexion du roman sur soi-même éclaire le romancier sur ses véritables intentions, et grace à la médiation d'oeuvres insérées, le romancier va être capable de prendre conscience et d'éclairer pour nous ce qu'il est en train de faire."[15] Morcos continues saying that for the analogy (here quilt: book) to be helpful, its meaning must be narrow and precise. *Mise en abyme* objects must function as "miroirs plus ou moins correctifs."[16]

Butor does more in this passage, however, than give us a modest-sounding ("*un peu" comme un quilt*) helpful hint. In the same offhand "I'm-only-a-visitor-here" tone, he introduces us to the Shelburne Museum as an American phenomenon which for him is surprising ("*singulier*" and "*étonnante*"). Any museum, be it as grand as the Louvre or as intimate as a Left Bank gallery, is a quiltlike construct of disparate individual art objects. But there's something uniquely American about Shelburne, something that smacks of our indifference to high-art/low-art distinctions. Butor mentions the old houses brought together to form Shelburne. What he doesn't mention, but seems to imply by his adjectives of surprise, is the incredibly hodgepodge (a disloyal American might even say "tacky") nature of a museum of Americana. Shelburne includes (and here I borrow from the Shelburne Museum brochure and visitor's guide) "37 period homes and historic structures," a lilac garden, a printing shop, a sawmill, the recreation of the "plush New York City apartment of J. Watson and Electra Webb," a carousel, a covered bridge, a locomotive, big game trophies, Native American artifacts, the SS *Ticonderoga* ("last vertical beam sidewheel steamship intact"), plus a "525-foot-long miniature circus parade." Electra Webb, who founded the museum in 1947, was the daughter of "Sugar King" H. O. Havemeyer, a collector of (of all things) French Impressionist art. Electra's first art acquisition, at age eighteen, was not, however, a Monet but a cigar store Indian. No wonder Butor found her museum "*singulier*"!

My guess is that Butor refrained from ironic description of the Shelburne out of respect for its "serious" art holdings, including the quilts. Butor also implicitly makes the point about our hodgepodge American tastes in the

14. "*Mobile* de Butor," 73.
15. Ibid.
16. Ibid.

Freedomland sections of *Mobile* and indeed throughout the book. The reason the Shelburne, Vermont, material on page 29 is located in a chapter on Connecticut is clear only if one knows Butor's intricate rules for the mentioning of place names. It so happens that none of the quilt material is found in the Vermont chapter itself.

The second mention of quilts in *Mobile* does not occur until 152 pages later, in the New Hampshire chapter. (After the mention on page 29 all remaining quilt material is directly from the Shelburne catalog.) The following shows the original entry and Butor's version:

Jacob's Ladder

This quilt design recalls the Biblical dream of the wandering Jacob who lay down on the ground with stones for his pillow and dreamed of a ladder which was "set up on earth, the top reaching to heaven, with angels of God ascending and descending."

The slanting chains in this design are made up of red calico patches printed with flower sprigs. The eighteen ladders are composed of the same design of calico, but here the squares are separated by plaid cotton triangles set off by white squares.

The large maple leaf sewed on one of the white blocks of this quilt is of interest for it demonstrates a quilting superstition of uncertain origin, but one probably inherited from the old Oriental conviction that only supreme gods could create perfection, and man was presumptuous to attempt to produce things without blemish or fault. With this superstition in mind and in order to avert punishment for her bold forwardness in trying to imitate the diety [*sic*], the early quilter sometimes deliberately spoiled the perfect symmetry of her design, thus averting evil and misfortune. Today this seems amusing, but we have a similar superstition of our own. We "knock on wood" after uttering vainglorious speech, and this irrational action is certainly akin to the old quilting superstition.

77 x 93 No. 182

Third quarter 19th century

(*Pieced Work and Appliqué Quilts at Shelburne Museum*)

Quilts du Shelburne Museum

No. 182: l'Échelle de Jacob:

"Le dessin de cette courtepointe rappelle le rêve de Jacob pendant son errance, qui s'étendit sur le sol avec un oreiller de pierre et rêva d'une échelle qui était 'dressée sur la terre, le sommet atteignant au ciel, avec les anges de Dieu qui montaient et qui descendaient' . . . La grande feuille d'érable cousue sur l'un des carrés blancs vient d'une superstition d'origine incertaine, mais probablement héritée de la croyance orientale que seuls les dieux suprêmes peuvent créer la perfection, et que l'homme serait présomptueux d'essayer de produire des oeuvres sans défaut. Afin d'éviter la punition de son audace en prétendant imiter la divinité, celle qui composait autrefois un quilt détruisait parfois délibérément la symétrie de son dessin, détournant ainsi le malheur." (181)

Jacob's Ladder

Butor's version begins with a heading that is an inexact (shortened) version of Carlisle's catalog title. He then gives the art object's catalog number and, after a colon, the individual quilt's title. (This number appears at the bottom of the original Carlisle entry.) Butor omits the dimensions of the quilt (also at the bottom in the original) but moves the object's number to a more prominent place, probably to assure that his readers get the "object-from-a-museum" idea. Butor's first paragraph, introduced by quotation marks, is a faithful word-for-word translation, down to the internal quotation marks around the Biblical portion. The quilt is nonnarrative; indeed it is the most geometric and nonrepresentational of Butor's three selections. Butor omits Carlisle's second paragraph, a description of the colors and material of the Jacob's Ladder piece. The third paragraph of the original is then included (without indentation on Butor's part) but rather loosely translated. Whereas the original says, "The large maple leaf sewed on one of the white blocks of this quilt is of interest for it demonstrates . . . ," Butor simply says "La grande feuille d'érable . . . vient d'une superstition." He apparently feels he doesn't need to tell the reader that something is interesting. While the original says "without blemish or fault," Butor elides the phrase to "sans défaut." He likewise elides "with this superstition in mind."

For Carlisle's "the early quilter," Butor writes "celle qui composait autrefois un quilt" echoing the verb "composer" from the first mention of quilting 152 pages back: "*Ce 'Mobile' est composé . . .*" (29). Again avoiding our Anglo-Saxon penchant for redundant pairs of words, Butor translates "evil and misfortune" as simply "le malheur." Left out entirely is Carlisle's excursus into how a modern mind might view the old quilting superstition: "Today this seems amusing, but we have a similar superstition of our own. We 'knock on wood' after uttering vainglorious speech, and this irrational action is certainly akin to the old quilting superstition." Butor evidently found this little analogy between one superstition and another either too cutely editorial on Carlisle's part or too obscurely idiomatic for French readers.

Butor, one suspects, does not find the old quilting superstition "amusing" at all. Indeed he takes the idea of purposeful asymmetry quite seriously as an element of the "open-ended" work of art. As critic Seda A. Chavdarian and others have pointed out, with the possible exception of "Le Froid à Zuni" in *Où: Le génie du lieu 2*—a highly symmetrical piece that's been likened to a geometric Indian weaving[17]—almost all of Butor's works are imperfect "failures" of one sort or another: "They all begin with a definite goal that disintegrates as we proceed and ends in apparent defeat. Yet this failure is always projected to be a positive experience."[18] What Chavdarian implies, and what I think is true, is that the typical Butorian work—no matter how carefully structured—contains intentional "crazy" patches or flaws. Since, for Butor, all books are merely phases of the Book (or *Livre Futur*) this always-in-process, nonhierarchical, composite work I mentioned before, then symmetry or "perfection" would be worse than an unwise challenge to the gods. It would be a betrayal of art.

The Jacob's Ladder quilt, created, according to the catalog, in the third quarter of the nineteenth century (Butor omits the date) was an anonymous work, executed, one assumes, according to a preexisting or traditional pattern (the Jacob's Ladder pattern). Butor assumes the quilter was a woman, as is shown by his choice of the pronoun "celle" in "celle qui composait autrefois un

17. Dean McWilliams, "Butor's American Texts: The Writer as Red Indian," 263.
18. "Images of Chaos," 49.

quilt." The eastern connection ("la croyance orientale") was probably also of interest to a Frenchman whose career has been built on drawing connections between world cultures (especially in his trilogy of works with "le génie du lieu" in their titles). The connection with the Orient is also implied by Butor's initial explanation of a quilt (back on page 29) as a "*mosaïque* (my emphasis) *d'étoffes*."

As for the thematic relevance of the "Jacob's Ladder" Bible story, Butor is clearly interested in the intense religiosity of many Americans, a theme throughout *Mobile* but most fully brought out in the Clifton's Cafeteria sections. (Clifton's serves up fundamentalism with its food.) In Butor's America, even the monks make and market a product (Trappist jams). What better place for a vision of angels going up and down a calico ladder linking heaven and earth?

The third mention of quilts is still in the New Hampshire chapter beginning on page 184 (not numbered) and continuing on 185. Here is the catalog description Butor "lifted," followed by his French rendition:

Civil War Counterpane
    This spread, illustrated and described in "American Quilts and Coverlets" by Florence Peto, was found in New Jersey and shows textiles much older than the Civil War period–chintzes, Scotch ginghams, paisley-patterned calicoes. Colors are soft browns, cream, blue, rose and dull reds. A homespun linen backing has been turned to face, the two edges have been folded in on each other and stitched together.
    Traditionally this counterpane was made by a Civil War veteran whose nerves had been shattered by his wartime experiences. After he was invalided home, he started this quilt as a therapeutic measure. He has used a variety of geometrical shapes, including squares, triangles, demi-circles, crescents and shaped eight-point cut-out stars. The two wide borders of pieced squares and triangles have been set off with small sharply pointed calico triangles. A rectangular white section depicts appliqued mounted soldiers grimly followed by marching infantrymen. The center square, enclosed by scallops, shows a diversity of forms. Here the foot soldier figure is repeated, but other appliqued forms have been added which make this portion of the spread of absorbing interest. A female figure offering refreshments (copied from the trademark of a well-known brand of chocolate, which in turn was adopted from a 1780 French painting called "La Chocolatière") appears in each of the four corners. There are fat, peaceful doves—symbol of femininity and conjugal felicity—and oak leaves, symbolic of continuing life and strength. But it is the hearts in the corners that tell the story. The heart was reserved for the bridal quilt, and one can surmise the rest of the love story the veteran has immortalized in his quilt. The foot soldier? Surely he was the war veteran who fashioned the spread. And the lovely lady with the tray? Was she not the sweetheart who nursed him back to health?
96 x 111 No. 10 Third quarter 19th century
(*Pieced Work and Appliqué Quilts at Shelburne Museum* 42–43)

Civil War Counterpane

Quilts du Shelburne Museum:

No. 10: la Guerre de Sécession:

"Cette courtepointe fut exécutée par un vétéran de la Guerre de Sécession, dont les nerfs avaient été ébranlés par ses expériences militaires. De retour, il entreprit cet ouvrage pour se guérir. Cadre en motifs géométriques: carrés, triangles, demi-cercles, croissants, étoiles à 8 branches . . . Une section rectangulaire, reprise 4 fois, contre des cavaliers sabre au clair, suivis de fantassins prêts à tirer. Dans le carré central, on retrouve ce fantassin 4 fois, mais il est accompagné de 4 figures féminines plus grandes que lui, apportant des rafraîchissements, copiées sur l'étiquette d'une marque de chocolat qui reproduisait la Chocolatière de Liotard. Au centre, une étoile à 8 branches. Faisant guirlande avec la Chocolatière autour du quadruple fantassin, des feuilles de chêne, symboles de virilité, des colombes grasses, des croissants de lune. Aux 4 coins de ce carré central, comme aux 4 coins des carrés aux 4 coins, autour d'autres étoiles à 8 branches accompagnées de croissants de lune, des coeurs, motif qui était réservé aux courtepointes de la nuit de noces." (184–85)

Butor begins with the same heading: "Quilts du Shelburne Museum." He follows his now established format, putting the number of the quilt and title right afterwards: "No 10: la Guerre de Sécession." But Carlisle's first paragraph is this time omitted, referring as it does to merely curatorial interests, such as the fact that the quilt has been included in another book, "was found in New Jersey" and was made of textiles "much older than the Civil War Period." These technical details obviously don't interest Butor. He goes straight for Carlisle's paragraph number two, which begins, "Traditionally this counterpane was made by a Civil War veteran." When Butor translates this line, however, he leaves out the element of doubt (the word *traditionally*) and states, as if it were a known fact, "*Cette courtepoint fut executée par un vétéran de la Guerre de Sécession, dont les nerfs avaient été ébranlés par ses expériences militaires.*" It is this idea of a man, a soldier no less, making a quilt that has undoubtedly drawn Butor to this particular selection from the Shelburne. And why would a veteran choose to sew a quilt? As Carlisle puts it, "as a therapeutic measure" for shattered nerves. Butor translates it "*pour se guérir,*" the French verb "guérir" (to cure) sounding ironically close to "guerrier" (soldier) or "la guerre" (war), the very source of the sickness afflicting the quilter/soldier. Butor proceeds with most of Carlisle's visual description of the guilt, the quilt's pictorial components being this time significant to him. The putative male quilter has included in his work soldiers "*prêts à tirer*"—ready to shoot. They stand next to, however, larger female figures offering food and hospitality, plus some fat doves who are also larger than the soldiers and traditional symbols of peace. Carlisle notes that the female figures are copied from "the trademark of a well-known brand of chocolate, which in turn was adopted from a 1780 French painting called 'La Chocolatière.'" Butor has no need to tell his French readers about their own familiar painting. He simply calls the female figure "*la Chocolatière de Liotard.*" He likewise mentions Carlisle's fat doves, but he elides her remark that they are "peaceful" and a "symbol of femininity and conjugal felicity." He does include her remark that the oak leaves on the soldier's quilt are "symboles," but he says "*de virilité*" (my emphasis) instead of, as in the original, "symbolic of continuing life and strength." Moreover, Butor has taken the liberty of mentioning the virile oak leaves first in his sentence, modifying Carlisle's word order. Butor concludes his version with a matter-of-fact statement that hearts were a motif "*réservé aux courtepointes de la nuit de noces.*" He completely omits Carlisle's yarn at the end of her description: "One can surmise the rest of the love story the veteran has immortalized in his quilt. The foot soldier? Surely he was the war veteran who fashioned the spread. And the lovely lady with the tray? Was she not the sweetheart who nursed him back to health?"

This "happy ending" for the shell-shocked quilter must have struck Butor as a bit much, a bit too romantic. The veteran's quilt as it stands in *Mobile* can, however, be legitimately seen to symbolize the hoped for marriage of former enemies. Butor does, after all, leave in the part about hearts being used on bridal quilts. And throughout *Mobile,* Butor implicitly calls for a marriage of all the warring factions in American culture: males versus females, whites versus blacks, European Americans versus Native Americans. This implicit hope for America's salvation (also conveyed by the frequent mention of Abraham Lincoln in *Mobile*) lies at the very heart of the author's work, beneath even his most bitter implied criticisms of the U.S. The specific lessons, therefore, of this particular quilt patch within the grand design of *Mobile* are that quilting (1) can be done by men (like the author himself) and (2) can be an essential healing experience. In this sense, Butor's veteran stands for the author himself and all other Americans—male and female—in search of sanity. He can also be seen as an odd precursor to Alice Walker's fictional Albert (who learns to sew from Celie late in *The Color Purple*) or to Walker's male Olinka quilters in the same novel.[19]

The fourth and final mention of quilting in *Mobile* is 18 pages later in the chapter on New York. This time Butor cites a quilt that bears its creator's name—Ann Robinson—and even the date of its composition.

Ann Robinson Spread

Ann Robinson of Connecticut started her spread on October 1st of 1813 and finished it exactly three months and twenty-seven days later, for she cross-stitched this information into her counterpane for posterity so that we would have a record of her work. She also appliqued a matching bolster cover measuring 37 x 20" in a similar design of calico patches.

This spread shows a saw tooth border of blue and white triangles and laurel branches of vari-colored calicoes. Cornucopias spill out a profusion of tulips and other flowers, and additional floral bouquets fill in the intermediate spaces. Two trees grow out of calico hummocks at the bottom of the spread and a sleek cat is bounding over another small mound with two dogs in hot pursuit. Other dogs are baying at birds (which have been carefully cut from printed chintzes) preening themselves in the tree branches.

Ann used hexagons of parti-colored calicoes, poinsettia blooms, laurel branches

---

19. For discussion of Alice Walker's quilt metaphors I'm indebted to M. Teresa Tavormina's "Dressing the Spirit: Clothworking and Language in *The Color Purple*" (1986) and the admirable essay by Houston A. Baker, Jr., and Charlotte Pierce-Baker, "Patches: Quilts and Community in Alice Walker's 'Everyday Use'" (1985). Tavormina (225) cites a very Butorian statement by Alice Walker discussing her quiltlike structuring of *Meridian:* "A crazy quilt story is one that can jump back and forth in time, work on many different levels, and one that can include myth" (originally in Claudia Tate, ed., *Black Women Writers at Work,* 176).

Ann Robinson Spread

and a four-looped curvilinear interlacement motif in the spaces between the outside border and the laurel-enclosed center portion of her spread. The gingham crown at the top of the spread with its three circles of calico probably represents the Triune Deity (Father, Son and Holy Ghost) who reigns over all. 95 x 100 No. 140 Dated 1814

(Pieced Work and Appliqué Quilts at Shelburne Museum 64–65)

Quilts du Shelburne Museum:
No. 140: Ann Robinson:
"Ann Robinson du Connecticut commença cette courtepointe le 1er octobre 1813 et la termina exactement trois mois et vingt-sept jours plus tard, comme elle a pris soin de l'inscrire au point de croix sur son ouvrage. Bordure de triangles bleus en dents de scie sur le fond blanc. Rameaux de laurier de calicots multi-colores. Des cornes d'abondance déploient une profusion de tulipes et autres

fleurs, d'autres bouquets remplissent les intervalles. 2 arbres s'élèvent de talus de calicot dans le bas; entre eux 2 un souple chat bondit sur un autre petit talus, poursuivi par 2 chiens. D'autres chiens aboient à des oiseaux soigneusement découpés dans un chintz imprimé, qui lissent leurs plumes dans les branches. . . . Au sommet, les 3 cercles surmontés par une couronne impériale évoquent sans doute la trinité." (202–3)

In translating this description, Butor follows the same pattern as before, omitting things extraneous to his concerns (he does not care that there's a matching bolster), and omitting (without an ellipsis) some of the visual detail such as "Ann used hexagons." He makes one of Carlisle's complete sentences ("This spread shows . . .") into two punchier sentence fragments (*"Bordure de triangles . . ."* and *"Rameaux de laurier. . ."*). He also removes an element of doubt that doesn't suit him (Carlisle's statement that the circles and calico crown probably represent the "Triune Deity [Father, Son and Holy Ghost] who reigns over all"). This becomes Butor's decisive more laconic statement: *"Au sommet, les 3 cercles surmontés par une couronne imperiale évoquent sans doute la trinité"* (my emphasis).

This final quilt with its lush floral motifs, cornucopias and its bounding cats and dogs is the most difficult to analyze as to purpose. Perhaps Butor was intrigued by the naming and dating. It is, after all, a work of art that alludes to its own composition. Perhaps the bounding dogs and cats reminded Butor of medieval tapestries at Cluny or elsewhere. Perhaps the cornucopia is, for him, a particularly evocative symbol of America's riches.

Fortunately, determining Butor's exact intentions is not central to this study. What matters are the incontrovertible changes and alterations he has made in his original "old cloth." He is remarkably consistent in his treatment of Carlisle, removing what seems to be excess visual description and many of her editorial or interpretive remarks. He does include quotation marks and sometimes (though not always) ellipses to indicate he has cut his source. Other times he silently emends, changing "probably" to *"sans doute"* or omitting the word *traditionally* when it doesn't suit him. These activities leave behind "marks" in the old text just as pinking shears leave a jagged edge when they cut. And the marks are not difficult to interpret. Butor is clearly after the mythic truth embodied in the quilts at Shelburne. Historical accuracy or exact faithfulness to his catalog source are only secondary concerns.

Butor has chosen quilts to fit larger thematic concerns of his book which is not, after all, a treatise on quilting. How much Butor "really" knows about the art form or its history is not in question. He has altered his source materials in order to place them beside the other mythic elements that comprise his text. Elaine Showalter notes that quilting as an art form has its own myths. She cautions feminist enthusiasts that viewing the quilting bee as some ideal, nonhierarchical coming together of creative women may be a poor idea.[20]

20. "Piecing and Writing," 227–28.

Not every quilt was created at a quilting bee; not every quilter was an equal at
such affairs. Sometimes expert seamstresses would be brought in to execute an
amateur's design; sometimes an expert designer would be brought in to create
a work to be executed by less skilled sewers. Some quilts were done entirely by
individuals. Laurel Horton, author of "Nineteenth-Century Quiltmaking Traditions in South Carolina," offers similar caveats about romanticizing the
quilters of yore. She points out that in the early nineteenth century, many
quilters were accomplished, recognized women of means who did "fine needlework on fine materials." Only later in that era did the outlet become common
among poorer rural women: "The mythology of humble but resourceful
women in their drafty cabins painstakingly stitching bits and scraps of rags
together, gradually discovering they could make pretty patterns, does more
than ignore the circumstantial evidence. The myth demeans and denies the
existence of a well-documented and important women's tradition of fine
needlework that extends back into prehistory."[21] Butor may be quite guilty of
romanticizing the history of American quilting in his mind. Myths are, after
all, his stock and trade. But regardless of his degree of expertise in art history,
what strikes the American reader of *Mobile* is Butor's profound interest in the
quilting art. He happens to choose quilts in a museum, two anonymous and
one whose creator is known. All have obviously been preselected by experts for
some striking quality. Jacob's Ladder must have been a particularly fine rendition of a standard pattern. At first glance its geometric shapes tell no story in
and of themselves, but when the quilt is named and the reason for the asymmetrical maple leaf is understood, the quilt becomes, for Butor, charged with
narrative (that is, "mythic") possibilities.

The Civil War quilt was chosen for the reasons discussed above: it's by a
man and was created for therapeutic reasons. These points, likewise, belong to
the prehistory—the "mythology" of the piece, if you will—and only indirectly
to its visual content. The quilt in question does depict soldiers and is certainly
more narrative than the geometric "Jacob's Ladder." One can, in effect,
construct a story about soldiers and ladies and doves and hearts. And Butor
omits Carlisle's little story as if to encourage us to work on our own. The same
thing can be done with the pictorial elements found in Ann Robinson's quilt:
dogs, cats, trees. But the story will be radically different for each imaginer,
given the nonlinear nature of the narrative elements. Butor doubtless could
have found true "storyquilts" at Shelburne analogous to Faith Ringgold's
Color Purple piece or Tar Beach. A number of antique quilts told Bible
stories, for example, the building of "Noah's Ark," incident for incident and
patch for patch. But Butor does not choose quilts that directly tell a tale. He
prefers those whose pictorial elements are either nonrepresentational (as in
Jacob's Ladder) or nonlinear (as in the other two). Why? Because Butor's

---

21. "Nineteenth-Century Quiltmaking Traditions in South Carolina," 113–14.

Mobile works, in a sense, the same way, with its ideas "distributed" rather than "developed" in linear narration.

Showalter, in her useful discussion of the quilt in feminist criticism, cites Radka Donnell-Vogt, "the Kristeva of quilting," and Rachel Blau Du Plessis, both of whom offer sophisticated explanations of how this art form relates to current feminist theory.[22] Du Plessis, for example, uses the quilt metaphor to describe a "pure women's writing" which would be "nonhierarchic . . . breaking hierarchical structures, making an even display of elements over the surface with no climactic place or moment, having the materials organized into many centers."[23] Du Plessis, here, is not worried about the facts of quilting history. She is mythologizing the quilt, making it a metaphor. And ironically, Du Plessis has perfectly described our male author's *Mobile* or, at the very least, his ideal of a "Livre Futur."

Mobile might best be likened to certain modern "art quilts"—it is not a "comfortable" read, not a book for "everyday use." It requires so much effort to follow the disparate threads of Butor's America text, that perhaps a modification of the quilt analogy is in order.

In 1976 Butor collaborated on something called a "Bicentenaire Kit," an homage to both the U.S. on its birthday and to Marcel Duchamps. This limited edition work consisted, according to Léon Roudiez, of "found" objects, plus silkscreens, plus Butor's text, all packed in a blue plastic box ("Text and Graphics," 14). Perhaps the "kit" analogy should be combined with the quilt one. The reader of *Mobile* is, in effect, presented with an enormously complex quilting "kit." On page 303 of *Mobile*, Butor mentions a sewing machine one can order from Sears, Roebuck & Company. Perhaps he intends us (figuratively) to put in such an order. For to make something out of *Mobile* requires active readers to carefully (sometimes painfully) stitch Butor's proffered patches onto the backing of their own experience. Not everyone has the skill, time, or patience for such a project, but the rewards can be great. The activity is not only therapeutic in and of itself, it might help heal American nerves shattered by racism, consumerism, and all the other ills exposed in *Mobile*. In that sense, Butor's "quilt kit," if faithfully and creatively executed by an active reader, may yield an object beautiful enough for a museum wall and useful enough to be an everyday comforter for the American soul.

22. "Piecing," 226.
23. Ibid., 226–27.

Census, Consensus, and the Commodification of Form

The NAMES Project Quilt

Van E. Hillard

> *Who decided what is useful in its beauty*
> *means less than what has no function besides beauty*
> *(except its weight in money)?*
>
> Marge Piercy, "Looking at Quilts"

As cultural forms, quilts readily lend themselves to rhetorical scrutiny. Their material composition permits us to witness symbolic action at work, most often in the ways quilts reclaim and recast the material of everyday existence into new forms, resonant with personal and social significance. Quilt production processes also have rhetorical import, enacting powerful models of cooperation, collaboration, and communal making. As a recognizable cultural sign, the quilt may be America's most knowable representation of the form and function of collective relationships. Finished quilts are emblems of successful community. Moreover, quilts are instruments for examining the efficacy of and application of socially construed metaphors significant to human culture; they are synonymous with goodness, protection, warmth, and caring. Quilts give us bright visual enactments of the working metaphor of stitching as creating unity, of collage as purposefully reclaiming old forms. In short, quilts and quiltmaking deliver up unique exemplifications of rhetorical art—art that is centered in social action, employs culture-specific forms as its text, and seeks to transform a previous social order.

As rhetorical forms, many quilts transform and enrich our notions of the agents, actions, purposes, and scenes of art production and individual creativity. Occasional quilts especially highlight the relationship of form to idea, of medium to meaning. Mourning quilts, victory quilts, autograph and friendship quilts, celebratory quilts, and quilts created to cast social and political significance (such as the antislavery, women's suffrage, and temperance quilts of the nineteenth century as well as the peace and environmentalist quilts in our era) may all be studied according to their effects upon social and political situation, and are all instances of rhetoric as they are constructed to do work in the world: to alter, to transform, or to solidify a position, not by physical force, but by symbolic action.

Not only are their final forms rhetorical, but also the forms of their production may be examined rhetorically—as the study of cooperative making. The scenes of quiltmaking help us to understand the dialogics of artistic production. Sewing and quilting bees are not only rich collaborative communities, but they also counterpoint the romanticized ideal of the individual artist, working isolate in her studio. Traditional quilt production, where individually created tops were brought to the social scene to be completed and brought to life as quilts, permits us to witness the workings of the individual/community dynamic in an especially clear way, as anyone who created a quilt top anticipated the moments when the work would undergo its "reading" by the group, who would cast their interpretations by stitching into the top's fabric, thoroughly transforming its individual character. Quilts provide us occasions for understanding how the everyday world can be written and read to new order, especially since quilters often employ socially construed constructions that occupy a formulaic aesthetic space, making rhetorical purposes predominate the "grammar" of quilting.

The rhetorical perspective I use to examine quilts and quilt production is pieced from sociologists of art, material culturists, Neo-Marxists, and contemporary rhetoricians. Quilting seems best explored and most profitably discussed utilizing art production theory, which valorizes the communal scene of production and configures symbolic forms as predominant forms of idea. The sociological view pays attention to the social conditions of making, to the way symbolic forms operate in society.[1] The material culturist perspective reclaims the objects of popular culture as emblematic of artistic and creative impulses woven through everyday life.[2] Neo-Marxists concern themselves with the

---

1. This perspective is based on the assumption Max Kaplan makes that "the work of art can never be completely grasped without sensing and bringing to consciousness the multitude of personal elements, cultural aspects, and historical relations that it contains." *The Arts: A Sociological Perspective*, 10. To create a sociology of art is to situate a community at the heart of art-making, to realize that artists act as agents of particular cultures. As Vera Zolberg puts this, "From a sociological standpoint, a work of art is a moment in a process involving the collaboration of more than one actor, working through certain social institutions, and following historically observable trends." *Constructing a Sociology of the Arts*, 9.

2. Similar to the sociological perspective, the material culturist viewpoint is especially well-suited to examining quilt production. Historically devalued as "women's work," quilting has been reclaimed by material culturists for whom quilts constitute significant forms of knowing the world. Simon J. Bronner repositions the material forms of everyday life by defining objects as "references people use to tangibly outline the worlds they know, the one they try to cope with, and those they aspire to or imagine. Creative objects . . . become markers for the physical and intellectual surroundings with which people identify. Such

scenes of production as they are dialectically held to the sites of distribution—useful concepts to employ, particularly in discussing twentieth-century quilt-making.[3] These perspectives examine art production with a consistent focus on ideology, allowing historical, social, political, psychological, and economic threads to constitute a contextual web within which particular works gain significance. Moreover, each perspective resituates and thereby works to heal disabling dichotomies fostered by much art criticism—rifts between aesthetics and politics, between the personal and the social, between solitary artists and nameless communities, between the popular and the elite.

In attempting to change the social order, rhetorical art is committed to addressing ideologic concerns more than aesthetic demands, is social-directed rather than self-referential, and envisions artist and audience in a working dialectic. Rhetorical art employs visual forms that may be read as texts, making use of recognizable presentational and/or discursive forms, accessible to a particular community, but contextualized to cast new meanings. Most importantly, rhetorical art is created in response to situation, and gains its power addressing what Lloyd Bitzer terms an "exigence": "an imperfection marked by urgency . . . a defect, an obstacle, something waiting to be done, a thing which is other than it should be." Bitzer's understanding of what he terms "the rhetorical situation" is helpful in defining how rhetorical art functions in getting us to ideology and to political or social purpose. For him, "a work of rhetoric is pragmatic; it comes into existence for the sake of something beyond itself; it functions ultimately to produce action or change in the world; it performs some task. In short, rhetoric is a mode of altering reality, not by the direct application of energy to objects, but by the creation of discourse which changes reality through the mediation of thought and action."[4]

Many quilts are instances of rhetoric in Bitzer's sense, not only because they were created to change political, social, or historical meanings, but also because they emerged in collaborative, collective settings and are themselves icons of rhetorical modes of thought—representative of debate or discussion or conversation or purposeful agreement by a number of interlocutors. By recognizing rhetorical quilting, we may locate a significant ritualized tradition in American life—one which has been marginalized at times, mythologized at others, and, in recent times, borrowed from and appropriated, as in the

---

objects reify intangible, abstract human and spiritual relations in those surroundings." "The Idea of the Folk Artifact," 14.

3. Neo-Marxist interpretations of art share with sociologists and material culturists the necessity of situating any created forms within the complex webs of historical, political, ideological, and socio-economic contexts, but, as Janet Wolff points out, replace "the vocabulary of 'creation', 'artist', and 'work of art' with that of 'cultural or artistic production' . . . 'cultural producer'." *The Social Production of Art*, 138. With this perspective, we can account for art as instrumental for recognition as well as for liberation.

4. "The Rhetorical Situation," 3, 2.

NAMES Project quilt, the focus of my exploration of rhetoric and quilt production.

Both in its creation and its display (with an eye to the complexities of production and consumption), the NAMES Project quilt represents a provocative instance of postmodern cultural politics—powerful in the intentions of its individual contributors, yet perplexing in the realization of its distribution and display. The NAMES Project quilt allows us to glimpse just how the traditional meanings of American quilting have been recast in contemporary contexts—with what loses, with what metaphoric change—not to lament changed meanings, but rather to explore how the postmodern conflation of politics and media can effect the social production of symbolic forms. As is the case with the NAMES Project quilt, such a conflation can result in what Orrin Klapp has termed the "inflation of symbols": a tendency to reduce the agency of a once authentically construed cultural symbol, through mass production and/or mass display, with the resultant increase in production inflating and thereby eroding originative significance. The quilt is an easily inflated symbol because of its recognizability, and also because patchwork symbolization can be replicated so facilely by different media. More to the point, the appropriation of quilts from the intimate space of the home to the public space of advertising display has permitted corporate America to use the quilt's iconography to readily purchase viewers' sentiments. A patchwork or pieced representation easily stimulates a thin aura of family, economy, and home. As Klapp points out, "Increasing the number of times a symbol is displayed in exchange tends at some point to reduce its display value," such that once-authentic meanings surrounding the personal creation and private use of quilts erode into mere euphemism with commercialized display.[5]

To grasp the rhetorical condition of the NAMES Project quilt it is necessary to place it within the historical frame of American quilting practices. Such contextualization throws into relief the ways in which the significance of the NAMES Project quilt runs parallel to and diverges from American quilting's traditional values. Many traditional American quilts are rhetorical both in the messages they conveyed in response to social and political circumstances and in the dialectic of their production and consumption—as the rhetoric of their making and use reveals relationships of power and contested meanings. To examine the rhetoric of their production and consumption, we should keep in mind that quilts have long been created by marginalized groups: by European-American women, who had few opportunities to express themselves in public discourse and employed their quilts to give expression to private thought and feeling; by African American women who, carrying forward African traditions, practiced the art of salvage and reclamation for utilitarian and expressive purposes; and by African American "quilting slaves," trained to

5. *Inflation of Symbols: Loss of Values in American Culture*, 108.

produce quilts for members of the oppressive culture.[6] Quilting has been steeped in tiring labor, meticulous skill, and the kind of thoughtful creation that emerges from maximizing the effect of limited resources. Quilting is emblematic of clever frugality, and is a metaphor of survival in the face of oppression and neglect. Ironically, such economic and political pragmatism has become synonymous with the ideal of motherhood and maternal care—a woman creator judged competent because she makes the most of the limitations the dominant culture of men have placed on her. As Elaine Hedges puts this, "Our response to quilts as art forms rooted both in meaningful work and in cultural oppression will therefore be inevitably complex; a combination of admiration and awe at limitations overcome and of sorrow and anger at limitations imposed."[7] We value quilts because we sense the efforts of their production and because we admire beauty wed to utility. Geometric quilt forms are particularly American because they appear so aesthetically practical, even parsimonious.

We can imagine, however, that for most women, quilting, needlework, and sewing went beyond both practical and aesthetic concerns; stitching became a habit of mind, a ritualized practice of connection-making, unification, and harmonizing. Many quilts—especially pieced and patchwork forms—are icons of a working community. They offer complex visual solutions for deriving unity from diversity; they represent the enactment of co-existence, the value of differences acting together to shape a new whole, greater than the sum of its parts. Some quilts are conceptual maps of the intense interplay of dialogue and dialectic—as one element and a diverse other together transcend differences to create a new solution. Allied to the symbol of community, quilts have become visual metaphors of the stabilized democracy that arrives after reasoned argument, purposeful debate, and productive conversation. Quilts demonstrate agreement and the possibilities of shared belief and in this way are the perfect realizations of form and idea: "A quilt is a map of devotion to doing and using as well as to completion, and the coexistence of these ways of seeing results in the narrative pleasure of its art."[8] The method of production (by individual and collective means, inventing new solutions from scarce resources) is echoed in the final product of the quilt. This quilt character is imbricated in form, process, and function.

Like few other production processes, the social production of quilts evinces the working of collaborative making and catalyzes community itself, permitting women to assemble as discussants in a public forum. As Miriam Schapiro and Faith Wilding remind us:

6. Eva Grudin has pointed out that "slave seamstresses often furnished the bedding for entire plantations." "The Exquisite Diversity of African-American Quilts," 41.

7. "Quilts and Women's Culture," in *In Her Own Image: Women Working in the Arts,* ed. Elaine Hedges and Ingrid Wendt, 17.

8. Jeff Weinstein, "Names Carried into the Future: An AIDS Quilt Unfolds," 44.

Quiltmaking was one of the most important female domestic activities for many centuries. In the collaborative, community-oriented art of the quilt, lapwork gives way to an ambitious multi-layered work. Transcending the boundaries of class, race, country of origin, and history, the quilt is a humanized, democratized art form. Even its subject matter—weddings, commemoration, friendship, freedom, political loyalties, family records—reflects rituals of community life.[9]

Such an opportunity was especially significant, given that women were excluded from the dominant forms of public discourse and address. The quilt was a vehicle for initiating conversation and for casting the symbolic form of such action—for bringing collective meanings back into public forum, as quilts were returned to the home or were auctioned and sold, often to raise funds for social or political causes. Demonstrating the centrality of the quilting bees to women's culture, Elaine Hedges has remarked, "Quilting bees were usually festive occasions, with opportunities to renew and cement friendships, to reestablish social bonds among women otherwise isolated . . . to exchange news and ideas and to express feelings. Where men had the tavern or the saloon, the marketplace or the courthouse square for bonding together, women had the quilting bee."[10] As such, the quilting bee was a spatial and temporal metaphor of productive and promising conversation, similar in form to dialectic, where meanings were shaped and shared with increasing vitality and intimacy:

> When the twelve women—arranged three on a side of the quilt frame—started out to quilt, they were wide apart; indeed, they were nine feet apart. But as the sides were rolled up, they came closer and closer together until, when the quilt was finished, they were face to face. The conversation would be very general when the quilt was started—the crops and the weather were safe subjects, also politics, which . . . actually entered into the names of quilts. At first the talk was loud enough to be heard by all but as the quilters came closer and closer together, the conversation became correspondingly more intimate. Small events were magnified and many an individual reputation was made or marred.[11]

Often, the quilting bee became an explicitly political forum where social issues were debated and quilts were made to address political exigencies such as suffrage or slavery.[12] This complex tradition of rhetorical art has been outlined in Karla Friedlich's "Quilts of Conscience," which documents the fact that "for as long as women in this country have been making quilts they have made quilts . . . that express their concern about the important moral, social, and ethical issues of their time. In the early years of this nation, when women had few rights, quiltmaking allowed them to participate in history, sometimes

9. "Cunts/Quilts/Consciousness," 13.
10. "Quilts and Women's Culture," 15.
11. Elizabeth Wells Robertson, *American Quilts,* 57.
12. Elaine Hedges reminds us that "Susan B. Anthony's first talk on equal rights for women was at a quilting bee" (17).

in a symbolic, and sometimes very real, manner."[13] Often, rhetorical effect came by way of metaphoric manipulation, as quilt patterns "which had for years Biblical or domestic referents were given new, more relevant names by women who had current social concerns on their minds. . . . [One] quilt pattern, which had been known as Jacob's Ladder, came to be called, by many women, Underground Railroad."[14] Similarly, the Drunkard's Path design was enlisted to serve new purposes by temperance movement quilters.

Creating a form that would later be appropriated by American advertising and utilized by other American artists, quilters wove textual and visual elements together, thereby solidifying a powerful pictorial form of public meaning-making. The combination of discursive and presentational forms led to the quilt's emergence as a banner of participation, a flag of citizenship. Suffragette quilters would often, for instance, embroider the names of the community's women across a powerful visual field; anti-slavery quilters commonly emblazoned an admonition across a delicate design. As Friedlich documents: "At a Ladies Anti-Slavery Fair . . . a cradle quilt containing the following inscription was among the items offered for sale: 'Mother! When around your child / You can clasp your arms in love / and when with grateful joy you raise / Your eyes to God above— / Think of the Negro mother / When your child is torn away— / Sold for a little slave—oh then, / For that poor mother pray!'"[15]

The use of quilts as textual sites is also generously evident in much African American quilting, where complex visual forms were wedded to both Nsibidi symbology and to natural or cultural remnants. In some quilts, Biblical narrative is retold in quilt form; in others, ancestral religious symbols are documented. African American quilts often acted as historical, cultural, and religious maps, directing the way from the past to the present. These quilts "revived a past cultural environment which emphasized religious symbols with meanings which could not always be put into words, and thereby provided an immensely important instrument for teaching, for enlivening tradition, for providing protection in an otherwise hostile world."[16]

More importantly, they provided a vehicle for subverting dominant ideologies; quilted texts enacted alternate readings of the world. As Elsa Barkley Brown has shown, the form of much African American strip quilting is a conceptual metaphor for the worldview of African American women who typically create a "polyrhythmic, 'nonsymmetrical,' nonlinear structure in which individual and community are not competing entities."[17] African American quilters also transformed their textiles into texts that subverted the Euro-

13. "Quilts of Conscience," 47.
14. Pat Ferrero, *Hearts and Hands: The Influence of Women* and *Quilts on American Society*, 69.
15. "Quilts of Conscience," 47.
16. Maude Southwell Wahlman, "Religious Symbolism in African-American Quilts," 36.
17. Elsa Barkley Brown, "African-American Women's Quilting: A Framework for Conceptualizing and Teaching African-American Women's History," 926.

pean-American aesthetic of controlled, tedious, lace-like stitching. Cast-off fabrics and discarded quilts of the masters were reinscribed by slaves, who preferred looser, broader, and more forceful "strokes" of the needle to the fussy and somewhat obsessive stitching preferred by white women. These reconfigured quilts and coverings provided an important rhetorical space for writing African American culture, cast against the dominant ideology and European aesthetic—the needle intruding into and thereby transforming what was most often, a field of white fabric.

Quilts have a rhetorical purpose, then, in providing a public space for naming and renaming the world. Permitting a reality to be known, defined, and communicated through shared visual code, they mediate the position of private person and public world. In the nineteenth century, when women were not only denied a representative voice in politics, but were also largely un-named in public records of ownership, friendship quilts provided a vital record of existence, acting as an instrument of census-taking. As Linda Otto Lipsett has pointed out, prior to 1850 "only the names of 'heads of families' were listed on government census records. . . . A woman's name was listed on the census only if she herself were the head of the household, generally due to the death of her husband. . . . Genealogies and county and town histories, written in usually great detail, listing persons living in that place during the time of publication or in the recent past, rarely mention a man's wife." The friendship quilt worked to name a woman's society as it reclaimed community from the margins. As Lipsett goes on to remind us, "In many instances, friendship quilts are the *only* remaining records of the women whose names are inscribed on them."[18] We can imagine that the power of signature as seal of promise, commitment, and authority—a power held by men—was transcribed onto friendship quilts as the sign of cooperation and accomplishment by women. Again, the quilt acts as mediator between the individual and the social realm, as an embroidered or stamped name was brought to public consciousness. The quilt's intimate yet public nature makes it an especially appropriate space for nominal inscription; upon a quilt, a woman's name marked a place of protective care as it represented a social identity.

Naming is also the constituent symbolic act for the NAMES Project quilt, a quilt that combines elements from both traditional friendship and memory quilts. The project's aim has been to assemble a massive collection of individual panels, each commemorating the life of someone who has died of AIDS. Thousands of panels have been created so far by companions, friends, relatives, and other interested people. The quilt takes shape whenever several panels are sewn together. These eight-panel arrangements are then displayed, either alone or alongside as many as hundreds of other eight-panel squares—as they have three times been laid out on the mall in Washington D.C. and

18. *Remember Me: Women and Their Friendship Quilts,* 29, 28.

once displayed in Central Park. The NAMES Project quilt is a powerful instance of public art. It allows us to see just how the highly individualized, personal symbology of one's life—sewn and appliquéd onto cloth—resonates with other individual symbolizing practices, allowing the personal to regain and reclaim its public representation.

Yet, the AIDS quilt is also both an appropriation and commodification of traditional quilting forms. As such, we may look to the AIDS quilt as an instance of postmodern cultural politics, as contemporary art that transmutes the historical scene of quilting—the quilting bee, especially, with its specialized community—into a mere "collective" of production. It may be also be argued that the NAMES Project quilt, though visually similar to pieced and patchwork forms, does not result in the deliberate unity in variety seen throughout quilting's history. With the AIDS quilt, the demands of consumption, distribution, and display have colored and dominated the mode of production, resulting in a commodified form, vaguely similar to quilt forms, but entirely different in its artistic unity and its rhetorical effectiveness. The AIDS quilt has been produced, in other words, by a collection rather than an authentic community of makers, and this distinction is echoed in its final product—in the varied, but non-unified diversity of its assemblage of individual panels. The AIDS quilt isn't so much composed as it is accumulated. Unintentionally, the quilt's form reveals, that is, the fragmented state of the community of persons with AIDS and HIV disease and those concerned about them. And, although individual commemorative panels speak clearly to the pathos of persons and powerfully articulate personal cries of pain, loss, and memory, as a unit—brought to its public rhetorical purpose—the NAMES Project quilt does not partake of a most vital aspect of traditional quilt-making: the working unification of diverse elements, stitched together to create a new whole, the finished quilt a constituent metaphor of consensus. It operates, that is, at the level of discrete "information" and statistic rather than deliberate, collective "idea."

In its production and distribution, the AIDS quilt gains significance in two realms—in the intimate and the public. The impetus to memorialize a person's death comes from an individual or group of individuals who form a community that collaboratively creates an individual panel. Typically, the panel contains personal symbology, drawn from significant aspects of the person's life. Objects are represented in embroidery or appliqué, text is drawn or sewn to the background, and meaningful objects—photos, scraps of significant cloth, badges, buttons—are glued or sewn on as well. And, in the production of individual panels, the symbolic actions of traditional quiltmaking survive: collaborative decision-making, work by an interested community to determine the shape of public representation, the application of textual, tactile, and visual forms to signal ideologic significance. Like memorial quilts of the nineteenth century (especially those that doubled as shrouds when coffins, because of expense or scarcity, could not be had) individual AIDS quilt panels contain the representations or names of persons important to the life of the deceased. These and letters appended to the backs of panels, written by panel-makers, richly contextualize the works, giving them a complex texture of community within which an individual panel gains social significance. Socially constructed, the panels represent person as socially construed. In memory, the self is remade as social self—reconstituted from the fragments of others' memories, other selves.

Yet, demands of distribution, display, and consumption constrain such creative promise and erode rhetorical effect. Once produced, individual panels are warehoused until they are indiscriminately sewn next to other panels and here, the "quilt" begins to take shape in a way no other traditional quilt had—in the very moment when authentic memorializing use delivers itself into the hands of politicized, mediated display. Since the central desire seems to have been the need to visually quantify the statistical toll of AIDS on America, the public display of panels is a gigantic sea of eight-panel squares. At its original display in 1987, "As the three-by-six foot cloth panels made by friends, family, and admirers of the dead were carefully unfurled, 1,920 names were solemnly read to a crowd of weeping spectators. Though representing only a small percentage of the people who have died in the epidemic, the seemingly endless litany of names, together with the astonishing size of the quilt, brought home the enormity of our loss so dramatically as to leave everyone stunned."[19]

The quilt gains its power from its sheer size, from its vast numbers of individual panels. The public context of the quilt's display places a high demand on the quantity of items produced. Thus, the concern for successful distribution overwhelms all other concerns of production so that the traditional form of quilts and quiltmaking are adumbrated under a blanket of postmodern cultural form—a form responsive to the constraints of marketing, product regularity, and random juxtaposition as in bricolage. This has the effect of diminishing or erasing the representational and ideological power of any individual panel, as each is subsumed under the consuming category of "display."

As social art, then, the AIDS quilt functions on two levels. As intimate emblems, individual panels are intensely rhetorical. By a process of reinscription, individual panels reclaim forgotten names from the margins of American consciousness. As friendship quilts operated to empower and reposition women in the past, the AIDS quilt is a valuable "census-taking" form, articulating the shape of a personal life as it acknowledges the number of dead—this especially important in the face of the marginalized status of those with HIV disease and AIDS. Most panels seem celebratory—affirming rather than somber, joyful rather than sad. Many are explicitly rhetorical, asking that we not forget the nameless dead. Others question official silences, inaction, and un-

19. Douglas Crimp, "How to Survive Promiscuity in an Epidemic," 257.

derfunding. Signification forwards significance as individual lives are config-
ured in material reclaimed from the everyday: "Whether drawn, painted,
appliquéd or stitched, the panels are spectacularly varied in style, materials
and sensibility. Humble little stick figures in crayon and the unsteady hand-
writing of a child are sewn to stunning, sophisticated renditions by a professional artist. Materials ranging from Brooks Brothers tweed to denim, polyester and black leather strive to create a true sense of person remembered."[20] As
public commodity, however, the power of individual panels becomes over-
shadowed by the predominant concern for massiveness. Since "more is better," vast combinations of panels dominate the sanctity of any single tribute.
The final form resembles Flanders Field or the view of any large cemetery
from a distance—a collection of bits, the totality of a census.

The Names Project quilt, then, is produced according to a dominant
consumption/distribution ideology located in a postmodern aesthetic. Its plan
and structure are echoed in Todd Gitlin's description of constituent postmodern form: "Instead of a single center, there is pastiche, cultural recom-
bination. Anything can be juxtaposed to anything else. Everything takes the
place in the present 'here' that is nowhere in particular. . . . The implied
subject is fragmented, unstable . . . it is finally nothing more than a crosshatch
of discourses . . . Beauty deprived of its power of criticism in an age of
packaging, has been reduced to the decoration of reality."[21] This principle of
distribution, fostered by contemporary media, is to saturate an audience with
as many informational bits as often as possible—quantity subsuming quality,
fact dominating idea. To distribute with ease and greatest effect, repeatability
and replicability of discrete units is sought. For instance, in their directions to
individual panel-makers, the NAMES Project mandates: "Choose your materials. Remember that the Quilt is folded and unfolded many times, so durability is crucial. A medium-weight, non-stretch fabric such as cotton works
best. The finished panel must be 3 feet by 6 feet." More than anything, these
are concerns for commodity, and even though the dimensional restrictions, for
instance, may not constrict individual creativity, they signal an overriding
structural principle of alignment and conformity; with these in place, any
panel can be joined to any other. The eight-panel assemblage, however reminiscent of patchwork forms, constitutes a mere collection of "bits." The
amassed parts of the AIDS quilt are not designed, in other words, to hold
together. In fact, their coexistence is altogether temporary, meeting the site-
specific demands of display.

This is entirely different from traditional pieced, patchwork, and crazy
quilts that were deliberately designed to appear random, cluttered, and spon-

20. Cindy Ruskin, *The Quilt: Stories from the NAMES Project,* 12.
21. "Postmodernism: Roots and Politics," in *Cultural Politics in Contemporary America,* ed.
Ian Angus and Sut Jhally, 350.

taneous, but were, in fact, intricate structural solutions to effect unity from great variety. As collage, such quilts are emblems of the rhetorical action of assembling old forms to create new, dialectically sought wholes. Crazy quilts were, in effect, metaphors of consensus—diverse elements agreeing to interact and hold together, to coexist for a synthetic, greater good. In contradistinction to this, the AIDS quilt is uncentered, working by the structural principles of accumulation and random combination, as the census-like juxtaposition of single panels, such a form mirrors the great diversity of AIDS deaths: a toll. When the quilt was unfurled in Washington, D.C. in October of 1992, there were more than 25,000 panels as compared with the 1,920 displayed in 1987. As more and more panels are warehoused at the quilt distribution site, as more and more panels are shipped to display sites (already, there have been over six hundred discrete displays mounted) the original purpose of the quilt survives—to announce "the humanity behind the statistics," but perhaps its political and rhetorical effects erode. As the quilt becomes an ever-increasing commodity, the collaborative efforts of individual panel-makers threaten to be lost, individuals becoming smaller and smaller parts in a more and more massive display. The originative play of diversity and differences thus becomes muddled, confused. The sum of the parts cannot be seen because the whole cannot be grasped. The quilt becomes a vast text that asks, simply to be "consumed" rather than "read."

At the level of single panel, then, the NAMES Project quilt is authentically folkloric—enlivened by the highly interpersonal interactions of a community of makers striving to inscribe the exigencies of mourning, grief, and remembrance. Similar to the pattern and structure of traditional rhetorical quilts and quiltmaking, each panel is a metaphor of care and concern, cast by a group of creators, acting consensually. But these qualities disappear as the drive for size increases, and the AIDS quilt mimicks the form of commercial media distribution, where, as Angus and Jhally point out: "The tendency of the contemporary commercial form of communication is toward a sequence of juxtaposed images without an explicit internal form of connection. . . . The production of cultural artifacts as commodities squeezes the maximum number of images into the shortest space of time . . . and, in so doing, pushes increasingly more of the context necessary for interpretation to the side of the audience."[22] As an instance of postmodern cultural politics, the AIDS quilt represents a society of persons who, assembled together, simply exist together. The AIDS quilt's "community" is merely geographic, a shared locale.

So far, AIDS awareness has taken the form of fact-finding and information-gathering. What the media offers the public is newsy knowledge about the pandemic: populations effected, methods of transmission, all the breakthroughs that come with scientific and medical investigation. What's generally

22. "Introduction," *Cultural Politics*, 9.

been absent are ideas and working ethics for addressing the complexities of AIDS and HIV disease: represented ideas about pain and suffering, discrimination, and prejudice—ideas that will bridge the vast divide between acquiring information (as in appraising statistics) and changing behavior and belief. In its final form, the NAMES Project quilt mirrors the factual, informational paradigm of AIDS knowledge most prevalent in the culture. Since the production/distribution construct is tied to numbers, to mounting statistics, it shall continue to grow and show, simply, "Here are more deaths!" The quilt itself is a commodity to be assembled, disassembled, and reassembled as needed.

As America's most recognizable form of public response to AIDS deaths, the NAMES Project quilt settles for the mandates of postmodern cultural commodity as it mostly "advertises" a message, confirms what is already known, newly packaged: that a horrendous pandemic continues, that inattention to it has resulted in the deaths of a great variety of people. What needs to be rewoven back into the texture of American life is a communal responsibility and response-ability for care, concern, and compassion—of the very kind represented by traditional American quilting.

Quilt-Value and the Marxist Theory of Value

Nora Ruth Roberts

An idea came to me while I was mending my grandmother's quilt with, appropriately enough, a scrap of shirt that had belonged to my now grown son when he was in kindergarten. I hope to restore the quilt to good condition, despite hard use, so I can pass it down to some future daughter-in-law. Just that thought set me to thinking about the Marxism that was the catechism in my socialist household while I was growing up. I thought about the value my grandmother's quilt has for me—almost illimitable—the value it has on the market, as it is in poor repair and was never anything fancy—almost nil—and I wondered where in the Marxist scheme of things I would find an expression for a theory of value that would cover grandma's quilt—quilt-value, I have come to call it.

In the Marxist lexicon, my son now assures me, the concept of private or sentimental value is covered under the concept of use-value as against exchange value. All commodities must have use-value or they will not have exchange value, and use-value can be interpreted broadly to mean any value at all that one gives to an item, regardless of its relation to labor time—the usual determinant of the concept of value that will ultimately lead to market value. This, to me, seems to beg the question, rather than answer it.

Marx, in his discussion of the use-value concept, argues against the notion that bases value in desire, as much a desire of the mind as of the body. Marx cites John Locke in a footnote: "The natural worth of anything consists in its fitness to supply the necessities or serve the conveniences of human life."[1] And he treats the economist Nicolas Barbon to another footnote: "'Desire implies want' it is the appetite of the mind, and as natural as hunger to the body. . . . The greater number [of things] have their value from supplying the wants of the mind." Against this idealist concept, Marx posits his thesis:

> A commodity is, in the first place, an object outside us, a thing that by its properties satisfies human wants of some sort or another. The nature of such wants, whether, for instance, they spring from the stomach or from fancy, makes

1. *Capital,* 1:42.

no difference. Neither are we here concerned to know how the object satisfies these wants, whether directly as means of production. . . . The utility of a thing makes it a use-value. But this utility is not a thing of air. Being limited by the physical properties of the commodity, it has no existence apart from that commodity. . . . Use-values become a reality only by use or consumption: they also constitute the substance of all wealth, whatever may be the social form of that wealth. In the form of society we are about to consider, they are, in addition, the material depositories.[2]

This, like most of Marxism, seems a necessary but insufficient guide to understanding the problem at hand. The value my grandmother's quilt has for me serves not in its usefulness as a blanket or spread, although I do use it as such on special occasions. It is almost entirely a matter of the sentimental value the bourgeois economists and philosophers were discussing before Marx took them on. The quilt itself is cotton, made of scraps and bits of dresses my grandmother wore every day to work on the farm, and blouses my favorite young aunt wore to high school. In my mind's eye, I can see both women when I look at the quilt. Unfinished by my grandmother at the time of her death, backed in no-nonsense washable cotton and polyester by my mother, the quilt links me through the female line to my own childhood and to precious memories of my grandmother standing close beside me or showing me how to do some chore or other. I can only pray that whatever daughter-in-law I do wind up with will understand the sacredness this quilt has for me, for all its tattered and patched and even blotted condition, or that, failing daughters-in-law in my lifetime, one of my sons will accept the quilt with due reverence. Yet I must face the fact that my most prized possession would not fetch twenty dollars on the open market. To anyone outside the family, its only use-value is as a covering or perhaps a quaint curiosity. Marx's use-value definition in and of itself seems inadequate to explain in economic or sociological terms the special value I find in the quilt. I think I am not alone. I note that in most families, real estate and investment values may be handed down through the male line, but heirlooms and family goods are more often passed from mother to oldest daughter. Thus, the theory of value I am looking for— quilt-value or heirloom-value—may well be a feminine theory of value, or at least, a feminine take on the sentimental theory of value charted by Adam Smith and John Locke.

One is hard put to find justification for this theory in Marx's analysis. In his early work, *The Critique of Political Economy*, Marx wrote,

Thus, entirely apart from their natural forms and without regard to the specific kind of wants for which they serve as use-values, commodities in certain quantities equal each other, take each other's place in exchange, pass as equivalents, and in spite of their variegated appearance, represent the same entity. . . . Use-

2. Ibid., 42–43.

values are primarily means of existence. These means of existence, however, are themselves products of social life, the result of expended human vital power, *materialized labor.* (italics in original)[3]

Marx clearly is addressing himself to the root source of value, labor time, the thrust of his campaign against the idealists. He argues that it is their function as the products of materialized labor, not as satisfaction of mind-wants, that gives use-values their value. This seems not sufficient to explain the memory-value of my grandmother's quilt to me or of heirlooms in general.

In his seminal thesis "The Work of Art in the Age of Mechanical Reproduction," the Frankfurt school theorist Walter Benjamin discusses the special quality of the work of art in a slightly different context. He uses the term *aura* to define the special quality of the work of art—a quality I maintain can be applied as well to the sentimental value I am associating with quilts and female-descendant heirlooms. Benjamin argues,

> The uniqueness of a work of art is inseparable from its being imbedded in the fabric of tradition. This tradition itself is thoroughly alive and extremely change-able. An ancient statue of Venus, for example, stood in a different traditional context with the Greeks, who made it an object of veneration, then with the clerics of the Middle Ages, who viewed it as an ominous idol. Both of them, however, were equally confronted with its uniqueness, that is, its aura.

In his discussion of the fate of this aura in the period of mechanical reproduction by such means as photography and film, Benjamin says, "One might generalize by saying: the technique of reproduction detaches the reproduced object from the domain of tradition."[4] I would go further and suggest that the very fact that modern-day quilts and personal items can be mechanically reproduced so easily confers all the more "aura" or sentimental value upon the hand-crafted heirlooms our foremothers passed down to us.

This concept of "aura" in Benjamin's terms is closely related to two concepts that have bearing on our case: Marx's theory of the fetishistic character of money and to the anthropologist's view of primitive gift giving, which sheds some light on the problem of the special quality of heirlooms.

The standard work in the anthropological field on theories of gift giving is *The Gift* by Marcel Mauss, first published in French in 1950. Mauss identifies gift giving, or potlach, as the essential form of exchange and treaty arrangement in primitive society in the absence of capitalist relations and parliaments. Gifts confirm social agreement, seal bonds, and, most of all, imply obligations. As Mary Douglas points out in her foreword, "There are no free gifts; gift

3. *A Contribution to the Critique of Political Economy*, 21–22.
4. *Illuminations*, 221–23.

cycles engage persons in permanent commitments that articulate the dominant institutions. . . . I give so that you may give."[5]

I find this concept fascinating in the context of the heirloom tradition I am pursuing, but it is a little outside the immediate concern of the problem of the theory of value. What obligation my grandmother meant to impose on me by passing along to me her final quilt is unguessable. Certainly the act carried with it an injunction to revere and treasure the quilt, its components, and with it my memories—an obligation freely returned. But was there something more? Did my grandmother, in the true feminine fashion typical of her generation, in the absence of written work or commercial enterprise, pass down to me a bit of her soul, her being, her essence, which she meant me to continue as a sacred trust and pass down in turn to the next generation, sons if willing, or my own granddaughters if any materialize?

There is an oral tradition that goes with heirloom transmission. I see it—or hear its expression—from my mother and aunts as well as in my recollections of my grandmother. My aunt knows just how all her heirlooms were used by her progenitors and can relate brief anecdotal reminiscences, which have been passed down from mother to daughter, to go with each one. An oral tradition accompanies my bits and pieces of memorabilia—the family Bible brooch I inherited from my paternal grandmother, the candy dish bought at a fair in Pennsylvania the year my mother was born. According to Mauss, the Maori have a word for this variation of Benjamin's "aura"—*taonga*.

Mauss's analysis is heavily freighted with contemporary economic equivalents—he sees in the system of the *taonga* a primitive system of barter and stresses the obligatory aspect of the exchange and the return. While Mauss may very well be reporting accurately, I am hard put to apply the concept of obligation to modern heirlooms. The obligation involved is not to return a like gift but to cherish and continue the gift itself and its oral "aura." In contemporary society, it is difficult to analyze here how these items fell into female rather than male hands and why women seem to feel instinctively that another woman—a daughter, daughter-in-law, or granddaughter—will be more likely to respect the implied *hau* than will a male heir.

That the question goes beyond merely economic obligation to return can be seen in Mauss's discussion of fellow anthropologist Brown's report on Australian tribes:

> Brown again reports on the rituals of meeting after a long separation, the act of embrace, the greeting made in tears, and shows how the exchange of presents is their equivalent, and how feelings and persons are mixed up together.
>
> In short, this represents an intermingling. Souls are mixed with things; things with souls. Lives are mingled together and this is how, among persons and things

5. *The Gift,* ix.

so intermingled, each emerges from their own sphere and mixes together. This is precisely what contract and exchange are.[6]

Marx gives passing acknowledgment of the power of a commodity to confer an "aura" in his discussion of the fetishistic character of money. In so doing, he would seem to be answering Adam Smith, who, in his 1759 discussion of "The Theory of Moral Sentiments," says:

> Though it is in order to supply the necessities and conveniences of the body that the advantages of external fortune are originally recommended to us, yet we cannot live long in the world without perceiving that the respect of our equals, our credit and rank in the society we live in, depend very much upon the degree in which we possess, or are supposed to possess, those advantages. The desire of becoming the proper objects of this respect, of deserving and obtaining this credit and rank among our equals, is perhaps the strongest of all our desires; and our anxiety to obtain the advantages of fortune is, accordingly, much more excited and irritated by this desire than by that of supplying all the necessities and conveniences of the body, which are always very easily supplied to.[7]

It goes without saying that the "we" Adam Smith refers to are men, and that the credit of equals he discusses as essential is the good opinion of other men, bought by show of commodities. No doubt women of all commercial ages have been affected by the same desire to display what their husbands can provide for them. But the *hau*, the soul mingling of the passing down of heirlooms, appears to have another quality that, in this context, seems peculiarly feminine. Outside the sphere of getting and spending, women pass down their soul-bits and oral traditions as life forces, as traditions, more in keeping with a feminine take on Benjamin's "aura" than the social-prestige–conferring qualities of the commodity inherent in Adam Smith's and Marx's concept of the fetishistic quality of the commodity.

Marx answers Adam Smith by arguing that all commodities derive their value from abstract human labor, and it is that quality that underlies the so-called mystery of the social prestige inherent in owning them.

> A commodity is therefore a mysterious thing, simply because in it the social character of men's labour appears to them as an objective character stamped upon the product of that labour; because the relation of the producer to the sum total of their own labour is presented to them as a social relation, existing not between themselves, but between the products of their labour. This is the reason why the products of labour become commodities, social things whose qualities are at the same time perceptible and imperceptible by the senses.[8]

6. Ibid., 20.
7. K. William Kapp and Lore L. Kapp, *History of Economic Thought*, 112.
8. *Capital*, 82.

By reducing the factor of "aura," or *hau* or fetish, to a matter of determinable labor time, Marx seems to have explained the inexplicable. Markers of the human soul are nothing more than the use-value aspects of commodities, whose market value can be socially determined in verifiable terms. This seems to be the very problem Henry James was conjuring in his depiction of the entrepreneur Adam Verver in *The Golden Bowl*. As an American from a historically deprived culture, but with plenty of cash, Verver sets out to buy all the artifacts and goods and castles—and even princes—he can to confer upon himself the aura of a prestigious feudal overlord. In Marx's terms, his acquisitions—including the prince he buys for his daughter—may be determinable in terms of the fetishistic quality of labor time. Verver has exploited labor back home in his factory, and that labor time and surplus-value now take on the expression of golden bowls, English country houses, and Italian princes. Where Marx closes off the discussion with a finality, James leaves the door open for the entry of the irrational—of love, of humanity, of the soul, all questions left in problematic form by the onslaught of the Ververs with their money and commodity and aura fetishes.

It is at the point in the discussion of the fetishistic character of the commodity that Marx seems to come the closest to providing an answer for the mystery of the *hau* or the quilt-value I have defined as a feminine system of value. And yet it is at this point that the two concepts seem most to diverge. While Marx's answer to Adam Smith may sufficiently reduce the gilt of social prestige to a matter rationalized in labor time that can be commanded, that answer seems inadequate to address the question of the soul-mingling aura of my grandmother's quilt and of heirlooms in general.

The cleavage widens when we consider the question of how many imponderables of the human soul cannot be sufficiently answered by Marx's theory—even his theory of the fetishistic quality of commodities. Why does advertising work? Marx postulates the concept of socially necessary labor time; it is the use-value quality of the commodity that determines if it is socially necessary. The concept of social necessity is a matter of community determination—in the capitalist context, of free-market values. If it will sell, it has, ipso facto, a use-value, either socially or as determined by the market. This goes as well for gilded hula hoops and mass-produced imitation antique quilts, as for wheat, milk, or soybeans. The only hope for rationalism, it would seem, is to reenter consciousness into the concept of use-value and social necessity and to determine in idealist rather than in production terms what is worth producing and consuming. The concept of use-value, therefore, contains within it the very germ of antimaterialist protosocialist idealism, the intervention of rational conscious control of the market system.

This argument admittedly throws us back to the antimaterialist utopianism of the nineteenth-century transcendentalists, continuing in a line up to the German Marxist Ernst Bloch. Of the two, Bloch is the more convincing. While

Bronson Alcott's Fruitlands Community was a dismal failure and Louisa May Alcott's *Little Men* may seem unrealistically smarmy, Bloch posits a role for utopianism that can conceivably be integrated into a Marxist or materialist enterprise. Bloch suggests an essential function for Utopianism as "a critique of what is present."[9] To translate this in terms of quilt-value, as I have defined it, or heirloom-value, the very fact of keeping alive the reverence for family artifact and an individually humane history postulates a time that, in the Marxist lexicon, can only come when all goods are produced for use rather than for exchange. By reverencing these values in the here and now, reified in the goods and items passed on from one generation to the next, the female keepers of these vessels of human history postulate the utopia that criticizes inherently the overly materialistic present. Heirlooms serve as the antithesis of the insistent newness of TV commercialism and magazine ads. As Bloch quotes Oscar Wilde, "A map of the world that does not include utopia is not worth glancing at."[10]

While Bloch discusses advertising as trading on a certain utopianism for material intent, it is clear that heirlooms embody a peculiarly human value. Commercial items may embody human values of time and labor and, as Marx discusses in the fetish chapter and Henry James illustrates, such values may signify one person's control over other men and women (and children), who labor to produce the goods he flaunts. The human value embodied in heirlooms and quilts is of a more personal, if you will, more human quality. In that way, this human value posits the possibility of a more humane, more rational way of calculating what to produce and what to spend our laboring hours doing. In suggesting the possibility of an "aura" of human potential, heirlooms suggest in their very existence the superseding of capitalism and the market economy. Of course, such a notion is in itself somewhat utopian. As Bloch says, "It has become clear that capitalist society is based on the unlimited profit motive and price quantification of all of its objects, and thus it is the commodity category that rules all relations, including the mathematical natural sciences and even all the 'irrational' diverging ideologies."[11]

Commenting on Bloch, speaking of a Derridean concept of "trace," which suggests the pure signification of the sort I have been discussing, Fredric Jameson says, "For the trace in Bloch is both an external object and an immediate experience: its authenticity is certified, before any conscious intellectual interpretation, by the sheer glowing emblems in which some urgent yet utterly personal secret seems to be concealed."[12]

---

9. *The Utopian Function of Art and Literature,* 12.
10. Ibid., 17.
11. Ibid., 23.
12. *Marxism and Form,* 122.

Here again the Marxist philosophers are addressing themselves to the "utterly personal secrets,"—*hau*, perhaps—that stand in defiance of the reduction of all human activity to the commodity form.

Central to Bloch's argument is the notion that if we could not conceive of noncommercial values in the here and now, we could not conceive of them in some socialist future. *Hau* values, heirloom-values, seem a perhaps peculiarly feminine means of posing the possibility of a future noncapitalist world of relations based on use-value and human value rather than profit.

Marx, himself, in his early, preliminary work, saw that this idealist determination was possible. First of all, he saw that the subversion of subjective determination was a phenomenon of private property or what he called alienated labor. Writing in the early manuscripts of 1844, he said,

> Because men making exchanges do not relate to one another as men, *things* lose the significance of being human and personal property. The social relationship of private property to private property is a relationship in which private property has alienated itself. The reflexive existence of this relationship, money, is thus the externalization of private property, an abstraction from its *specific* and personal nature. (italics in original)[13]

Marx then projected an image of unalienated labor, which he thought might yet come to pass in some future de-materialized society with the abolition of marketplace private property:

> Suppose we had produced things as human beings; in his production each of us would have *twice affirmed* himself and the other. (1) In my *production* I would have objectified my *individuality* and its *particularity*, and in the course of that activity I would have enjoyed an individual *life;* in viewing the object I would have experienced the individual joy of knowing my personality as an *objective, sensuously perceptible*, and *indubitable* power. . . . In my individual life I would have directly created your life; in my individual activity I would have immediately *confirmed* and *realized* my true *human* and *social* nature. (italics in original)[14]

In this theorizing, Marx suggests the unalienated labor of the communist future. In point of fact, it is difficult to imagine that computers or microwaves or fastbacks will ever be the product of individualized nonmass labor, or that the producers of helicopters will know personally the passengers of helicopters. Similarly, it seems unrealistic to suggest, as did William Morris and such socialist leaders as James P. Cannon, that a return to the arts and crafts movement in the future utopia will somehow obviate alienated labor.

Nonetheless, the fact that we have the capacity to treasure nonmarketable relics of family history and travel memorabilia and can, in this generation,

13. Loyd T. Easton and Kurt H. Guddat. *Writings of the Young Marx on Philosophy and Society*, 267.
14. Ibid., 281.

hope to convey such values to our sons as well as to our daughters, suggests that noncommercial humanistic determinations may not need to wait for the future nirvana. We can, even now, as our foremothers did before us, experience ourselves as significant players in the drama of human continuity just by passing down our quilts.

A Quilt Is an Art Object when It Stands Up like a Man

Susan E. Bernick

Most feminists predicted that the elevation of quilts to fine-art status would be a positive development for women in both the male-dominated art world and in traditional women's quilting circles. I would like to present the results of an investigation into who has, in fact, benefited from this elevation; the inquiry suggests that the increase in status for some quilts was bought at the cost of women's control over quilting as an art form, the creation, reception, and preservation of their quilts, and at the cost of deep divisions between traditional quilters and art quilters, including some feminists, which resulted from a splintering of what had been a fairly unified artistic tradition.

This analysis was originally a case study within a larger work on the political and ontological ramifications of recent developments in aesthetics.[1] In that work, I criticized as overly simplistic the account given by Marcia Eaton of the way in which artifacts may become, or cease to be, works of art.[2] While contemporary work in the philosophy of art, including Eaton's, acknowledges that art, particularly in the twentieth century, has taken inspiration from nonart artifacts (for example, Picasso's *Les Demoiselles d'Avignon*), utilized them in the making of new works of art (see my discussion of Robert Rauschenberg's *Bed* below), and even occasionally treated them as works of art on their own terms (as in Jonathan Holstein's 1971 Whitney show of American patchwork quilts), aestheticians have insufficiently noted or appreciated the extent to which these artifacts *were already* seen as works of art within the various traditions from which they were appropriated. More careful attention to the place of quilts and quiltmaking in what I will call traditional quilt culture reveals the presence of a woman's artworld, coexisting with those institutions and practices we usually designate by that term. Drawing on my earlier work, I will utilize the convention of referring to the high art culture as the artworld,$_1$ and to any oppositional or marginalized

---

1. Susan E. Bernick, "How an Artifact Becomes or Ceases to Be a Work of Art: Artworld Category Changes as a Possible Model for Feminist Politics."
2. *Art and Nonart: Reflections on an Orange Crate and a Moose Call.*

artistic tradition as an artworld.$_2$[3] That the referent of the term *work of art* cannot be fixed, on this account, is the result not only of the evolutionary and transgressive nature of the artworld,$_1$ but is also due to the presence of artworlds$_2$ that coexist, overlap and occasionally compete with it.

If one reads the material on quilts published in the last twenty-five years in the United States, including not just art books but scholarly monographs and, most importantly, articles in women's magazines and the women's pages of American newspapers, it becomes clear how complex and contested is the current status of quilts. The popular view, which is also the view with which I began this research, has it that quilts, lined up in neat rows like suffragettes, have now achieved acceptance as a uniquely American, uniquely female art form.[4] This picture is not just incomplete; it's inaccurate. There are at least three distinct quilt cultures. Although more or less independent, each culture overlaps and influences the others, and each culture can plausibly claim credit for quilts being or becoming works of art. None of these quilt cultures alone has done, or perhaps can do, justice to quilts' multiplicity of meanings.

In descending order of social legitimacy, the cultures I have identified are what I will term the art quilt tradition or culture, the feminist quilt culture, and the traditional quilt culture. It should be noted at the outset that each of the three quilt cultures considers at least some quilts to be works of art, and there are individual quilters from each of the three cultures who are seen as artists within that culture. The following brief summary may help in navigating the distinctions I will draw out more fully below.

3. I will not utilize this notation throughout the text, as it becomes distracting for the reader. I will use it selectively to underscore the status of quilts *as works of art on their own terms within an autonomous women's artistic tradition* in those places I believe the evidence allows me to make the point.

4. Quilts are not uniquely American. Quilted clothing and bedcovers are found in a number of cultures and historical epochs other than American ones. Quilts have probably been made almost exclusively by women; their status as works of art is less clear. The murkiness of the actual geographic and aesthetic status of quilts notwithstanding, some version of this sentiment can be found in nearly every recent publication on quilts. A representative sampling from each of the three quilt cultures I will discuss below: "Hood River Arts & Crafts Society's Columbia Art Gallery is saluting the Bicentennial with an exhibit having a uniquely American art form, the patchwork quilt." Jeannie Senior, "Quilts Dating from 1860s in Show," *Portland Oregonian*, September 12, 1976. "Quilts have endured for centuries to take their rightful place as one of the most universally recognized American art forms, an art of the people, an art that speaks of love with every stitch—love of beauty, love of life, love of work, love of family." Karoline Patterson Bresenhan and Nancy O'Bryant Puentes, *Lone Stars: A Legacy of Texas Quilts, 1836–1936*, 11. "The contrast between the utilitarian necessity of patching and quilting and the beautiful works of art which women made of it, and the contrast between the traditions of patchwork and quilting as brought to America and the quilts made here from colonial times to the present, give ample evidence that quilts are The Great American Art." Patricia Mainardi, "Quilts: The Great American Art," 1982, 331.

The traditional quilt school is composed of the vast majority of women who have quilted in the past and most of the women who quilt now. Their story is complicated by the fact that traditional quilters have been, historically, the makers of the quilts now theorized about and bought by both feminist and non-feminist art critics and collectors. If an art collector buys a quilt made after 1940, however, odds are that the quilt was not made by a member of the traditional quilt culture, since quilts made by traditional quilters after that date are generally considered to be less aesthetically valuable.[5]

One way to describe the relationship between the traditional quilt culture and the others is to say that the traditional quilt culture is the trunk from which the other quilt culture branches grew. The traditional quilt culture has a branch of its own, however; it is not merely an ancestral or stock culture. The art quilt and feminist quilt cultures, both of which sprouted in the early 1970s, attend to the quilters of the trunk, but they generally ignore, when they do not actively denigrate, the traditional quilters in the branch of the tree growing alongside their own.

The feminist quilt culture is diverse. It includes women's studies scholars who are interested in women's art, feminist historians who use quilts as documents of social and domestic history, and a handful of feminist artists who are making quilts directly for the art market. Some of the state-by-state efforts to document quilts have been informed by feminist concerns, but they rely heavily on traditional quilters and their social organizations to locate the quilts they will document, photograph, and exhibit.[6] The art quilt group includes a few gallery directors and curators, but its main constituents are collectors, artists who make quilts, and art book publishers.

---

5. There are no doubt innumerable exceptions to this generalization and the 1940 date is somewhat arbitrary; it is, however, consistently used as a demarcation between "good" and "bad" quilts made within the traditional quilt culture. It reflects not just a perceived decline in the artistry of American quiltmakers but more crucially the beginning of the wide-spread availability and use of synthetic fabrics, which for complex reasons are considered a mark of an aesthetically inferior quilt.

6. I would cite the Kentucky and Eastern Pennsylvania projects in particular. The usual procedure for a quilt project is for a small group of women to hold "quilt documentation days" in as many regions of the state as possible. Information is collected about the fabric in each quilt and the technique used to make it. When possible, information about the quilter and her family history is also noted. The quilt is measured and a photograph of it is taken. The process of collecting this information about a state's quilts typically takes from eighteen months to two years. At the conclusion of the work, a show of the best quilts is held in an art gallery or historical society museum, and a large glossy art-book-format text is published. Minnesota completed its state quilt project in 1990. Women in Oregon, North and South Carolina, and Texas have also documented their state's quilts. No doubt these projects have been undertaken in other parts of the country as well.

The Art Quilt Culture

The story of the art quilt tradition begins in July of 1971, when Jonathan Holstein guest-curated a show of quilts at the Whitney Museum of American Art in New York. This event is considered the single most important in the certification of quilts as full-fledged art objects.[7] Holstein is also, more than any other single individual, responsible for the fact that quilts have been accepted in the highest reaches of the artworld₁ *only* to the extent that they have been taken away from traditional quilt culture and defeminized.

> At this time [pre-Whitney], normal criteria for judging the importance of quilts was [*sic*] age, historical associations, workmanship and beauty. . . . We were . . . interested . . . solely in how well they worked as visual phenomena. While no one who collects quilts can remain unaware of their extraordinary meaning as social documents, we managed to stick ruthlessly to our criteria, feeling that was the only way we could reach our goal [of having an exhibition in a major art museum]. . . . The emphasis on the visual aspects of quilts over their other intrinsic qualities, a position which characterized the Whitney exhibition and others, was a necessary step in freeing quilts from their bedspread/craft/mythology baggage.[8]

His insistence on evaluating quilts on only the narrowest of visual criteria, and his presentation of quilters as "anonymous women," even when many quilts in his collection are signed and dated, have been criticized at length by other feminist writers.[9] My criticisms will be directed at two other features of the art quilt culture less-often discussed: documentation and money.

Holstein and Gail van der Hoof had been collecting quilts throughout the eastern United States for a number of years before the Whitney show. If the labels on the quilts in the catalog of the exhibit and in his 1973 book are any indication, the only data he collected on any quilt he bought were the state in which it was purchased and the approximate date it was made. Having set such a poor example for those who would follow, he acknowledged in 1986, "as the quilt collecting craze gathered force during the 1970s, it became apparent that many textiles were leaving the social matrix in which they had been embedded since they were made. As a result, much valuable information was being lost."[10] "*Were leaving* the social matrix," he said, not "were being taken," as if the quilts ran away from home, yearning to be free of the "baggage" of their social matrix, namely women's traditional quilt culture.

---

7. I follow custom in identifying Holstein as the only curator despite the fact that his wife, Gail van der Hoof, was centrally involved. She has written a few pieces on appraising quilts, but he has generally been the more public member of the couple. Davey Packer, interview with author.

8. "The Whitney and After . . . What's Happened to Quilts," 81–83.

9. Mainardi, "Great American Art," passim.

10. "The Whitney and After," 83.

There is no way to recover this information once the connection between the quilt and its "social matrix" has been severed; I would suggest we should view the treatment of quilts collected in this way as a form of cultural theft.

Despite the deserved reproach feminists have leveled against quilt collectors for their sloppy documentation practices, few scholars have asked hard questions about why families have sold quilts that had been passed down through generations, and no one has drawn attention to the fact that Holstein and others have made fortunes on their collections while the individuals from whom quilts were bought made a few hundred dollars at most. While I have not been able to find any accurate information on the size of Holstein's profits, there is another large quilt collection for which numbers are available.

In 1977 David Pottinger left his Detroit plastics manufacturing job and moved to Honeyville, Indiana, where he bought the general store serving a small Amish community. In addition to selling goods to the Amish, he also bought their quilts, some seven hundred in all.[11] He donated one hundred of them to the Museum of American Folk Art in New York. In order to keep the rest of the quilts in the state, the Indiana State Museum had to raise the $650,000 Pottinger was asking for the collection. The Lilly Endowment put up $400,000 and "the Indiana State Museum Society volunteers [worked] to raise the remaining $250,000."[12] The cost to Indiana was more than $1,000.00 per quilt; at the time Pottinger was collecting, even the finest examples of Amish quilts could be bought for only a few hundred dollars.[13]

The Traditional Quilt Culture

The traditional quilt culture is the most difficult to write about, in part because of its remarkable unselfconsciousness. There is an additional problem created by contemporary traditional quilters having been cut off from their own history by the appropriation of their past by the two other quilt cultures. In addition, the traditional quilters of the past and the quilts they made are the raw materials for theories about quilts and quilting constructed by the other quilt cultures. Contemporary traditional quilters, on the other hand, who don't often theorize about or document their own work, are denigrated by the art culture and too often ignored by feminists.

The 1976 Bicentennial was the impetus for a renewed interest by working and middle class Americans in America's folk arts and craft heritage. Although some women had continued to quilt between 1940 and 1976, quilting, in its richest social, artistic, and psychic complexity, had nearly ceased being prac-

11. Joseph Harriss, "The Newest Quilt Fad Seems to Be Going Like Crazy," 120.
12. Sally Falk, "Donors Sought to Keep Amish Quilt Collection," *Indianapolis Star,* June 21, 1987.
13. Harriss, "Newest Quilt Fad," 124.

ticed. Fifteen years later, there has been a rebirth of quilting activity, especially among women of the middle class. Projects such as the Boise Peace Quilt Project[14] and the efforts of a Milwaukee quilting teacher to have quilts made for the local Ronald McDonald House[15] testify to a renewed appreciation of quilts as community-building events as well as aesthetic objects. Younger women are once again making quilts for exhibition at the state fairs that have often served as established gallery spaces for quilts made as works of art$_2$ by traditional quilters.

In contrast to the art quilt culture, women who make quilts value not just their beauty as designed objects, but also the evenness and size of the stitching used in piecing and quilting them. Quilters also consider the reason a quilt was made to be a fact about its history of production that can direct the viewer's attention to intrinsic properties of the quilt that are worthy of contemplation (in Eaton's view, the mark of an aesthetic property). They especially value quilts made to express affection or concern for a family member. Beyond these general properties, the specific aesthetic choices quilters make depend greatly on class, race, and region. One attempt at distinguishing differences among quilters has been to divide them into plain quilters and fancy quilters.[16] These categories have the virtue of being used by women who quilt, but the line between the two is not hard and fast, and different regions and racial groups have made the distinction using different criteria.

Historically, traditional quilters were primarily plain quilters; some quilters never attempted a fancy quilt. A privileged few made only fancy quilts. The fancy/plain quilt distinction is in part an art/non-art distinction; that is, traditional quilt culture typically only counts fancy quilts as works of art.$_2$ The distinction may sometimes instead be used to describe class distinctions among quilters. Plain quilts were, above all else, made to be used. In one Appalachian community, pieced, strip, and string quilts made of remnants, which were often synthetic, and quilted in a fan pattern with long stitches or tacks were considered "plain." The thread used contrasted with, rather than blending with, the cloth.[17] Black quilters are usually, but not always, plain quilters, and the improvisational style said to be typical of African American quilters can be found in the compositions of poor white quilters as well.[18]

14. Elizabeth Kolbert, "Quilters Making an Appeal for Peace," *New York Times,* October 10, 1985; Natalie Gittelson, "The Peace Quilt," 95.

15. Charlene Gaynor, "Quilters Piece Together Gifts of Love, Comfort," *Milwaukee Journal,* May 6, 1984.

16. Geraldine N. Johnson, "'Plain and Fancy': The Socioeconomics of Blue Ridge Quilts"; Joanne Farb, "Piecin' and Quiltin': Two Quilters in Southwest Arkansas."

17. Johnson, "'Plain and Fancy,'" 14–18.

18. While there is considerable similarity between quilts made by black and white working-class or poor plain quilters, some scholars have argued that African Americans have a distinctive quilting aesthetic of their own, one which includes fancy quilts. See John

Fancy quilts are made "'for the beauty and not really for the service,'"[19] in other words, for other than strictly utilitarian reasons. The fancy quilters in the Appalachian community discussed above have a stereotypically feminine conception of what counts as beauty and value floral appliqué quilts more than rectilinear pieced ones. While plain quilts are made for a family's utilitarian needs, fancy quilts are often made to symbolize and sanctify relationships. Family members often encourage fancy quilters "to spend long hours at the quilting frame producing an item they know will eventually be theirs."[20] The quilting and piecing stitches are done with thread that blends with the fabric, and both piecing and quilting are usually executed using smaller stitches than those found in plain quilts.

Another plain/fancy distinction was made on the basis of the size of the pieces used in constructing the top; the smaller the pieces, the fancier the quilt.[21] In addition, the distinction has been used to differentiate between shapes and elaborateness of the quilting stitches (rather than in reference to the quilt as a whole). Fancy quilting in this sense is used to refer to the complex and curvilinear shapes used to quilt open spaces in a pieced design, while plain quilting is quilting done in straight rows, either outlining the pieces or straight across an appliquéd or geometric pieced top.[22]

Quilters use both the plain and fancy quilts they make, although fancy quilts may only be used sparingly. Quilts represent home, family, and community values rather than monetary ones, even to women who sell their work, which is probably why they are willing to part with their quilts for such staggeringly low sums. What I find significant, however, is that quilters express less conflict between utilitarian and aesthetic values than they do between the cluster of associations they attach to quilts and money. That a quilt is useful, in other words, is part of what makes it beautiful. That a homemade artifact, embedded in the history of a family, might have a high monetary value, on the other hand, is often not a welcome or even salient feature of quilt-ownership within the traditional quilt culture. Contrast this with the assumption made by most participants in the artworld₁ that utility *detracts* from aesthetic value, may, indeed, even disqualify an artifact as a work of art, while monetary value,

---

Michael Vlach, *The Afro-American Tradition in Decorative Arts,* and Maude Southwell Wahlman, "African Symbolism in Afro-American Quilts." On the other hand, which aspects of quilting are black and which ones white can be difficult to determine, particularly in the South. Black women made many of the Southern quilts counted today as part of the white quilting tradition. Even when made for whites, under white supervision, they may bear some resemblances to the quilts black women made for themselves. More recently scholars have begun to recognize the complexity of these questions. See Cuesta Ray Benberry, *Always There: The African-American Presence in American Quilts.*

19. Lura Stanley Johnson, quoted in "'Plain and Fancy,'" 26.
20. Ibid., 27.
21. Merikay Waldvogel, *Soft Covers for Hard Times: Quiltmaking and the Great Depression,* 55.
22. Marilyn Lithgow, *Quiltmaking and Quiltmakers,* 47–49.

when it is not considered irrelevant, is seen as enhancing its value as a work of art.₁

Over and over women say that the purpose of making a quilt is to express love. Rather than demonstrating mastery over what is by any standard a difficult medium, the effort and time required to make a quilt beautiful are valued not for their own sake, but as tangible evidence of an abiding affection for a family member, a desire for world peace, or concern for a community of children with cancer.

All of this suggests that for traditional quilters, the term *work of art* has a more complex meaning than it has in the artworld.₁ For example, "x is a painting," or "x is a sculpture" is typically considered to imply "x is a work of art." The distinctions that are made amongst paintings and sculptures are usually made in terms of quality, not membership in the class of works of art. Quilting as a medium does not work in the same way. For traditional quilters, a quilt, *simply by virtue of its membership in the class,* is not necessarily either a work of art₂ or not a work of art.₂ Despite the fact that quilting as an activity does not always result in a work of art, there are, nevertheless, quilts that are made to be art works and that are treated as such within the community of women who share quilting as, among other things, an artistic tradition.

The Feminist Quilt Culture

The development of a specifically feminist approach to quilts can be dated from the publication, in 1973, of Patricia Mainardi's article, "Quilts: The Great American Art."[23] In her essay, Mainardi presented the first feminist art historical treatment of quilts, complete with an analysis of the interweaving design traditions of African American, Native American, and European quilters and the role quilting played in women's social and emotional lives. In other words, Mainardi treated the artistic tradition of quilts as an artistic tradition in its own terms, although she also used the language of the artworld₁ in speaking of the evolution of quilt design. Mainardi also excoriated Jonathan Holstein and other members of the artworld₁ for their sexist treatment of quilts, citing, in particular, the presentation of quilt artists as anonymous, self-effacing women who in no way saw what they were doing as art.

The second landmark event in the history of the feminist quilt culture was the creation of Judy Chicago's *The Dinner Party*, first exhibited in 1979. The table runners for Trotula, an eleventh-century midwife and gynecologist who lived in southern Italy, Sojourner Truth, and Susan B. Anthony all contain quilted sections. In their text, *Embroidering Our Heritage: The Dinner Party Needlework*,[24] Chicago and Susan Hill summarized quilt lore found in books written by traditional quilters; through them, the traditional lore became part of

23. "Great American Art."
24. *Embroidering Our Heritage: The Dinner Party Needlework.*

feminist lore about quilts. Mainardi's and Chicago's approach to the reclamation of quilts as art, while not identical, is similar; both attempt to envision quilts as art on their own terms.

The other approach to quilts taken by feminists has been concerned less with the aesthetics of quilts than it has been with quilts as texts of social history. Because women have left few documents with which historians can reconstruct our past, feminist scholars have turned to quilts as one source of information about women's lives. The difficulty with this approach is that explicitly reducing even narrative quilts to their textual content fails to challenge and may even buttress the categories of text, history, and art that have excluded women from participating in all three.[25]

Probably the lowest point in the history of feminist involvement with quilting was Charlotte Robinson's *The Artist and the Quilt*,[26] conceived in the early 1970s and finally completed and shown in 1982. Twenty famous women artists,$_1$ not all of them feminists, were recruited by Robinson. Each artist was paired with a quilter, most of whom were unknown in the artworld$_1$ at the time the project began. The artists, in some cases without consultation with the quilters, made works of art$_1$ that were then "translated" by the quilters into their medium.

Some of the women who quilted for the project expressed pleasure in both product and process and stated that working with professional artists had stretched them in ways they liked. Some of the quilters felt they were treated as the second-class member of the partnership, although these voices are muted in the self-congratulatory text on the project published by Robinson. Up until the sale of the entire collection to Phillip Morris, only the quilters had been paid for their work. Each of the quilters received $2,000, which Robinson had generated through grants. Ironically, this added to, rather than diminished, their exploitation. It is true that the artists$_1$ could better afford to do the work without pay, but it made the quilts, waiting for a buyer, the product of the artists;$_1$ the quilters, like materials, were purchased to realize the artists' intentions.

Middle-class and/or educated feminists have sometimes had difficulty reconciling our desire to valorize our female past with the day-to-day reality of women who are still enmeshed within the confines of women's traditional lives. Feminists have a vested interest in presenting quilting foremothers as strong, independent, and self-consciously creative women. Miriam Schapiro, an artworld$_1$ artist, has been in the forefront of the effort to claim women's traditional arts$_2$ as part of the high art$_1$ tradition. She has written,

> What is a quilt? Among other things, it is the history of women, a receptacle of passions, attitudes, largess, and anger. It is a reassembling process, which in itself

25. Pat Ferrero, Elaine Hedges, and Julie Silber, *Hearts and Hands: The Influence of Women and Quilts on American Society;* Linda Otto Lipsett, *Remember Me: Women and Their Friendship Quilts.*
26. *The Artist and the Quilt.*

may embody a solution to human problems. It is inspiration, a connection with self, the dogged will to make something extraordinary in the midst of family routine, a sense of wholeness, the wish to please, to succeed, pleasure in the act of working and knowing the power of "making."[27]

What should such a feminist say to a woman who

> seems to feel that the quilting, although it is nice to do and she enjoys it tremendously, has little real worth. . . . She bases her belief that she isn't artistic on the fact that she can't draw a straight line; she doesn't consider her ruler as a tool to be used in helping her achieve her goals; rather, she considers it cheating. She therefore does not consider her quilts to be an art, but nevertheless is not at all embarrassed or reticent to have pictures taken of them or to answer questions about them.[28]

If the materials published by feminists are any indication, mostly we say nothing and ignore women who do not fit our preconceived notions of what a quilter should be like. Judy Chicago is at least honest about feeling disillusioned by some aspects of her apprenticeship to a china-painter, which she undertook in preparation for painting the porcelain plates for *The Dinner Party*. Chicago expresses admiration that the china-painters teach and work in public, rather than living their artistic lives in private, shut away from the uninitiated but curious who might want to learn from them. She continues,

> My learning experience with the china-painters was not totally positive, however. Many of them viewed me suspiciously, were outright hostile, or thought of me as someone who wanted to exploit them—despite all my efforts, both public and private, to honor them. This kind of reaction forced me to confront the conservatism and fear which, along with generosity and warmth, typify the 'subculture' of women's crafts. . . . They did not take themselves seriously nor did they believe that their experiences were important enough to express. This lack of self-esteem resulted not only in a continual dependence upon preformed patterns and designs, but also in a resistance to new ideas and unfamiliar thoughts. All this only reinforced my belief in the importance of addressing women's lack of self-worth as a crucial step in creating change and my determination to achieve this through art.[29]

Chicago is herself trained in the high-art tradition of the isolated and private artist. She felt that tradition oppressed her as a woman; surely one response to the oppressiveness of the artworld,[1] which the china-painters have undoubtedly also felt, is to choose not to identify oneself as an artist at all.

Rozsika Parker and Griselda Pollock have tried to reconcile these apparent conflicts by arguing that the contrast between heroic quilting grandmothers and simpering quilting granddaughters is due to historical changes that have

27. "Geometry and Flowers," 26.
28. Farb, "Piecin' and Quiltin'," 372–73.
29. *Embroidering Our Heritage*, 10.

their source outside the sphere of women's artistic traditions. In particular, they cite "the intersection in the eighteenth and nineteenth centuries of the development of an ideology of femininity, that is, a social definition of women and their role, with the emergence of a clearly defined separation of art and craft."[30] Lucy Lippard describes the rift in terms of the general decline of domestic arts, and attributes it to the process of de-skilling that accompanied the rise of industrial production and the consumer ethic that concurrently replaced working class artisans' pride in a job well done.[31]

While social history, particularly feminist social history, goes some way toward providing a framework within which to place these developments, the economic and social context doesn't answer all the questions posed by the history of quilting. In particular, feminists have to acknowledge the extent to which we have contributed to the gulf between traditional artists$_2$ and art$_1$ quilters, both feminist and not.

The tensions between traditional and feminist quilters are not often discussed openly, in part because the two groups to some extent live in separate worlds. It is significant that the fragments of conversation about the rift that have leaked into print take the feminist quilters' side of the story.

> As an increasing number of contemporary [feminist and/or art] quilters' works are reviewed in arts publications, some of these artisans are disassociating themselves from the traditional roots of quilting, Partee and Westfall say. "The stakes might be higher in the contemporary quilt art movement, but contemporary and traditional quilts are not mutually exclusive. They're part of a continuum. And we see ourselves as a necessary part of that continuum," Partee says. . . . "The contemporary, innovative quilt maker is not saying 'What I do is better,'" she says. "What this artist is saying is, 'I appreciate what the traditional quilt maker did. I understand the medium. Now I want to use the medium to express something different.'"[32]

Ruth McDowell, a contemporary feminist artist who makes quilts for the art market, complains that it is difficult for quilters like herself not to be bitter about the extent to which their work as artists is not considered as valuable as it might be had they chosen a different medium in which to work. She acknowledges that there is a tendency to blame traditional quilters for this, which she also says is a tendency that must be resisted.

On the other hand, she is angry at traditional quilters for being resentful of the relatively large sums art quilters make for their work. She is also angry that traditional quilters take exception to the unwillingness of art quilters to stay within the confines of established patterns and methods of construction. "Choosing her words carefully, she continues. . . . 'Unfortunately, there's a lot

30. *Old Mistresses: Women, Art and Ideology*, 58.
31. "Up, Down, and Across: A New Frame for New Quilts," 39.
32. Ann Beckmann, "Quilt Craze," *Everett [Washington] Daily Herald*, August 7, 1987.

of controversy that goes on between the traditional people and the ones who say, ". . . to copy exactly what they did 100 years ago is not getting us anywhere." . . . And I wish these traditional people would not feel so threatened by these new things.'"[33]

The Processes of Quilts Becoming Art_1

I hope thus far to have demonstrated, or at least made plausible, that quilts are part of an artistic tradition that was less privileged than the $artworld_1$ but nonetheless an $artworld_2$ in its own right. Both the feminist quilt tradition and the art quilt tradition have laid claim to the recent certification of quilts as works of art_1 but even feminists at times overlook the reality that quilts were works of art_2 before feminists discovered them as such. Broadly speaking, the art quilt culture claims to have made quilts into art while the feminist quilt culture claims only to have discovered that they were art all along. The former is arrogant as well as erroneous; the difficulty with the latter is that it presumes that *no one* knew quilts were works of art_2 before the feminist discovery that they were, which is also false. Nonetheless, each of the quilt cultures, including the traditional quilt culture, contains a narrative of certification. Not surprisingly, each culture tells the story of quilts-become-art quite differently, and these differences can help us distinguish between cultures yet further.

Discussions of the certification process of quilts by the $artworld_1$ typically ask, When did quilts become works of art? Was there a single identifiable moment when these homecrafted objects left the arenas of kitchen and bedroom and arrived, appropriately attired, for the gala gallery opening? Most of the writers who express an opinion on this subject acknowledge that there was a transformation, a process occurring over a space of several years, rather than a single event in time. Nonetheless, there are certain identifiable moments that have been consistently mentioned as crucially significant. The 1971 Whitney show, "Abstract Design in American Quilts," is the one usually pointed to by the art quilt culture, while the American Bicentennial in 1976 and Robert Rauschenberg's 1955 mixed media piece *Bed* are foregrounded in discussions by the traditional quilt culture and the feminist quilt culture, respectively. In comparison with the other events, the Bicentennial is usually credited with stirring renewed interest in *making* quilts, rather than in their aesthetic appreciation; in this sense it does not mark the certification of quilts as works of art in the same way as the 1971 Whitney show and *Bed* have been thought to do. Since I have argued that at least some quilts were already works of art within the traditional quilt culture, this is to be expected. If this is right, the Bicentennial marks, then, the *rebirth* of an artistic tradition, rather than the *creation* of one.

The writers who mention the American Bicentennial as a central event in

33. "Designing Woman," *Boston Herald,* June 28, 1987.

the new appreciation of quilts are, for the most part, reviewers for local newspapers and authors of how-to-quilt articles that appear in the women's pages of newspapers and in women's magazines. "Interest in quilting surged dramatically after the 1976 Bicentennial. Many communities, stirred by thoughts of pioneer folk art and America's past, made commemorative Bicentennial quilts, reviving the idea of the old quilting bee."[34] Within the world of dealers, collectors, and gallery curators, Jonathan Holstein's show of quilts at the Whitney Museum in July of 1971 is generally credited with being the single most important event in the transition of antique quilts from "mere" craft to high art. Robert Bishop, Director of the Museum of American Folk Art, wrote in a 1983 article, "'Abstract Design in American Quilts,' an exhibition assembled by collectors Jonathan Holstein and Gail van der Hoof at the Whitney Museum of American Art, changed all that [underappreciation of and low prices for quilts] and encouraged the public to perceive the extraordinary sense of color and design inherent in these early American textiles."[35] Similarly, Elizabeth Warren, a curator at the same museum, wrote, "[Since the Whitney] American quilts have been appreciated for their visual appeal as art, as well as for their functional value as bedcovers, and their historical importance as fabric documents of the lives of American women."[36] The clear implication is that quilts were not appreciated for their visual appeal before the Whitney show.

Despite the modest tone Holstein occasionally adopts, no one has insisted as loudly as he that the Whitney show, more than any other single event, was responsible for the revolution in the valuation of quilts. In fact, much of his subsequent career as a collector, writer, and quilt-show judge has been dependent on the supposed centrality of his role in the process of artistic elevation. "From this exhibition, it has generally been said, stemmed an international awareness of American quilts as designed objects. But it would be more accurate, perhaps, to say that the Whitney exhibition was the first in a series of events which changed forever the way quilts were seen."[37]

The centrality of Holstein's role in the re-valuation of quilts and the significance of the Whitney show in particular have been adopted as articles of faith by the popular press as well as by the art press, despite the fact that the popular press has been the only forum for the traditional quilt culture. A contemporary review of the Whitney show was headlined "Art: Quilts Find a Place at the Whitney."[38] Newspapers from communities as diverse as San Diego, Louisville, Kentucky, and Philadelphia have all credited the Whitney show with, at a minimum, effecting a new appreciation of quilts as designed

34. Harriss, "Newest Quilt Fad," 115.
35. "Robert Bishop on Quilts as Art," 32.
36. "Amish Quilts in the Museum of American Folk Art," 514–15.
37. "The Whitney and After," 80.
38. Hilton Kramer, "Art: Quilts Find a Place at the Whitney," *New York Times,* July 3, 1971.

objects; some explicitly lay the credit for the creation of quilts as art objects at the door of the Whitney.

> The explanation for why these quilts [at the Institute of Contemporary Art in Philadelphia] are being presented as "high art," which would have been unthinkable as little as six or eight years ago, reflects the success the Whitney Museum of American Art had with its trend-setting "Abstract Design in American Quilts" exhibition in 1971.[39]

> [The Whitney show] elevated the homely quilt to fine art.[40]

> [The Whitney show] didn't result in quilts being accepted as art but it had a major impact on fine craft since it emphasized the quilts' decorative characteristics independent of their function as blankets.[41]

All these accounts explicitly or implicitly credit the Whitney show with the *invention* of quilts as designed, decorative, and artistic objects. The authors of these articles come close to treating quilts as if they were naturally occurring objects, made without benefit of human skill, intelligence, or aesthetic sensibility.

Feminist quilt scholars have adopted one of two approaches when it comes to the question of how quilts are to be seen as art. Some agree with Holstein that modern art was a catalyst for a new, aesthetic valuation of quilts, but they have attempted to combine this insight with research into the role of quilts as social documents of women's history. One of the first feminist book-length pieces to be published on the subject of women and quilting was *The Quilters: Women and Domestic Art* by Patricia Cooper and Norma Bradley Buferd. A review of this book by Melinda Frye includes the following comment:

> Although the title suggests that this is an art book, it is more a work of cultural and oral history, arrived at through the medium of a craft. . . . While inspired by the Whitney Museum show that presented quilts as optical art in 1972 [*sic*], Cooper and Buferd have dug beneath the obvious attractive patterning to study the lives of women and have learned a deeper meaning to the art of "piecing." They have studied quilts as interpretations of life.[42]

More radical feminist writers reject the claims of Holstein and others to have discovered or created quilts as art,$_1$ and insist that quilts have been art$_2$

39. Victoria Donohoe, "Amish Quilts and Abstract Art Blended at ICA," *Philadelphia Inquirer,* August 8, 1976.

40. Diane Heilenman, "Blend of Old and New 'To Be Admired, Not Slept Under,'" *Louisville Courier-Journal,* July 8, 1984.

41. David Lewinson, "Quilts—Are They Art or Craft?" *San Diego Union,* August 2, 1984. It should be noted, however, that sometimes the writers are merely repeating what the local curators, dealers, or quilt artists have told them in the course of a background interview.

42. Review of *The Quilters: Women and Domestic Art,* 53.

all along, unappreciated at best, denied any status as works of art in their own terms at worst. These feminists have joined forces with the traditional quilters. Mainardi goes so far as to suggest that quilts were a crucial source of inspiration for modern art itself, and she rejects as male appropriation of female creativity the view that it was modern art that lay the foundation for seeing quilts as art.[43]

For the second sort of feminist writer, an event that took place in 1955 is more seminal than the 1971 show at the Whitney. In 1955 Robert Rauschenberg incorporated a Log Cabin quilt into a mixed media "painting" entitled *Bed*. The quilt was glued or nailed to a bed-shaped form, and portions of the surface of the quilt were painted. Both Rauschenberg's use of this quilt and the circumstances surrounding his use of it have been the subject of commentary by a number of authors. Radical feminists point to *Bed* not because they think it made quilts into works of art, but because it symbolizes how quilts as art$_1$ are often destroyed as quilts and, hence, as art.$_2$

I will contend, in agreement with Mainardi, that this work set the boundaries within which quilts could be viewed as art.$_1$ This early piece allowed for a new appreciation of the design elements of a particular range of quilts, but it also connected quilts-as-art-objects with male permission for their being seen as such. Rauschenberg was the first to publicly appropriate this female art form. On this view, Holstein's decision to collect quilts and his success in getting the Whitney to show them were continuations of that process.

Although Holstein's entire career is dependent on the apparent similarities between quilts and modern art, he has warned that one should be cautious about identifying them too closely:

> Any direct linking of the two mediums would be demeaning to the history and presence of both quilts and paintings. Implicit in the act of creating a painting is the intellectual process which ties the work of an artist to his aesthetic ancestors and his peers, and places it in the history of objects specifically made to be art. This is precisely the quality which was absent in the making of pieced quilts.[44]

In other words, art is smart, and quilts *qua* quilts are dumb, and therefore not art. The footnote to this passage discusses *Bed* as a paradigmatic instance of art as intellection; the fact that it incorporates a quilt does not demean the work because the reasons for its incorporation are entirely artistic and/or intellectual in nature. The text of this note reads, in part:

> The quilt was taken from a bed, where it had no doubt served to warm sleeping householders. Were they all-unsuspecting sleeping under "art," or did the quilt become that only when Rauschenberg made his bed on the wall? Thus stated, the answer would have to be that Rauschenberg made the quilt into art by

43. "Great American Art," 1982, 344.
44. *The Pieced Quilt: An American Design Tradition*, 115.

incorporating it in his painting, even though the quilt itself, extracted and put on the wall, would, like many of its fellows, be visually similar to paintings of some of Rauschenberg's contemporaries.[45]

Penny McMorris and Michael Kile have jointly authored a book in which they discuss the history of quilting in the context of the history of popular culture. Their perspective differs from the approaches of both the modernist Holstein and the feminist Mainardi.[46] They mention Rauschenberg's piece in the context of post–World War II art, which they claim (contra Holstein) was *less* intellectual and more open to popular and technical cultural influences than was pre–World War II art.

Art of the late 1940s and 1950s experimented with new media, including fabric. In 1955, *two* new works of art incorporated Log Cabin quilts: I have already discussed one; the other was made by Anne Wilson.[47] McMorris and Kile provide a bit more information about the householders from whom Rauschenberg took his quilt.

> The *Log Cabin* quilt used in *Bed* once belonged to artist Dorothea Rockburne. She recalls, "It was kind of special to me because I had it at the time my daughter Christine was born, and she used to spend a lot of time on it. I didn't actually give Bob the quilt, it just sort of appeared in the work one day. We were living at Black Mountain College then, and when you sent the wash out things had a way of appearing and disappearing. I remember when I first saw the painting he had made of it I thought, 'Oh! That's the quilt that I had.' It was a wonderful experience seeing it."[48]

Patricia Mainardi is the only consistently radical writer on the history of the creation and appropriation of quilts. As such, she has a much less benign interpretation of this event.

> The elevation of quilts from folk art to contemporary craft to contemporary art has been marked by distinct stages of acculturation. Retrospectively, Robert Rauschenberg's *Bed* of 1955 can be seen to have enacted a paradigmatic masculine attitude towards feminine cultural production; he stated: "When I did *Bed,* I had just literally run out of things to paint on. There was a quilt that I didn't need and I thought it would be good." *Bed* reflected accurately the place women's traditional arts held before the feminist movement of the 1960s. It is as raw material or support for the "art," namely Rauschenberg's painting, that the *Log*

45. Ibid., 115, n. 4.
46. McMorris and Kile are attempting, fairly successfully, to create a middle ground between the high art and the feminist quilting traditions. Penny McMorris and Michael Kile, *The Art Quilt.*
47. Holstein ignores her entirely. McMorris and Kile mention her work, but only provide a reproduction of Rauschenberg's piece. Lucy Lippard, in her essay "Up, Down, and Across: A New Frame for New Quilts," is alone in illustrating Wilson's work.
48. *Art Quilt,* 54, n. 104.

Cabin quilt in his work is used, transformed, and destroyed. The precedence of male over female, high art over low, is graphically illustrated. And yet Rauschenberg and many other male artists of his generation collected and admired traditional quilts, although not quite as "real art" and certainly not as the work of "real artists."[49]

By way of conclusion, I would like to make two points, one general, and one more specific. The general point is that if feminists are to have an account of quilting that does full justice to its considerable complexity, we will have to do better than we have done so far at including all the women who quilt in our analysis. The particular point has to do with what I think the complexity of quilting, and the story of its status as both art_1 and $art_{,2}$ can tell us about the ongoing struggle of women to define ourselves simultaneously as both participants in society and oppositional outsiders to its institutions. Women's art_2 forms

> can be experienced as a source of strength, joy, expression and as an affirmative badge of pride. [They] remain nonetheless stigmatic in the sense of a brand, a restriction, a definition as less. This is not because of any intrinsic content or value but because the social reality is that their shape, qualities, texture, imperative, and very existence are a response to powerlessness. They exist as they do because of lack of choice. They are created out of social conditions of oppression and exclusion. They may be part of a strategy for survival or even of change—but, as is, they are not the whole world, and it is the whole world that one is entitled to.[50]

As long as contemporary traditional quilters are divided from feminists—whether artists, quilters, collectors, critics, or historians—the full story of quilts as an art form created and maintained by generations of women must wait to be told.

---

49. "Quilt Survivals and Revivals," 50, footnote omitted. I find it curious that of the few sources that mention Rauschenberg's piece, most limit their discussion of it to the footnotes rather than incorporating it into the text. It's as if the incident can only be alluded to. Also, none of the authors mention one another's interpretations. Although Mainardi is quick to challenge Holstein on a variety of other issues, and while chronologically both Mainardi and McMorris and Kile could have commented on Holstein's account, neither do so. For another discussion of this event and for a color reproduction of *Bed*, see Helen Dudar, "The Artist Who Wants to Embrace the Whole World," 64–66.

50. Catharine A. MacKinnon, "Sexuality, Pornography, and Method: 'Pleasure under Patriarchy,'" 343, footnote omitted. I have used this quotation in a different context than the one MacKinnon intended.

◆ Preserving the Social Fabric ◆
Quilting in a Technological World
Susan Behuniak-Long

I didn't know that when I first looked at an Amish quilt and felt my heart pounding that my soul was starving, that an inner voice was trying to make sense of my life.

. . . .

I thought I was going to learn more about [Amish] quilts, but the quilts were only guides, leading me to what I really needed to learn, to answer a question I hadn't yet formed:
Is there another way to lead a good life?

Sue Bender, *Plain and Simple:*
A Woman's Journey to the Amish

In an age in which the inexhaustible power of scientific technology makes all things possible, it remains to be seen where we will draw the line, where we will be able to say, here are possibilities that wisdom suggests we avoid. I am convinced that any philosophy of technology worth its salt must eventually ask, How can we limit modern technology to match our best sense of who we are and the kind of world we would like to build?

Langdon Winner, *The Whale and the Reactor: A Search for*
Limits in an Age of High Technology

The ubiquitous nature of technology indicates a society driven by the pursuit of speed, efficiency, and production. Technological innovations are developed, sold, and embraced in the name of progress. The acclaim, however, is not universal. Scholars are producing a body of literature that ques-

This essay was inspired by my participation in the Le Moyne College Values Program's 1991 Summer Institute on Science, Technology, and Values. I am indebted to all of the participants for sharing their ideas and enthusiasm. I also acknowledge and thank the Le Moyne College Faculty Senate Committee on Research and Development for its support.

tions whether technology can truly buy us time, release us from boredom, and unleash our creativity.[1] These critics are not technophobes; rather, they are raising the question of whether technology, in eliminating the traditional way of doing things, fails to fully replicate all the social functions of the previous method.[2] A substitution of technique may result in a loss of social patterns and community values. Are we aware of the point when this occurs? Do we know where to stop the advancement of technology?

Given the social import of these questions, it may seem odd to seek answers through the study of quilting. Quilts are, after all, anachronisms of a preindustrial world. Painstakingly cut, pieced, and sewn, they move in slow motion as the rest of the world reels ahead in fast-forward. But this is precisely the source of their value. In a highly mechanized world, quilts stand as statements about social values and technological limits. While we grapple with the task of defining technological boundaries, quilters use a needle to stitch the line beyond which technology should not tread.

Like a quilt, this essay is constructed of three layers. The first section examines the degree and kind of impact that technology has had on the craft of quilting. While quilting may appear to be an act of resistance in the face of technology, quilters have, in fact, integrated elements of technology within their work, and indeed, technology has transformed the meaning of the activity itself. The essay's second layer applies theoretical critiques of technology in the workplace to the craft of quilting in order to illustrate the political dimensions of technology. The essay's third section returns to the question of what is lost when one technique is substituted for another. As applied to quilting, the answer also indicates what is preserved by the practice of this craft.

How Technology Touches Quilting

It is important to see quilting not as outside of the technological world, but as a part of it. It is the rare quilter who is impervious to the impact of technology; both the theory and the practice of the craft are influenced, even shaped, by technology. First, the political significance of quilting has changed as the activity has evolved from an economic necessity to an art form, a transformation rooted in the industrialization of textiles. Second, technology has also changed the practice of the craft through the introduction of new quilting tools, machines, books, and methods.

1. See Albert Borgmann, *Technology and the Character of Contemporary Life: A Philosophical Inquiry;* Bernard Gendron, *Technology and the Human Condition;* Michael Goldhaber, *Reinventing Technology: Policies for Democratic Values;* Winner, *Whale and the Reactor,* 103.

2. Langdon Winner, *The Whale and the Reactor: A Search for Limits in an Age of High Technology,* 48.

Technology and the Meaning of Quilting

The history of American quilting is inextricably bound to the history of technology. Prior to industrialization, quilting was a necessity. Little girls learned the craft at so young an age that many had completed their first quilt by the time they were five. But this was no childish hobby; it was work. Needlework was taught through use of the "stints"—"the assignment of a specific amount of work to be done each day."[3] Young white girls labored for years to complete twelve quilts before work on their marriage quilts began.[4] Black women (and men) bound in slavery sewed late into the night, producing quilts to cover their families.[5] Women who relocated to America's frontier depended on their quilts not only to warm their beds but also to cover windows and doors and shut out the cold and the blowing dust.[6]

In that preindustrial age, women labored to weave and dye fabrics, collected cotton or wool to make the batting, and sewed until their hands cramped too badly to hold needles any longer. Such labor elevated the value of each item produced. Fabric was so highly valued that frugality demanded patchwork over the more wasteful technique of appliqué which layers fabric over fabric. While quilting did serve as a much-needed outlet for creativity[7] and political expression,[8] and while it did provide occasions for social contact through the quilting bees,[9] quilting was also oppressive in its attempt to answer the urgent need of survival.

With the rise of industrialization, quilting took on new meaning. The mass production and low cost of fabrics, clothing, and bedding might have freed at least middle- and upper-class women from the oppressive needle. Instead, the bondage continued in a new form. The creation of quilts was used to further the development of new standards of femininity. No longer were large quantities the goal; now the quality of the quilt was highly prized. Elaborate designs, extravagant use of fabrics, and tiny and profuse quilting stitches became the marks of quilting excellence. The model wife or daughter was one who sewed, quilted, embroidered, knitted, crocheted, and tatted items worthy of admiration. Not so coincidentally, she was also a woman who sat quietly, modestly, and patiently, and selflessly engaged in the repetition, monotony,

3. Elaine Hedges in Pat Ferrero, Elaine Hedges, and Julie Silber, *Hearts and Hands: The Influence of Women and Quilts on American Society*, 18.

4. Carter Houck, *The Quilt Encyclopedia Illustrated*, 34.

5. Gladys-Marie Fry, *Stitched from the Soul: Slave Quilts from the Ante-Bellum South*, 39.

6. For the first hand accounts see, Patricia Cooper and Norma Bradley Allen, *The Quilters: Women and Domestic Art, An Oral History*; Grace Snyder, *No Time on My Hands*.

7. Carolann Barrett, "Quiltmaking: Telling the Truth of Women's Lives"; Radka Donnell, *Quilts as Women's Art: A Quilt Poetics*; Fry, *Stitched from the Soul*; Mainardi, "Great American Art."

8. Robert Bishop and Carter Houck, *All Flags Flying: American Patriotic Quilts as Expressions of Liberty*; Fry, *Stitched from the Soul*; Hedges, *Hearts and Hands*; Mainardi, "Great American Art."

9. Cooper and Allen, *The Quilters*; Fry, *Stitched from the Soul*; Hedges, *Hearts and Hands*.

and routine of the women's sphere.[10] Her role was to create a home that was "a warm, comforting and beautiful sanctuary away from the harsh world of trade and commercialism." Quilting (and femininity) was encouraged with the marketing of patterns and the prizes offered by contests.[11] It was in contributing to the cult of the feminine that needlework also became "the expression of femininity" itself.[12]

Perhaps not so ironically, some women were able to spend their days creating delicate objects of beauty because other women continued to labor out of necessity. Whether bonded to a master and his plantation, or to a master and his machine, slave women and factory women experienced a different effect of industrialization than did middle-class women. Some slave women suffered under the demand from northern mills for more and more cotton. Other slave women worked as "sewing women" who crafted quilts for their masters' houses. Use of women as "living machines" was also employed in the textile mills of the North. Describing their circumstances in such terms as "white slavery," and "slave labor," the "mill girls" made clear how their oppression connected them with the black women of the South.[13] Working twelve-hour days, six days a week, lodged in crowded boardinghouses with strictly enforced rules, exposed to unsanitary working conditions and deadly epidemics, and devalued even more by pay cuts, the mill girls struggled to reform this oppressive construction of technology.[14] Thomas Hood's "Song of the Shirt" movingly captured their plight:

Oh men, with sisters dear!
Oh men, with mothers and wives!
It is not linen you're wearing out,
But human creatures' lives!
Stitch—stitch—stitch!
In poverty, hunger, and dirt,
Sewing at once, with a double thread,
A shroud as well as a shirt![15]

In the wake of further mechanization and labor reform, the position of textiles as a product of industry, rather than of home, was solidified.

The 1940s witnessed yet another change in the meaning of quilting—its loss

10. Hedges, *Hearts and Hands,* 26.

11. Susan Jenkins and Linda Seward, *The American Quilt Story: The How-To and Heritage of a Craft Tradition,* 32, 96, 102.

12. Rozsika Parker, *The Subversive Stitch: Embroidery and the Making of the Feminine,* 5.

13. Fry, *Stitched from the Soul,* 18–19; Hedges, *Hearts and Hands,* 33; Benita Eisler, ed., *The Lowell Offering: Writings by New England Mill Women,* 159.

14. Eisler, *Lowell Offering.*

15. Thomas Hood, "Song of the Shirt," in *Feminism: The Essential Historical Writings,* ed. Miriam Schneir, 59–62.

of significance in the public realm. During World War II, women left their homes to enter the work force; their new occupations left them little time or inclination for quilting. Even when the women workers were displaced by the returning troops, quilting did not regain national prominence. While quilting was still practiced locally, interest in it faded until a national revival in the early 1970s.[16] Certainly contributing to the resurgence of enthusiasm for the craft was the preparation for celebrating the Bicentennial of the Declaration of Independence. In 1976, communities and individuals alike honored the occasion by creating commemorative quilts depicting the history of the nation, a specific community, or a concept illustrative of two hundred years of liberty.[17]

However, this rebirth was not a mere replication of the past, but a "reinvention" of the meaning of quilting. Once regarded as utilitarian artifacts of the past, quilts were reborn both as women's art and political artifacts.[18] While changes in the art world and the feminist movement served as two of the catalysts for this dramatic transformation, the technological world provided the necessary environment.

While quilts have always been displayed—on beds, sofas, walls, dolls, and even people—their first display as "art" came in a 1971 exhibit at the Whitney Museum of American Art, "Abstract Design in American Quilts." Organizer Jonathan Holstein presented quilters as fabric artists.[19] While this elevation of a "common" household item might appear to be unique, it is a rather common phenomenon of popular culture. While Jeff Ferrell suggests that economics guides an item's passage through the four stages of degradation and rehabilitation (new, old, used, and vintage), technology plays a role as well. This process, "being more social than physical," is related to the item's scarcity as well as its age.[20] The quilt became valued again only when quilts became rarer and symbolic of an age distant enough to be regarded with nostalgia. Part of the charm of butter churns, washboards, spinning wheels, and quilts is that they are no longer necessary. They are also from a distant enough past that ownership of the item is indicative of good taste rather than of a financial inability to acquire the latest in technological devices.

But the art world's elevation of the quilt was also related to the quilt's changing status within the feminist movement. Painfully aware of how needlework had been used to confine women's lives and choices, feminists tended to regard quilting as another symbol of women's unequal status in society.[21]

16. Jenkins and Seward, *The American Quilt Story*, 102.
17. Joseph Harriss, "The Newest Quilt Fad Seems to Be Going Like Crazy," 115; for examples see Bishop and Houck, *All Flags Flying*.
18. Hedges, *Hearts and Hands*.
19. Harriss, "The Newest Quilt Fad," 115; Willow Ann Soltow, *Quilting the World Over*, 20; for a feminist critique of the biases of the exhibit see Mainardi, "Great American Art," 22.
20. Jeff Ferrell, "Degradation and Rehabilitation in Popular Culture," 89–100.
21. Barrett, "Telling the Truth," 14.

However, with the maturation of feminist discourse in the 1970s, feminism expanded to include a recognition and celebration of women's difference. Rediscovery of women's history and women's voice was furthered by the rediscovery of women's quilts. As Carolann Barrett writes,

> For me, quiltmaking blends and integrates feminism and spirituality. In the best sense, both feminism and spirituality seek to increase our awareness of ourselves and our sisters, empower us to our finest and strongest, connect us with each other, honor our differences, and appreciate the mysteries of life. All of these aspects can be present in our quilts.[22]

However, such a joyous reunion of women and craft was made possible not only by changes in gender roles, but also by changes in technology. Freed from the needle, women could embrace quilting as their history, their voice, and their art. Quilts, no longer a necessity, no longer used to enforce standards of femininity, could only now become a banner of feminism.

Technology and the Act of Quilting

While technology shapes the meaning of quilting, it also influences the act of quilting itself. Although the end product can appear remarkably like its ancestors, most quilts are crafted today in a dramatically different way than those made prior to industrialization. Quilts of yesteryear were designed with paper templates, constructed with homemade fabrics, cut with scissors, pieced by hand, layered on a wooden frame, and quilted or tied by a handheld needle. It was slow, painstaking work.

Enter technology. Quilters can buy a book or a magazine for inspiration, or use a computer to help them envision the plan. If the pattern needs to be reduced or enlarged, the copy machine makes this fast work. The fabric shop offers an abundance of manufactured bolts, and special fabric can be ordered from a catalog (just call 1–800, have your credit card number ready, and ask for Federal Express). Now fabrics are washed, dried, and ironed using the latest in appliances and cut using the cutting mat, rotary cutter, and gridded ruler. One can save time by cutting several layers of material at once. Quilts are chain pieced or strip pieced in assembly-line fashion on the sewing machine. Once the top is done, quilting lines are traced using precut plastic stencils and the latest in chalk/pencil/pen. The top, batting, and backing are connected with hundred of stainless steel safety pins. Those who opt for low-tech quilting snap a walking or darning foot onto their sewing machines and begin quilting. The technologically advanced use a "state of the art" quilting machine to complete a full-size quilt in two hours or less.[23] Edges are bound by machine. The finished product is often signed on quilt labels, using an

22. Ibid.
23. "Ultimate Quilting System," American Professional Quilting Systems (video).

indelible pen to record the quilter's name and city and the completion date. That is how many modern quilts are done.

Of course, being of an individualistic nature, not all quilters have adopted the technological approaches described above. Even so, contemporary methods, tools, and machines have brought to the forefront a concern shared by most quilters of the past and the present—that of time. Time is a consideration of every quilter. The more time spent on one quilt, the fewer quilts produced. Even within communities for whom time appears to stand still, there is recognition of temporal limitations. The Amish quilts, distinctive in their use of large pieces of fabric, are illustrative of a time-saving piecework tradition. Eschewing the wasteful, whether it is wasting fabric in appliquéing or time spent piecing, the Amish readily accepted the treadle sewing machine in the 1870s and 1880s. By the turn of the century, another group of people not usually associated with technology was also piecing fabrics on machine. The Seminole women used their sewing machines, along with strip-piecing methods, to develop a new form of patchwork that today bears their name.[24]

The conservation of time is also a dominant theme in instructional quilting books. Popular guides like Leslie Linsley's *The Weekend Quilt,* Anita Hallock's *Fast Patch,* Marti Mitchell's *Quilting for People Who Don't Have Time to Quilt!,* Eleanor Burn's *Quilt-in-a-Day* series, and Kay Wood's *Strip Quilting* series all emphasize shortcuts, use of modern tools, and machine construction. Even Georgia Bonesteel's *Lap Quilting* series emphasizes techniques to quicken hand quilting.

Conquering time constraints can also be accomplished by scaling back the size of the quilt. While wall-hanging and crib sizes are favorites, the miniature quilt is also gaining in popularity. A reflection of "the technological advances that have brought us ever-more complex devices in smaller and smaller packages, such as the computer chip and miniatured circuit boards in calculators and appliances,"[25] the trend toward miniature quilts is also supported by a fast-paced culture with limited hours of free time. A real attraction of a miniature quilt is that the quilter might actually be able to complete it in weeks rather than in years—even if making it entirely by hand.

Today's quilt, then, "comprised of spare time as well as excess material" is touched not only by human hands, but by technological innovations as well.[26] The meaning of quilting has evolved, and the craft of quilting has changed, due, at least in part, to the ever-shifting character of technology. How technology affects the crafter's relationship with her quilt constitutes the next layer of this study.

24. Eve Wheatcroft Granick, *The Amish Quilt,* 45; Soltow, *Quilting the World Over,* 49, 59.
25. Pat Flynn Kyser, "Pieces and Patches," 16.
26. Whitney Otto, *How to Make an American Quilt,* 9.

Quilts and the Politics of Technology

Since at least 1867 when Karl Marx published the first volume of *Capital,* the introduction of technology into the workplace has been viewed as a political phenomenon. Something happens when a machine or device becomes part of a production process. Time may be saved and output increased. New techniques may change the character of the product, and the value ascribed to the product may increase or decrease. Political thought, however, has focused on the impact that technology has on the relationship between the crafter and the product, and the ramifications of this changed relationship for society and humanity.[27] Does the technology further the crafter's ability to create or does it "usurp the crafter's control over the form of the product?"[28] This question is as relevant for quilting as it is for automobile manufacturing since the focus is on whether the technology enhances or undermines a crafter's work. The theoretical concepts of connection and commodification, which occupy a dominant place in political thought, become animated in the craft of quilting.

Connection

Since quilting today takes place in a technological world, the question here is not *whether* technologies should be used, but *how* technologies are, in fact, used by quilters. In considering technology as a practice, Ursula Franklin distinguishes between holistic and prescriptive technologies. Holistic technologies, exemplified by crafts, are individualistic in nature. The crafter is in control of the planning and creation of the product. Since the person works as an individual, changes in the original design can be made as needed or as desired. The worker specializes in a product (quilts), rather than in a process (cutting fabrics, piecing, or quilting). In contrast, prescriptive technologies are based on a division of labor, designs for compliance, and a mandate for precision and conformity. Because work is now divided according to specialization in a process, the process demands that workers follow specifications. Under prescriptive technologies, "there is only one way of doing 'it'." That one way is determined not by the worker, but by the supervisor or boss who is now in control of the product. The price, then, of increased efficiency and production is the loss of workers' control over their craft. Franklin advises that

27. See Hannah Arendt, *The Human Condition;* Jacques Ellul, *The Technological Society;* Herbert Marcuse, *One-Dimensional Man: Studies in the Ideology of Advanced Industrial Society;* Lewis Mumford, *The Myth of the Machine: The Pentagon of Power;* Theodore Roszak, *The Making of a Counter Culture: Reflections on Technocratic Society and Its Youthful Opposition;* Thorstein Veblen, *The Instinct of Workmanship: And the State of the Industrial Arts.*

28. Adrian Forty, *Objects of Desire,* 43.

"understanding the social and political impact of prescriptive technologies is . . . the key to understanding our own real world of technology."[29]

Within the world of quilts, manufactured bedcovers are clearly examples of both the strengths and weaknesses of prescriptive technology. They are made quickly and inexpensively and are often attractive. While they more than adequately serve their function of keeping sleepers warm, they fail to express the work of an individual crafter. The buyer's awareness of this lack of relationship between crafter and product is evident in the casual use and disposal of bedcovers. Inexpensively bought, mass produced items rarely engender care and sentimentality. In their mundaneness, they have no meaning or value beyond their limited use of covering and warming a bed. A product of a technological process, they are mere function.

While it may be tempting to evaluate a quilt on the basis of whether it was made by hand or by machine, Franklin's distinction between holistic and prescriptive forms suggests that the determinative factor should not be the absence of technology, but rather the presence of a connection between the crafter and her work. It is therefore a mistake to assign all handmade quilts to the category of holistic and all machine-made quilts to the category of prescriptive, since a closer look reveals varied patterns in the relationship between quilters and quilts.

For example, Amish quilts are often prized as models of personal workmanship, while quilts produced on sewing machines are devalued as technological products. Yet, an Amish quilt that is sold to the public is rarely the creation of one woman crafter.[30] Instead, the quilts are made in assembly-line fashion with the work divided among the quilters—illustrative, then, of prescriptive rather than holistic methods. In contrast, a quilter who uses her sewing machine to quilt relies on technology to preserve the finer qualities of holistic work. Freed of the demands of hand sewing, the quilter has more of an opportunity to explore her creativity.

Some women have simultaneously participated in both types of quilt technology. Slave sewers, who quilted designs determined by their mistresses, were not only participants in prescriptive technologies but were treated as if they were indeed sewing machines.[31] Yet, these same women, when freed from oppressive control, used fabric as a medium for expression,[32] a paradigm of holistic technology.

The distinction between holistic and prescriptive technologies is also useful in considering quilting as an individual versus a collective activity. The example of the slave sewers is again useful. Denied control, slave women were

29. *The Real World of Technology*, 24.
30. Houck, *Quilt Encyclopedia*, 14.
31. Fry, *Stitched from the Soul*, 31.
32. Eli Leon, *Who'd A Thought It: Improvisation in African-American Quiltmaking;* Fry, *Stitched from the Soul*.

engaged in a prescriptive technology even though they may have been working with another woman, the mistress, in the creation of the quilt. However,
when true collaboration occurred, both women were a part of holistic quilting.
There is a tendency, however, to view collective efforts as a blending of
women's expression rather than as support for the realization of one woman's
expression.[33] The quilting bee is a collective endeavor but the control is in the
hands of the woman who made the quilt top. It is she who determines where
the quilt lines will be sewn. While she engages in the holistic, her friends offer
their prescriptive labor. The line, then, between prescriptive and holistic technology wavers like a seam sewn by a child.

Quilting in a technological world demands that a quilter make choices. She
can design her own quilt, use someone else's design for inspiration, or buy a
quilt kit with preselected fabrics and pattern. She can sew by hand all, some,
or none of the quilt. She can work alone, with others, or for others. In defining
the circumstances under which technology will be allowed to enter the craft of
quilting, each quilter sets her own boundaries based on her conception of what
it means to create a quilt.

Commodification

Technology not only affects the degree of connection between quilt and
quilter, but also has an impact on the value ascribed to the process and
product of quilting. Indeed, as Marx argues, connection, commodification,
and technology are so closely related that the introduction of technology
results in greater productivity and greater profit but less connection between
the worker and the product.[34] Before industrialization, the crafter, working
alone, produced less and made less money but was intimately involved with
the craft. Each of the three phases of capitalism witnessed a breaking of the
connection between crafter and product in the interest of profit. During the first
phase of capitalism, there is cooperation among crafters; during the second
phase, labor is divided among workers; and during the third phase, machines
are introduced and the factory system is established. Therefore, while technology plays a fundamental role in advancing the third stage of capitalism, the
worker's control over the craft is already being threatened by the need to
produce and sell more of the product.[35]

This picture of diminished connection and increased commodification is
expanded by Thorstein Veblen's study of the "captains of industry."[36] While
Marx focuses on the *worker's* sense of connection to the product, Veblen adds
as well the *master's* sense of connection. Before industrialization, each master

33. Mainardi, "Great American Art," 20.
34. *Capital.*
35. Forty, *Object of Desire,* 44.
36. *The Engineers and the Price System.*

had practiced the craft as an apprentice. Upon learning the craft and acquiring a modest savings, apprentices could purchase the labor-saving devices necessary to allow them to work as individuals. But as specialization and the role of technologies increased, the impact was felt at two levels. First, the worker's use of technology became guided by "a logic of masses, velocities, strains, and thrusts, not of personal dexterity, tact, training, and routine."[37] Second, the master became the permanent employer since few workers could now afford the transition from apprentice to master. This new breed of employer ceased crafting to become business managers. Production shifted from quality to quantity; from workmanship to profits.[38] Today's industries are controlled by financiers who may have no grasp of the industrial arts, and whose connection to the work is not that of crafter but of profiteer.[39]

Many catalog companies today market quilts by selling nostalgia. The quilts are usually not antiques but newly sewn replications. The ads hawk these quilts as "hand sewn," "handcrafted," or "folk art," but it isn't usually clear just who the workers are who made these quilts or the degree of connection they have to their craft. Lands' End, Inc. serves as a good example of a company that mass markets quilts by downplaying their commodification and exaggerating their artistic dimensions. The August 1991 Lands' End catalog contains four pages on quilting that seem to deliberately obscure the distinction between the art of quilting and the mass production of quilts. Two pages display five quilts that can be purchased. They are of traditional designs (Bear Paw, Double Wedding Ring, Sunbonnet Sue, School House, and Sailboat), and they are touted as "handcrafted quilts." Yet these "Coming Home" quilts are also marketed as even better than those of yesteryear:

> You spread Great Aunt Sabina's antique quilt on your bed and it's wonderful! But look . . . it doesn't fold over the pillows, it doesn't cover the sides of the mattress, it just sits on top. It was made for smaller people, smaller beds.
>
> Today, people are bigger . . . and so are beds. Coming Home quilts are even larger than most modern quilts and completely machine washable (we urge commercial-sized washers) so they fit our beds *and* our rough-and-tumble lifestyles. Imported.

But Lands' End does not want to give the impression that these quilts are of lesser value. A buyer must believe that she is participating in the folk art tradition of quilting by making this purchase. Hence, Lands' End (along with *Good Housekeeping*) invites consumers to enter "The All-American Quilt Contest" to "celebrate the art of the quilter." Following the two page spread on the quilts for sale is an article, "Continuing the Thread: Quilter Kathleen Mc-

37. *Instinct of Workmanship*, 241.
38. *Engineers and the Price System*, 281–283.
39. *Instinct of Workmanship*, 40.

Crady." It is introduced by the statement, "Just as we're committed to fine workmanship in our 'cut and sewn' business, so we celebrate it in fields once removed from our own."[40]

These four catalog pages market mass-produced quilts by portraying prescriptive technologies as holistic. These quilts look like the old, but they are better than the old. They are handcrafted, but they are mass-produced. Kathleen McCrady is a quilter, but she is not the quilter of these mass-marketed quilts. Consumers can buy one of these quilts or enter their own quilts in a contest. These quilts are pieces of art, but they are inexpensive (the most expensive twin size is $139, and double size is $169).

The Lands' End catalog illustrates some of the concerns of Marx and Veblen. In the mass production of these quilts, the worker's control is gone. The profit made does not belong to the crafter. The inexpensive pricing of imported quilts by mail-order companies, such as Lands' End, L. L. Bean, J. C. Penney, Spiegel, and Domestications, raises the question of just who the foreign workers are who handcrafted these quilts, and what percentage of the profit they received for their labor. Sandra Hatch, editor of *Quilt World*, reports that according to MAQGNET (Mid-Atlantic Quilt Guilds Network), some of the imported quilts are made in China with forced prison labor.[41] If true, consider the sad irony of Chinese prisoners carefully sewing calico fabrics into Double Wedding Ring and Log Cabin quilts while fearing for their lives. This would be the ultimate perversion of an American heritage for the sake of profit.

It is indeed a clever marketing strategy to sell prescriptive products as holistic. A company can ride the tide of renewed interest in quilting but bank on the fact that few consumers have the time to engage in the craft. Given the recent "commodification of leisure," that is, the devaluing of free time as wasted time,[42] it is a good bet that workers will not be quilters. Hence, the companies fill a need they helped to create. Hidden, then, behind these mass-produced and mass-marketed quilts is industry masquerading as folk art.

The buying and selling of quilts is always problematic, given that quilts reflect not only the time and material invested, but also the crafter herself. It is more than fabric, stitching and time that is being bought—it is, as author Whitney Otto describes it, someone's story. As a character in her novel *How to Make an American Quilt* laments, "Anyone who could buy something like [a] quilt . . . [is] unabashedly immoral."[43] Yet, like some other precious items, quilts can be treated as commodities. Collectors strive to buy low and sell high.[44] The profit motive has even endangered their existence. For example,

40. Lands' End, Inc., *Direct Merchants Catalog*, 118–21.
41. "Editorial," 3.
42. Juliet B. Schor, "Workers of the World, Unwind," 28–29.
43. *Make an American Quilt*, 138.
44. Donnell, *Quilts as Women's Art*, 77.

Ralph Lauren collected antique quilts in order to cut them up to make designer jackets, vests, and skirts.[45] Someone's story, cut apart, rearranged, and worn, is flaunted for fashion's sake.

Yet, it is ironic that the commodification that separates the crafter from her quilt may also preserve the quilt for future generations. A dramatic illustration of this point is the story of Harriet Powers, a gifted slave quilter who sold one of her distinctive quilts to artist Jennie Smith for five dollars. Powers's quilts reflected her African heritage in both their appliqué style and story depictions. Smith carefully preserved not only the quilt but an eighteen-page narrative describing the sale and the symbols in the quilt; both quilt and narrative reside today in the Smithsonian. The only other surviving quilt of Powers's was one commissioned by "the faculty ladies of Atlanta University," which is now owned by the Museum of Fine Arts in Boston.[46]

Even the quilter who does not sell her quilts is subject to the dictates of commodification. Prescriptive technology's penchant for standardization has seeped over into the criteria used in juried quilt competitions. To win an award, a quilt must conform to certain expectations of quality. While quilts are judged on technique as well as on interpretation, standards of "quality" seem remarkably similar to those imposed on the assembly line: uniformity, precision, replication. Quilters who seek recognition and approval of their work are sometimes painfully disappointed when their quilts are not as highly valued as they expected.[47] A seam not straight enough, stitches not small enough, quilt patterns that don't fill a space, or "inappropriate" fabric selections can cost a quilter an award. Yet, if quilts are a form of women's expression, the imposition of standards stifles the voice of individuality.

But this is not the only implication of standardization. Rigid standards result in the assignment of a higher value to quilts of some heritages over others. For example, the traditional quilts of the American frontier favored the block setting.[48] Striving for uniformity, quilters employed templates for making blocks such as Bear's Paw, Ohio Star, Tree of Life, and Drunkard's Path. When the traditionally trained eye views the improvisational quilts stitched by African Americans, there is a clash in values. While the judge may view an upside-down block or a mismatched seam as a "mistake," the quilter may have welcomed it as "an integral component of craftsmanship."[49] Gladys-Marie Fry suggests as well that African American quilts were influenced by the belief that a perfect quilt, or one with unbroken straight lines, would bring bad luck.[50] Given that criteria, it is the Amish bars quilt that is of lesser value. Eli Leon's

45. Harriss, "The Newest Quilt Fad," 116.
46. Fry, *Stitched from the Soul*, 84–91.
47. Jim Leahy, "Quilt," 6.
48. Soltow, *Quilting the World Over*, 19.
49. Leon, *Who'd A Thought It*, 22.
50. *Stitched from the Soul*, 67.

comparison of the traditional frontier quilt with the improvisational African American quilt brings to mind again the difference between holistic and prescriptive technologies:

> If the standard-traditional American quilt is properly executed, its final appearance is largely predetermined by the choice of pattern and fabric. The quiltmaker has only to cut and sew the pieces correctly and they will fit together to make consistent blocks and relatively predictable quilts. This emphasis on precision piecing and exact pattern replication, often yielding splendid textiles, is not conducive to improvisation.
>
> The Afro-traditional quilter, on the other hand, when she is not measuring her pieces precisely, must make adjustments as she puts the pieces together if they are to fit, since each block may be different in size and/or shape. As she deals with the irregularities, drawing on a body of Afro-traditional techniques, she has opportunities to explore and excel in improvisational possibilities not open to the standard-traditional quilter.[51]

The Chilean arpillera, the Panamanian mola, the Hmong patchwork, and the Japanese sashiko are examples of other quilting heritages that offer elements not contained within the standards of the traditional frontier quilt.[52]

What becomes clear, then, is that quilts are illustrative of the politics of technology. The connection between the quilter and her craft, as well as the value ascribed to her quilt, are shaped by the interplay between technology and commodification. Yet, while quilters are influenced by both of these factors, most are not controlled by it. Quilters keep on quilting. The craft may be practiced differently over time, but there are some elements essential to quilting that are maintained. In this way, quilts serve as artifacts of social values. What, then, does quilting in a technological world tell us about our values, our society, and ourselves?

Preservation of Social Values

So far we have seen that quilters are affected by technology. The meaning of quilting has evolved, the craft of quilting has changed, the relationship between the quilter and her product has been threatened, and the value of her work has been influenced by technology. Yet, almost in defiance, the quilter continues her crafting. Rather than resist technological forces, she bends them to her will.

In choosing whether and how to draw upon technology, she preserves the holistic nature of her work. Aware of how technology can be used, she sees its presence in terms of option rather than mandate, choice rather than command. Freed from the needle, she returns to it, empowered to control it.

51. *Who'd A Thought It*, 28.
52. Soltow, *Quilting the World Over.*

Expression, rather than need, fuels the desire. Tools and machines are used to save labor, leaving more time for creativity. Rather than separate her from her craft, technology is used as an extension of herself, thus binding artist and art together. When mass-produced quilts are marketed as "just like" or "even better than" hers, she refuses to be drawn into competition. She is confident in the knowledge that her quilts are unique, that they represent something that a factory cannot replicate. She knows that in quilting, she preserves social values. These values are clear to the one who quilts, the companion who watches the quilter, and the loved one who lies beneath the quilt, stroking the patches and tracing the stitches.

Even if you are none of these, you too know the difference between using technology and being used by technology. Consider, for instance, the town and the shopping mall. Shopping malls attempt to replicate two of a town's functions, a sense of community and opportunities for commerce, but with an improved form of delivery.[53] Malls offer parking, bathroom facilities, eateries, banks, stores, and social functions (like fashion shows, Santa Claus, art exhibits), all in a climate-controlled, security-patrolled, and community-extolled environment. The elderly engage in fitness walking, teenagers hang out, and the families recreate in the malls. The demise of the downtown stands as a testimonial to the success of the shopping mall. Offering such diversity and convenience, they have everything an individual or a community needs—or do they? Are technologies interchangeable? Does the substitution of a mall for a town replace all the social functions performed by the town? If not, what is the social cost in terms of community values, patterns, and functions lost?

It is obvious that a town and a mall are not, in fact, the same. While a mall may improve on some of the town's commercial functions, it is an artificial town. It fails to create a real sense of community because as George Lewis explains, "Having the *perception* of a community feeling does not mean that it actually exists."[54] Neither does having quaint objects from the past, like carousels and gazebos, recreate the old-fashioned town. Unlike towns, malls are not unique. They are mass-produced by architects and builders who fulfill their own vision of community needs. Malls are, after all, a "marketing strategy."[55] The deliberative process focuses on what will draw consumers, not what will bind a community together or what will answer the community's social needs. Designed by an outsider, they are erected on the outskirts of town. Resistant to the natural forces of change, growth, or demise, they are also unable to adapt when consumers—lacking any real sense of community, connection, or loyalty—take their business elsewhere. They have no way to evolve, no way to

53. George H. Lewis, "Community Through Exclusion and Illusion: The Creation of Social Worlds in an American Shopping Mall," 121–136.

54. Ibid., 123.

55. Ibid., 121.

change stores into apartments, offices, parks, or schools; vacancies spread like an epidemic. The mall's strength is also its weakness.

Like towns, quilts are not a rejection of technology, time constraints, or convenience. These artifacts do indeed symbolize the impact of such considerations on our society. Instead of a rejection, towns and quilts are an affirmation of other social values: patience, connection, and expression. Shopping malls and manufactured bedcovers lack all these.

Patience may be a virtue but it is not celebrated in a technological world. It is ironic, but "despite all our time-saving devices, Americans say they feel more rushed than ever."[56] There is little time to still the mind. Instead, car phones, laptop computers, miniature tape recorders, fax machines, touch-tone phones, and microwave ovens give us little excuse to withdraw from work and chores. Every spare moment can be devoted to some type of work. Quilting is one way to make time serve rather than master us. The quilter embraces what technology strives (but fails) to end: the monotonous, the repetitious, the endless hours of hand work. "With the immediate focus on the hand work, the mind has the opportunity to quiet down and rest."[57] "Mindless," soothing work invites mindful, profound reflection. Some quilters claim that they find balance within the work. Quilting, then, is a reclamation of time, of reflection, and of self.

Connection is another social value. The act of quilting is the act of connecting. Pieces are stitched together, blocks joined, borders attached, and layers quilted and bound. A quilter has the ability "to see the whole in the pieces."[58] Quilting also binds her to women of different times or different nations who have used the quilt as a means of expression. Teaching the craft of quilting binds generations, friends, communities. Quilter Radka Donnell describes quilting as "the work of touch."[59] Quilts are touchable art that symbolizes the importance of connection. Quilts do not only cover people, they "hold" them. Donnell states, "Visibly and tangibly, quilts show us the innumerable and infinitesimal acts of women, acts we perform *to hold* ourselves together, *to hold* the elements of our lives together, *to hold* fast to the good life, to celebrate the persons we love and our imbeddedness in nature."[60] Onondaga Chief Oren Lyons knows as well the power of touch and the importance of interacting with things:

Things have a way of understanding and knowing. There's a need of every part to be used and to be needed. There's an interaction and if that interaction isn't carried out, things suffer.

56. Ralph Keyes, "Do You Have the Time?" 22.
57. Barrett, "Telling the Truth," 14.
58. Stacie Marinelli, "Art and Metaphor: The Language of Quilts," 40.
59. *Quilts as Women's Art*, 59.
60. Ibid., 68.

> It's like a house. A house that's not lived in decays. A house that's lived in somehow just stays on and on, it gets some sort of life from somewhere. The minute you leave a house, even for six months, it begins to decay. It's like that. *Things need to be interacted with.*[61]

What both Lyons and Donnell are referring to is love. Love is not frequently called upon to inform our scholarship or guide our use of technology. Yet, quilting is rarely done without emotion for the project, for the recipient, for the self. Quilts, then are not only the result of connecting, but are also artifacts of the social need for connection.

Expression is another value affirmed by quilting. "Quilts are one way in which women tell the truth of our lives."[62] When sexism prevented women's participation in public forums like book publishing, newspaper reporting, and speechmaking, "their needles became their pens and quilts their eminently expressive texts."[63] Some quilts are overtly expressive. For example, during the Civil War, the Jacob's Ladder block was renamed Underground Railroad. Log Cabin quilts containing black fabrics were often used to signal safe houses on the journey to freedom.[64] The blue and white Drunkard's Path quilt voiced the stance of the Women's Christian Temperance Movement.[65] Today, the AIDS memorial quilt mourns the passing of loved ones, celebrates their lives, and rages at public policymakers who refuse to see the enormity of the loss. Stories are also told by the fabrics used in abstract pictorial quilts.

The meaning of some quilts is derived from their "type." Marriage quilts, mourning quilts, friendship quilts, and freedom quilts are crafted with obvious intent. Other quilts are not so transparently expressive. One must look for clues. Quilted gardens bursting with color that were made by women on the dusty prairie speak volumes about their lives, their needs, and their dreams.[66] The plainness of Amish patchwork gives voice to the value of simplicity.[67] What is a quilter saying when she chooses to make a Log Cabin rather than a Baltimore quilt? When she changes the color of the chimney square from the traditional red to white? When she stitches some parts by machine and other parts by hand? Carolann Barrett concludes that "Each gesture of pure intent is a statement of what is important to us, a confirmation of something in our world, whether positive or negative, static or needing change."[68] Every quilt, then, is more than fabric. It is the preservation of a woman's voice.

Scholars who study the politics of technology are well aware that technology

61. "Amid Pollution and Strife, a Faithkeeper Endures," B4, emphasis is mine.
62. Barrett, "Telling the Truth," 13.
63. Hedges, *Hearts and Hands,* 11.
64. Fry, *Stitched from the Soul,* 52.
65. Hedges, *Hearts and Hands,* 82.
66. See Cooper and Allen, *The Quilters.*
67. See Bender, *Plain and Simple: A Woman's Journey to the Amish.*
68. "Telling the Truth," 14.

elevates some values at the cost of others. Particularly sensitive to the impact of technology on democracy, scholars are striving to find ways to ensure that technological innovations promote rather than impede political and social processes.[69] This analysis has been extended to include the workplace. Rather than allow technology to strip workers of control, innovative scholars and policymakers are striving to harness technology to serve democracy in the workplace.[70] These scholars are engaged in the important work of identifying social values and finding ways to preserve them through creative uses of technology. This is work that quilters understand well.

A technological world threatens what quilting affirms and preserves—the values of patience, connection, and expression. Knowing that there is a social cost in assuming that all techniques are interchangeable, the quilter identifies what a technology can and cannot do. She does not resist technology, but she applies it in ways that will serve her values. Patience and thinking, connection and caring, expression and creativity are the values protected by her needle. Quilts stand as examples of how to use technology without sacrificing social values. In their setting of technological limits, quilts act to preserve the social fabric.

69. See Borgmann, *Technology and Contemporary Life;* David Dickson, *The New Politics of Science;* Franklin, *Real World of Technology;* Goldhaber, *Reinventing Technology;* Pamela Varley, "Electronic Democracy," 43–51; Winner, *Whale and the Reactor.*

70. See Robert Howard, "UTOPIA: Where Workers Craft New Technology," 43–49; Harley Shaiken, *Work Transformed: Automation and Labor in the Computer Age.*

◆ Bibliography ◆
Virginia B. Broaddus

As Cheryl Torsney and Judy Elsley say in their introduction, this volume proposes to encourage its readers to "'think about it', it being the quilt: its mode of production, its value to its makers and owners, its meaning in culture." Accordingly, this bibliography is designed to aid its users in both thinking and reading about quilts, their manufacture, their history, and their cultural place.

The first section contains works cited in the text. The second section of the bibliography introduces other, recent texts that concern quilt culture. It is divided into broad sections, which are listed alphabetically, so that readers who are interested in specific aspects of quilt culture can more readily locate sources of use to them. This bibliography by no means includes all significant quilt scholarship; the texts listed here represent only pieces of what we might call a quilt in continuous production: the history and theorizing of quilt culture. The entries are provided so that readers might access some of the important texts concerned with quilt culture as it manifests itself ethnically, regionally, nationally, and internationally.

I. Works Cited

Abel, Elizabeth. "(E)Merging Identities: The Dynamics of Female Friendship in Contemporary Fiction by Women." *Signs* 6 (1981): 413–35.

Adams, Hazard, and Leroy Searle, eds. *Critical Theory since 1965*. Tallahassee: University of Florida Press, 1986.

Angus, Ian, and Sut Jhally, eds. *Cultural Politics in Contemporary America*. New York: Chapman, 1989.

Arendt, Hannah. *The Human Condition*. Chicago: University of Chicago Press, 1958.

Auerbach, Nina. *Communities of Women: An Idea in Fiction*. Cambridge: Harvard University Press, 1978.

Austen, Jane. *Northanger Abbey*. 1818. Vol. 5 of *The Novels of Jane Austen*. 3d ed. Edited by R. W. Chapman. Oxford: Oxford University Press, 1933.

Baker, Houston A., Jr., and Charlotte Pierce-Baker. "Patches: Quilts and Community in Alice Walker's 'Everyday Use.'" *Southern Review* 21 (1985): 706–20.

Bakhtin, M. M. *The Dialogic Imagination*. Edited by Michael Holquist. Translated by Caryl Emerson and Michael Holquist. Austin: University of Texas Press, 1981.

Barker, Jane. *A Patch-Work Screen for the Ladies; Or, Love and Vertue.* 1723. *Foundations of the Novel,* edited by Josephine Grieder. New York: Garland, 1973.

Barret, Michèle. *Virginia Woolf on Women and Writing.* New York: Harcourt, 1979.

Barrett, Carolann. "Quiltmaking: Telling the Truth of Women's Lives." *Sojourner: The Women's Forum* 16 (1991): 13–15.

Barthes, Roland. "Littérature et discontinu." *Critique* 185 (1962): 817–29. Rpt. in *Essais critiques.* Paris: Seuil, 1964.

Battersby, Christine. *Gender and Genius: Towards a Feminist Aesthetics.* London: Women's Press, 1986.

Baudrillard, Jean. *For a Critique of the Political Economy of the Sign.* Translated by Charles Levin. St. Louis, Mo.: Telos, 1981.

Beasley, Jerry C. "Politics and Moral Idealism: The Achievement of Some Early Women Novelists." In *Fetter'd or Free?: British Women Novelists, 1670–1815,* edited by Mary Anne Schofield and Cecilia Macheski, 216–36. Athens: Ohio University Press, 1986.

Bell-Scott, Patricia, et al., eds. *Double Stitch: Black Women Write About Mothers and Daughters.* Boston: Beacon, 1991.

Benberry, Cuesta Ray. *Always There: The African-American Presence in American Quilts.* Louisville: Kentucky Quilt Project, 1992.

Bender, Sue. *Plain and Simple: A Woman's Journey to the Amish.* San Francisco: Harper, 1989.

Benjamin, Jessica. "The Bonds of Love: Rational Violence and Erotic Domination." In *The Future of Difference,* edited by Hester Eisenstein and Alice Jardine, 41–70. Boston: Hall, 1980.

———. "A Desire of One's Own: Psychoanalytic Feminism and Intersubjective Space." In *Feminist Studies/Critical Studies,* edited by Teresa de Lauretis, 78–101. Bloomington: Indiana University Press, 1986.

Benjamin, Walter. *Illuminations.* New York: Schocken, 1969.

Bernick, Susan E. "How an Artifact Becomes or Ceases to Be a Work of Art: Artworld Category Changes as a Possible Model for Feminist Politics." Ph.D. diss., University of Minnesota, 1990.

Bishop, Robert. "Robert Bishop on Quilts as Art." *Architectural Digest* (July 1983):32–38.

Bishop, Robert, and Carter Houck. *All Flags Flying: American Patriotic Quilts as Expressions of Liberty.* New York: Dutton, 1986.

Bitzer, Lloyd F. "The Rhetorical Situation." *Philosophy and Rhetoric* 1 (1968): 1–15.

Bloch, Ernst. *The Utopian Function of Art and Literature.* Cambridge: MIT Press, 1989.

Borgmann, Albert. *Technology and the Character of Contemporary Life: A Philosophical Inquiry.* Chicago: University of Chicago Press, 1984.

Bresenhan, Karoline Patterson, and Nancy O'Bryant Puentes. *Lone Stars: A Legacy of Texas Quilts, 1836–1936.* Austin: University of Texas Press, 1986.

Bronner, Simon H. "The Idea of the Folk Artifact." In *Material Culture and Folklife: A Prologue and Dialogue,* edited by Simon J. Bronner, 3–46. Ann Arbor, Mich.: UMI, 1985.

Brown, Elsa Barkley. "African-American Women's Quilting: A Framework for Conceptualizing and Teaching African-American Women's History." *Signs* 14 (1989): 921–29. Rpt. in *Black Women in America: Social Science Perspectives,* edited by Micheline R. Malson, et al, 9–18. Chicago: University of Chicago Press, 1990.

Buckler, Patricia P., and C. Kay Leeper. "An Antebellum Woman's Scrapbook as Autobiographical Composition." *Journal of American Culture* 14 (1991): 1–8.

Butor, Michel. *L'émploi du temps.* Paris: Minuit, 1956.

———. *La modification.* Paris: Minuit, 1957.

———. *Le génie du lieu.* Paris: Grasset, 1958.

———. *Degrés.* Paris: Gallimard, 1960.

———. *Mobile: Étude pour une représentation des Étas-Unis.* Paris: Gallimard, 1962.

———. *6 810 000 litres d'eau par seconde: Étude stéréophonique.* Paris: Gallimard, 1965.

———. *Où: Le génie du lieu 2.* Paris: Gallimard, 1971.

———. *Bicentenaire Kit.* Collaboration with Phillipe Lebaud. Jacques Monory: 1975–1976.

———. *Boomerang: Le génie du lieu 3.* Paris: Gallimard, 1978.

Callahan, Nancy. *The Freedom Quilting Bee.* Tuscaloosa: University of Alabama Press, 1987.

Carlisle, Lilian Baker. *Pieced Work and Appliqué Quilts at Shelburne Museum.* Shelburne, Vt.: Shelburne Museum Pamphlet Ser. 2, 1957.

Castle, Terry. *Clarissa's Ciphers: Meaning and Disruption in Richardson's "Clarissa."* Ithaca, N.Y.: Cornell University Press, 1982.

Charbonniers, Georges. *Entretiens avec Michel Butor.* Paris: Gallimard, 1967.

Chavdarian, Seda A. "Images of Chaos in Butor's *Mobile, 6 810 000 litres d'eau par seconde* and *Où.*" *Perspectives on Contemporary Literature* 10 (1984): 49–55.

Chicago, Judy, and Susan Hill. *Embroidering Our Heritage: The Dinner Party Needlework.* Garden City, N.Y.: Anchor, 1980.

Christian, Barbara. "Alice Walker: The Black Woman Artist as Wayward." In *Black Feminist Criticism: Perspectives on Black Women Writers, 81–101.* New York: Pergamon, 1985.

———. "The Race for Theory." *Feminist Studies* 14 (1988): 67–80.

Cixous, Hélène. "The Laugh of the Medusa." *Signs* 1 (1976): 875–93. Translated by Paula and Keith Cohen. Rpt. in *Critical Theory since 1965,* edited by Hazard Adams and Leroy Searle, 309–21. Tallahassee: University of Florida Press, 1986.

Clarke, Mary Washington. *Kentucky Quilts and Their Makers.* Lexington: University Press of Kentucky, 1986.

Cleveland, Richard L., and Donna Bister. *Plain and Fancy: Vermont's People and Their Quilts as a Reflection of America.* San Francisco: Quilt Digest, 1991.

"Continuing the Thread: Quilter Kathleen McCrady." *Lands' End: Direct Merchants Catalogue* (August 1991):120–21.

Cooper, Patricia, and Norma Bradley Allen. *The Quilters: Women and Domestic Art.* New York: Doubleday, 1977.

Cott, Nancy. *The Bonds of Womanhood: "Woman's Sphere" in New England, 1780–1835.* New Haven: Yale University Press, 1977.

Crimp, Douglas. "How to Survive Promiscuity in an Epidemic." In *AIDS: Cultural Analysis/Cultural Activism,* edited by Douglas Crimp, 237–71. Cambridge: MIT Press, 1989.

Cross, Mary Bywater. *Treasures in the Trunk: Quilts of the Oregon Trail.* Nashville, Tenn.: Rutledge Hill, 1993.

Dallenbach, Lucien. *Le livre et ses miroirs dans l'oeuvre romanesque de Michel Butor.* Paris: Minard, 1972.

Dickson, David. *The New Politics of Science.* New York: Pantheon, 1984.

Donnell, Radka. *Quilts as Women's Art: A Quilt Poetics.* North Vancouver: Gallerie, 1990.

Donnell-Vogt, Radka. "Memoir." In *Lives and Works: Talks with Women Artists,* edited by Lynn F. Miller and Sally S. Swenson, 37–56. Metuchen: Scarecrow, 1981.

Donovan, Josephine. "Towards a Women's Poetics." In *Feminist Issues in Literary Scholarship,* edited by Shari Benstock, 98–109. Bloomington: Indiana University Press, 1987.

Duke, Dennis, and Deborah Harding. *America's Glorious Quilts.* New York: Macmillan, 1987.

DuPlessis, Rachel Blau. "For the Etruscans." In *The New Feminist Criticism,* edited by Elaine Showalter, 271–91. New York: Pantheon, 1985.

Easton, Loyd T., and Kurt H. Guddat. *Writings of the Young Marx on Philosophy and Society.* Garden City, N.Y.: Doubleday, 1967.

Eaton, Marcia Muelder. *Art and Nonart: Reflections on an Orange Crate and a Moose Call.* East Brunswick, N.J.: Associated University Presses, 1983.

Eisler, Benita, ed. *The Lowell Offering: Writings by New England Mill Women.* New York: Harper, 1990.

Eliot, George. *The Mill on the Floss.* 1860. New York: Signet, 1981.

Elsley, Judy. "The Rhetoric of the NAMES Project AIDS Quilt: Reading the Text(ile)." *AIDS: The Literary Response,* edited by Emmanuel Nelson, 187–96. New York: Twayne, 1992.

Ellul, Jacques. *The Technological Society.* New York: Knopf, 1964.

Farb, Joanne. "Piecin' and Quiltin': Two Quilters in Southwest Arkansas." *Southern Folklore Quarterly* 39 (1975): 363–75.

Ferrell, Jeff. "Degradation and Rehabilitation in Popular Culture." *Journal of Popular Culture* 24 (1990): 89–100.

Ferrero, Pat, Elaine Hedges, and Julie Silber. *Hearts and Hands: The Influence of Women and Quilts on American Society.* San Francisco: Quilt Digest, 1987.

Ferris, William, ed. *Afro-American Folk Arts and Crafts.* Boston: Hall, 1983.

Finley, Ruth E. *Old Patchwork Quilts and the Women Who Made Them.* New York: Grosset, 1929.

Flax, Jane. *Thinking Fragments: Psychoanalysis, Feminism, and Postmodernism in the Contemporary West.* Berkeley: University of California Press, 1990.

Forty, Adrian. *Objects of Desire.* New York: Pantheon, 1986.

Franklin, Ursula M. *The Real World of Technology.* Montreal: CBC, 1990.

Friedlich, Karla. "Quilts of Conscience." *Clarion* (1991): 47–54.

Fry, Gladys-Marie. *Stitched from the Soul: Slave Quilts from the Ante-Bellum South.* New York: Dutton, 1990.

Frye, Melinda Young. Review of *The Quilters: Women and Domestic Art,* by Patricia Cooper and Norma Bradley Allen. *Museum News* 56 (July/August 1978): 53.

Gendron, Bernard. *Technology and the Human Condition.* New York: St. Martin's, 1977.

Gilbert, Sandra M., and Susan Gubar. *The Madwoman in the Attic: The Woman Writer and the Nineteenth-Century Literary Imagination.* New Haven: Yale University Press, 1970.

————, eds. *The Norton Anthology of Literature by Women.* New York: Norton, 1985.

Gitlin, Todd. "Postmodernism: Roots and Politics." In *Cultural Politics in Contemporary America,* edited by Ian Angus and Sut Jhally, 347–60. New York: Chapman, 1989.

Gittelson, Natalie. "The Peace Quilt." *McCall's* (May 1985):95+.

Goldhaber, Michael. *Reinventing Technology: Policies for Democratic Values.* New York: Routledge, 1986.

Granick, Eve Wheatcroft. *The Amish Quilt.* Intercourse, Penn.: Good Books, 1989.

Grudin, Eva. "The Exquisite Diversity of African-American Quilts." *Fiberarts* (November/December 1989):41–43.

Guest, Barbara. "Quilts." *Woman Poet* 2 (1981): 116–18.

Harriss, Joseph. "The Newest Quilt Fad Seems to Be Going Like Crazy." *Smithsonian* (May 1987):114–25.

Hatch, Sandra. "Editorial." *Quilt World* (June/July 1992):3.

Hawkins, Peter S. "The Art of Memory and the NAMES Quilt." *Critical Inquiry* 19 (1993): 752–79.

Hedges, Elaine. "Hearts and Hands: The Influence of Women and Quilts on American Society." In *Hearts and Hands: The Influence of Women and Quilts on American Society,* edited by Pat Ferrero, Elaine Hedges, and Julie Silber, 11–97. San Francisco: Quilt Digest, 1987.

————. "Quilts and Women's Culture." In *In Her Own Image: Women Working in the Arts,* edited by Elaine Hedges and Ingrid Wendt, 13–19. Old Westbury, Conn.: Feminist, 1980.

———. "'The Needle or the Pen': The Literary Rediscovery of Women's Textile Work." In *Tradition and the Talents of Women,* edited by Florence Howe, 338–64. Urbana: University of Illinois Press, 1991.

———. "The Nineteenth-Century Diarist and Her Quilts." *Feminist Studies* 8 (1982): 293–99.

Hedges, Elaine, and Ingrid Wendt, eds. *In Her Own Image: Women Working in the Arts.* Old Westbury, Conn.: Feminist, 1980.

Heilbrun, Carolyn. *Writing a Woman's Life.* New York: Ballantine, 1988.

Henderson, Mae. "The State of Our Art." Interview with June Jordan in *Women's Review of Books* 8.5 (February 1991): 23–26.

Hirsch, Marianne. *Beyond the Single Vision: Henry James, Michel Butor, Uwe Johnson.* York, S.C.: French Literature Publications, 1981.

———. *The Mother-Daughter Plot: Narrative, Psychoanalysis, Feminism.* Bloomington: Indiana University Press, 1989.

Holstein, Jonathan. "Curator's Statement: Abstract Design in American Quilts." In *Louisville Celebrates the American Quilt: A Guide to the Exhibits.* Louisville: Kentucky Quilt Project, 1992. 5.

———. *The Pieced Quilt: An American Design Tradition.* Greenwich, Conn.: Little Brown and Co., 1973.

———. "The Whitney and After . . . What's Happened to Quilts." *Clarion* (Spring/Summer 1986):80–85.

hooks, bell. *Ain't I a Woman: Black Women and Feminism.* Boston: South End, 1981.

———. *Yearning: Race, Gender, and Cultural Politics.* Boston: South End, 1990.

Horton, Laurel. "Nineteenth-Century Quiltmaking Traditions in South Carolina." *Southern Folklore* 46 (1989): 101–15.

Horton, Laurel, and Lynn Robertson Myers, eds. *Social Fabric: South Carolina's Traditional Quilts.* Columbia: University of South Carolina Press, 1986.

Horvitz, Deborah. "Nameless Ghosts: Possession and Dispossession in *Beloved.*" *Studies in American Fiction* 17 (1989): 157–67.

Houck, Carter. *The Quilt Encyclopedia Illustrated.* New York: Abrams, 1991.

Howard, Robert. "UTOPIA: Where Workers Craft New Technology." *Technology Review* (April 1985):43–49.

Hutcheon, Linda. *The Politics of Postmodernism.* London: Routledge, 1989.

Irigaray, Luce. *This Sex Which is Not One.* Translated by Gillian C. Gill. Ithaca, N.Y.: Cornell University Press, 1985.

Irwin, John Rice. *A People and Their Quilts.* West Chester, Penn.: Schiffer, 1984.

Jameson, Fredric. *Marxism and Form.* Princeton, N.J.: Princeton University Press, 1971.

———. *The Political Unconscious: Narrative as a Socially Symbolic Act.* Ithaca, N.Y.: Cornell University Press, 1981.

————. "Postmodernism, or the Cultural Logic of Late Capitalism." *New Left Review* 146 (July–August 1984): 53–92.

Jehlen, Myra. "Archimedes and the Paradox of Feminist Criticism." *Signs* 6 (1984): 575–601.

Jenkins, Susan, and Linda Seward. *The American Quilt Story: The How-To and Heritage of a Craft Tradition.* Emmaus, Penn.: Rodale, 1991.

Johnson, Geraldine. "More for Warmth than Looks: Quilts of the Blue Ridge Mountains." In *Pieced by Mother: Symposium Papers,* edited by Jeannette Lasansky and Mary Elizabeth Johnson, 35–47. Lewisburg, Penn.: Oral Traditions Project, 1988.

————. "'Plain and Fancy': The Socioeconomics of Blue Ridge Quilts." *Appalachian Journal* 10 (1982): 12–35.

Kaplan, Max. *The Arts: A Sociological Perspective.* Rutherford, N.J.: Fairleigh Dickinson University Press, 1990.

Kapp, K. William, and Lore L. Kapp. *History of Economic Thought.* New York: Barnes, 1966.

Kenyon, Jane. "Things." *New Letters* 51 (Spring 1985): 45–6.

Keyes, Ralph. "Do You Have the Time?" *Parade Magazine* 16 (February 1992): 22–24.

Klapp, Orrin E. *Inflation of Symbols: Loss of Values in American Culture.* New Brunswick, N.J.: Transaction, 1991.

Kyser, Pat Flynn. "Pieces and Patches." *Quilt World* (February/March 1992):16.

Lands' End, *Direct Merchants Catalog* (August 1991):118–21.

Lasansky, Jeannette. *In the Heart of Pennsylvania: Nineteenth and Twentieth Century Quiltmaking Traditions.* Lewisburg, Penn.: Oral Traditions Project, 1985.

————. *Pieced by Mother: Over 100 Years of Quiltmaking Traditions.* Lewisburg, Penn.: Oral Traditions Project, 1986.

————, ed. *In the Heart of Pennsylvania: Symposium Papers.* Lewisburg, Penn.: Oral Traditions Project, 1986,

Lasansky, Jeannette, and Mary Elizabeth Johnson, eds. *Pieced by Mother: Symposium Papers.* Lewisburg, Penn.: Oral Traditions Project, 1988.

Laws, Page R. "Mythic Images of America: Four Recent European Novels." Ph.D. diss., Yale University, 1979.

Leahy, Jim. "Quilt." *Quilt World* (August/September 1991):6.

Le Guin, Ursula K. "She Unnames Them." *New Yorker* 21 (January 1985): 27.

Leon, Eli. *Who'd A Thought It: Improvisation in African-American Quiltmaking.* San Francisco: San Francisco Craft and Folk Art Museum, 1987.

Lévi-Strauss, Claude. *The Savage Mind.* Chicago: University of Chicago Press, 1966.

Lewis, George H. "Community through Exclusion and Illusion: The Creation of Social Worlds in an American Shopping Mall." *Journal of Popular Culture* 24: 121–36.

Lippard, Lucy. *Mixed Blessings: New Art in a Multicultural America.* New York: Pantheon, 1990.

———. "Up, Down, and Across: A New Frame for New Quilts." Robinson, 32–43.

Lipsett, Linda Otto. *Remember Me: Women and Their Friendship Quilts.* San Francisco: Quilt Digest, 1985.

Lithgow, Marilyn. *Quiltmaking and Quiltmakers.* New York: Funk, 1974.

Lydon, Mary. *Perpetuum Mobile: A Study of the Novels and Aesthetics of Michel Butor.* Edmunton, Canada: University of Alberta Press, 1980.

MacDowell, Marsha. "Women, Quiltmaking, and Social Change in America." In *Quilted Together: Women, Quilts, and Communities,* edited by Joyce Ice and Linda Norris, 69–76. Delhi, N.Y. : Delaware County Historical Association, 1989.

McKay, Nellie. "An Interview with Toni Morrison." *Contemporary Literature* 24 (1983): 413–29.

MacKinnon, Catherine A. "Sexuality, Pornography, and Method: Pleasure under Patriarchy." *Ethics* 99 (1989): 314–46.

McMorris, Penny, and Michael Kile. *The Art Quilt.* San Francisco: Quilt Digest, 1984.

McPherson, Sandra. "Eve." In *Streamers.* New York: Ecco, 1988. 31–33.

McWilliams, Dean. "Butor's American Texts: The Writer as Red Indian." *World Literature Today* 61 (1982): 258–64.

Macheski, Cecilia. "Penelope's Daughters: Images of Needlework in Eighteenth-Century Literature." In *Fetter'd or Free?: British Women Novelists, 1670–1815,* edited by Mary Anne Schofield and Cecilia Macheski. Athens: Ohio University Press, 1986.

Mainardi, Patricia. "Quilt Survivals and Revivals." *Arts Magazine* (May 1988):49–53.

———. "Quilts: The Great American Art." *Feminist Art Journal* 2 (1973): 1, 18–23. Rpt. in *Radical America* 7 (1973): 36–78; *Feminism and Art History: Questioning the Litany,* edited by Norma Broude and Mary D. Garrard, 331–46. New York: Harper, 1982.

———. *Quilts: The Great American Art.* San Pedro, Calif.: Miles, 1978.

Marcuse, Herbert. *One-Dimensional Man: Studies in the Ideology of Advanced Industrial Society.* Boston: Beacon, 1964.

Marinelli, Stacie. "Art and Metaphor: The Language of Quilts." *Sojourner: The Women's Forum* 16 (1991): 40–41.

Marx, Karl. *Capital.* Edited by Friedrich Engels. Translated from the 3d German edition by Samuel Moore and Edward Aveling. Revised and amplified according to the 4th German edition by Ernest Untermann. New York: Modern, 1906; Chicago: Kerr, 1906.

———. *A Contribution to the Critique of Political Economy.* Chicago: Kerr, 1904.

Mauss, Marcel. *The Gift.* New York: Norton, 1990.

Meese, Elizabeth. *(Ex)Tensions: Re-Figuring Feminist Criticism.* Chicago: University of Illinois Press, 1990.

Miller, Lynn F., and Sally S. Swenson. *Lives and Works: Talks with Women Artists.* Metuchen: Scarecrow, 1981.

Milspaw, Yvonne J. "Jennie's Quilts: The Interface of Folk and Popular Tradition in the Work of a New York Quiltmaker." *New York Folklore* 8 (1982): 11–23.

Morcos, Gamila. "*Mobile* de Butor: typographie et justification." *Australian Journal of French Studies* 18 (1981): 56–76.

Morgan, Robin. "Piecing." In *Depth Perception: New Poems and a Masque.* Garden City, N.J.: Doubleday, 1982. 3–5.

Morrison, Toni. *Beloved.* New York: Plume-Penguin, 1988.

––––––. "Unspeakable Things Unspoken: The Afro-American Presence in American Literature." *Michigan Quarterly Review* 28.1 (Winter 1989): 1–34.

Mumford, Lewis. *The Myth of the Machine: The Pentagon of Power.* New York: Harcourt, 1970.

Munroe, Eleanor. "Breaking Stars: A Collaboration in Quilts." In *The Artist and the Quilt,* edited by Charlotte Robinson, 44–97. New York: Knopf, 1983.

Naylor, Gloria. *Mama Day.* New York: Vintage, 1988.

Norwood, Vera L. "Thank You for My Bones: Connections between Contemporary Women Artists and the Traditional Arts of Their Foremothers." In *New Mexico Women, Intercultural Perspectives,* edited by Joan M. Jensen and Darlis A. Miller, 357–75. Albuquerque: University of New Mexico Press, 1986.

Oates, Joyce Carol. "Celestial Timepiece." In *Celestial Timepiece: Poems by Joyce Carol Oates.* Illustrated by Paula George. Dallas: Pressworks, 1980.

Ostriker, Alicia Suskin. *Stealing the Language: The Emergence of Women's Poetry in America.* Boston: Beacon, 1986.

Otto, Whitney. *How to Make an American Quilt.* New York: Villard, 1991.

Ovid. *Metamorphoses.* Translated by Mary M. Innes. London: Penguin, 1986.

Owens, Craig. "The Discourse of Others: Feminists and Postmodernism." In *The Anti-Aesthetic: Essays on Postmodern Culture,* edited by Hal Foster, 57–77. Seattle: Bay, 1983.

Packer, Davey. Interview by Susan Bernick. Wild Goose Chase Quilt Gallery, Chicago, November 1987.

Parker, Rozsika. *The Subversive Stitch: Embroidery and the Making of the Feminine.* London: Women's Press, 1984.

Parker, Rozsika, and Griselda Pollock. *Old Mistresses: Woman, Art and Ideology.* London: Routledge, 1981; New York: Pantheon, 1981.

Petrides, George A. *A Field Guide to Trees and Shrubs.* Boston: Houghton, 1958.

Piercy, Marge. "Looking at Quilts." In *Living in the Open.* New York: Knopf, 1976. 86–87.

Pryse, Marjorie. "Zora Neale Hurston, Alice Walker, and the 'Ancient Power.'"

Conjuring: Black Women, Fiction, and Literary Tradition, edited by Marjorie Pryse and Hortense J. Spillers, 1–24. Bloomington: Indiana University Press, 1985.

Raillard, Georges. *Butor.* Paris: Gallimard, 1968.

Ricardou, Jean. "La Fiction Flamboyante." *Critique* 286 (1971): 210–28.

Rich, Adrienne. *Of Woman Born: Motherhood as Experience and Institution.* New York: Norton, 1976.

———. "When We Dead Awaken: Writing as Re-Vision." In *The Norton Anthology of Literature by Women,* edited by Sandra M. Gilbert and Susan Gubar, 2044–56. New York: Norton, 1985.

Richardson, Samuel. *Clarissa.* 1747. New York: Holt, 1901.

Roberson, Ruth Haislip, ed. *North Carolina Quilts.* Chapel Hill: University of North Carolina Press, 1988.

Robertson, Elizabeth Wells. *American Quilts.* New York: Studio, 1948.

Robinson, Charlotte, ed. *The Artist and the Quilt.* New York: Knopf, 1983.

Rogers, Michelle. "Interview avec Michel Butor." *French Review* 57 (1984): 509–16.

Ross, Daniel. "Celie in the Looking Glass: The Desire for Selfhood in *The Color Purple.*" *Modern Fiction Studies* 34 (1988): 69–84.

Roszak, Theodore. *The Making of a Counter Culture: Reflections on Technocratic Society and Its Youthful Opposition.* Garden City, N.J.: Doubleday, 1964.

Roudaut, Jean. "Parenthèse sur la place occupée par l'étude intitulée '6 810 000 litres d'eau par seconde' parmi les autres ouvrages de Michel Butor." *Nouvelle Revue Française* 14: 498–509.

Roudiez, Leon S. "Gloses sur les premières pages de *Mobile* de Michel Butor." *Modern Language Notes* 87 (1972): 83–95.

———. *Michel Butor.* New York: Columbia University Press, 1965.

———. "Michel Butor: Text and Graphics." *Columbia Library Columns* 36 (1986): 13–25.

Ruddick, Sara, and Pamela Daniels. *Working It Out: 23 Women Talk about Their Lives and Work.* New York: Pantheon, 1977.

Ruskin, Cindy. *The Quilt: Stories from the NAMES Project.* New York: Pocket, 1988.

St. Aubyn, F. C. "Entretien avec Michel Butor." *French Review* 366 (1962): 12–22.

———. "A propos de *Mobile.* Deuxième entretien avec Michel Butor." *French Review* 38 (1965): 427–40.

———. "Michel Butor's America." *Kentucky Foreign Language Quarterly* 11 (1964): 40–48.

Schapiro, Miriam. "Geometry and Flowers." In *The Artist and the Quilt,* edited by Charlotte Robinson, 26–31. New York: Knopf, 1983.

Schapiro, Miriam, and Faith Wilding. "Cunts/Quilts/Consciousness." *Heresies* 1988: 1–17.

Schneir, Miriam, ed. *Feminism: The Essential Historical Writings.* New York: Vintage, 1972.

Schofield, Mary Anne, and Cecilia Macheski, eds. *Fetter'd or Free?: British Women Novelists, 1670–1815.* Athens: Ohio University Press, 1986.

Schor, Juliet B. "Workers of the World, Unwind." *Technology Review* (November/December 1991):25–32.

Schweickart, Patrocinio P. "Reading Ourselves: Toward a Feminist Theory of Reading." In *Gender and Reading: Essays on Readers, Texts, and Contexts,* edited by Elizabeth A. Flynn and Patrocinio P. Schweickart, 31–62. Baltimore: Johns Hopkins University Press, 1986.

Shaiken, Harley. *Work Transformed: Automation and Labor in the Computer Age.* New York: Holt, 1985.

Shange, Ntozake. *Sassafras, Cypress and Indigo.* New York: St. Martin's, 1982.

Showalter, Elaine. "Feminist Criticism in the Wilderness." In *The New Feminist Criticism: Essays on Women, Literature, and Theory,* 243–70. New York: Pantheon, 1982.

———. "Piecing and Writing." In *The Poetics of Gender,* edited by Nancy K. Miller, 222–47. New York: Columbia University Press, 1986.

———. *Sister's Choice: Tradition and Change in American Women's Writing.* Oxford: Clarendon, 1991.

Shroder, Maurice. *Icarus: The Image of the Artist in French Romanticism.* Cambridge: Harvard University Press, 1961.

Shusterman, Richard. "The Fine Art of Rap." *New Literary History* 22 (1991): 613–32.

Snyder, Grace. *No Time on My Hands.* Lincoln: University of Nebraska Press, 1963.

Soltow, Willow Ann. *Quilting the World Over.* Radnor, Penn.: Chilton, 1991.

Spacks, Patricia Meyer. *Imagining a Self: Autobiography and Novel in Eighteenth-Century England.* Cambridge: Harvard University Press, 1976.

Spencer, Jane. *The Rise of the Woman Novelist.* New York: Basil, 1986.

Spender, Dale. *Mothers of the Novel.* New York: Routledge, 1986.

Spillers, Hortense J. "Mama's Baby, Papa's Maybe: An American Grammar Book." *Diacritics* 17 (1987): 65–81.

Spivack, Kathleen. "The moments-of-past-happiness quilt." In *Early Ripening: American Women's Poetry Now,* edited by Marge Piercy, 223–24. London: Pandora, 1987.

Suther, Judith D. "Apology for *Mobile.*" *Romance Quarterly* 32 (1985): 55–64.

Tate, Claudia, ed. *Black Women Writers at Work.* New York: Continuum, 1983.

Tavormina, M. Teresa. "Dressing the Spirit: Clothworking and Language in *The Color Purple.*" *Journal of Narrative Technique* 16 (1986): 220–30.

Thompson, Robert Farris. "From the First to the Final Thunder: African-American Quilts, Monuments of Culture Assertion." In *Who'd A Thought It: Improvisation in African-American Quiltmaking,* edited by Eli Leon, 12–21. San Francisco: San Francisco Craft and Folk Art Museum, 1987.

Tompkins, Jane. "Me and My Shadow." *New Literary History* 19 (1987). Rpt. in *Feminisms: An Anthology of Literary Theory and Criticism,* edited by Robyn R. Warhol and Diane Price Herndl, 1079–92. New Brunswick, N.J.: Rutgers University Press, 1991.

Toni Morrison. Produced and directed by Alan Benson. Chicago: Home Vision, 1987. Videocassette.

Torsney, Cheryl B. "The Critical Quilt: Alternative Authority in Feminist Criticism." In *Contemporary Literary Theory,* edited by G. Douglas Atkins and Laura Morrow, 180–99. Amherst: University of Massachusetts Press, 1989.

Tournier, Nan. "Sea Island Black Quilters." In *Social Fabric: South Carolina's Traditional Quilts,* edited by Laurel Horton and Lynn Robertson Myers, 41–46. Columbia: University of South Carolina Press, 1986.

Turner, Kay. "Mexican American Home Altars: Towards Their Interpretation." *Aztlan* 13 (1982): 310–23.

Twining, Mary Arnold. "An Examination of African Retentions in the Folk Culture of the South Carolina and Georgia Sea Islands." Ph.D. diss., Indiana University, 1977.

Ultimate Quilting Systems. Produced by American Professional Quilting Systems. Videocassette, n.d.

Varley, Pamela. "Electronic Democracy." *Technology Review* (November/December 1991):43–51.

Veblen, Thorstein. *The Instinct of Workmanship: And the State of the Industrial Arts.* New York: Macmillan, 1914.

———. *The Engineers and the Price System.* New York: Viking, 1921.

Vlach, John Michael. *The Afro-American Tradition in Decorative Arts.* Cleveland: Cleveland Museum of Art, 1978.

Wahlman, Maude Southwell. "African Symbolism in Afro-American Quilts." *African Arts* 20.1 (1986): 68–76.

———. "Religious Symbolism in African-American Quilts." *Clarion* (Summer 1989): 36–44.

Wahlman, Maude Southwell, and John Scully. "Aesthetic Principles in Afro-American Quilts." In *Afro-American Folk Arts and Crafts,* edited by William Ferris, 79–97. Boston: Hall, 1983.

Wagner-Martin, Linda. "Quilting in Gloria Naylor's *Mama Day.*" *Notes on Contemporary Literature* 18 (1988): 6–7.

Waldvogel, Merikay. *Soft Covers for Hard Times: Quiltmaking and the Great Depression.* Nashville, Tenn.: Rutledge Hill, 1990.

Walker, Alice. *The Color Purple.* New York: Pocket; New York: Washington Square, 1982.

———. "Everyday Use." In *In Love and Trouble.* New York: Harcourt, 1967. 47–59. Rpt. in *The Norton Anthology of Literature by Women,* edited by Sandra M. Gilbert and Susan Gubar, 2366–74. New York: Norton, 1985.

———. *In Search of Our Mothers' Gardens.* New York: Harcourt, 1983.

————. *Meridian*. New York: Simon, 1976.

————. "One Child of One's Own: A Meaningful Digression Within the Work(s)." In *In Search of Our Mothers' Gardens*, 361–83.

————. "Writing *The Color Purple*." In *In Search of Our Mothers' Gardens*, 355–60.

Waniek, Marilyn. "The Century Quilt." In *Mama's Promises*. Baton Rouge: Louisiana State University Press, 1985. 37–38.

Warren, Elizabeth. "Amish Quilts in the Museum of American Folk Art." *Antiques* 132 (1987): 514–23.

Waugh, Patricia. *Feminine Fictions: Revisiting the Postmodern*. London: Routledge, 1989.

Weinstein, Jeff. "Names Carried into the Future: An AIDS Quilt Unfolds." In *Art in the Public Interest*, edited by Arlene Raven, 13–21. Ann Arbor, Mich.: UMI Press, 1989.

Winner, Langdon. *The Whale and the Reactor: A Search for Limits in an Age of High Technology*. Chicago: University of Chicago Press, 1986.

Wolff, Janet. *The Social Production of Art*. New York: St. Martin's, 1981.

Yeats, William Butler. *Selected Poetry*. Edited by A. Norman Jeffares. London: Macmillan, 1965.

Young, Blanche, and Helen Young. *The Lone Star Quilt Handbook*. Oak View, Tx.: Young, 1979.

Zolberg, Vera. *Constructing a Sociology of the Arts*. New York: Cambridge, 1990.

II. Secondary Works

Because so many of the texts cited here could easily be categorized in more than one way, I have deliberately refrained from delineating sections too specifically. Further, because of the number of available articles concerning quilts, their makers, or the quilting process, I have generally included only book-length studies within this second section of the bibliography. Readers are encouraged to peruse individual volumes of some of the journals listed in the Journals section in order to acquaint themselves with the significant and important work contained therein.

By not including texts that are basically instructional in nature, that concern the history of specific quilt patterns, or that focus exclusively on the history of a particular quilt or its maker, I do not intend to suggest that such works are less important than those I do include here. Instead, limited by space, I have chosen to direct readers toward works of a more general nature, all sharing as their focus a broad historical or theoretical aspect of quilt culture: because of the wide interest in African American, international, and regional quilts, I have provided separate bibliographic sections for each of these categories. I have included also sections related to those topics that the essays in this volume discuss at length. Specifically, I offer a section that offers bibliographic information for literary works taking quilts as central images, so that those readers who are especially interested in this "use" of the quilt may familiarize themselves with texts other than those discussed in the preceding essays. Additionally, for readers who are particularly interested in the discussions centering on the NAMES Project, I offer a section listing texts that consider that project's sociocultural implications.

Finally, as quilt scholarship continues to play an important role in our understanding of culture, articles, books, catalogues, films, and even new journals are being produced at an exciting and rapid rate.

African American Quilts

In their important attention to the work of African American artists, scholars have also increasingly devoted consideration to the quilting traditions of the African American community. The texts listed below represent the groundbreaking work in this field, as do those by Cuesta Benberry, Leon Eli, Gladys-Marie Fry, Maude Southwell Wahlman, and John Vlach: bibliographical information for these authors' texts can be found in the Works Cited in this volume. Many of the texts listed here were conceived as catalogs to accompany museum exhibitions; they include both illustrations and the history of the quilts displayed.

Freeman, Ronald L. *Something to Keep You Warm: The Roland Freeman Collection of Black American Quilts from the Mississippi Heartland.* Jackson: Mississippi Department of Archives and History, 1981.

Fry, Gladys-Marie. "Harriet Powers: Portrait of a Black Quilter." In *Missing Pieces: Georgia Folk Art 1770–1976.* Atlanta: Georgia Council for the Arts and Humanities, 1976. 16–23.

MacDonald, Mary Anne. "Symbols from Ribbons: Afro-American Funeral-Ribbon Quilts in Chatham County, North Carolina." In *Arts in Earnest: North Carolina Folklife,* edited by Daniel W. Patterson and Charles G. Zug, III, 164–78. Durham, N.C.: Duke University Press, 1991.

McKinney, Nancy, ed. *Traditions in Cloth: Afro-American Quilts/West African Textiles.* Los Angeles: California Afro-American Museum, 1986.

McKinney, Nancy, and Nan Becker. *Black Quilters.* New Haven: Yale School of Art, 1979.

McKinney, Nancy, and Ella King Torrey. *Ten Afro-American Quilters.* Oxford, Miss.: Center for Study of Southern Culture, 1983.

Films Concerning Quilts

The films listed below include those that take quilt culture as their primary focus, such as *Hearts and Hands: A Social History of Nineteenth-Century Women and Their Quilts.* Also listed here are projects like *Anonymous Was a Woman* and *Images of Country Women: A Patchwork Quilt,* which include quilts as one example of women's creativity, and *Common Threads,* which documents the "story" of the AIDS quilt. Films like *A Stitch for Time,* on the other hand, offer the narrative of the Boise Peace Quilters and the political efforts expressed through their quilts.

Anonymous Was a Woman. Produced by Mirra Bank and WNET-TV. Films Inc., 1977. Videocassette.

Common Threads: The NAMES Project Quilt. Produced by Rob Epstein, Jeffrey Friedman, and Bill Couturie, 1989. Videocassette.

Hearts and Hands: A Social History of Nineteenth-Century Women and Their Quilts. Produced by Pat Ferrero and Julie Silber. Ferrero Films, 1987. Video-cassette.

Images of Country Women: A Patchwork Quilt. Produced by Lucyann Kerry and Blue Ridge Films. 16 mm, 29 minutes. Pennsylvania State University, 1976.

A Jury of Her Peers. Produced by Sally Heckel. 16 mm, 30 minutes. Films Inc., 1980.

Quilting: Patterns of Love. Produced by Larron Productions Ltd. 16 mm, 20 minutes. Toronto: Cinema Concepts International, Toronto, 1980.

Quilts in Women's Lives: Six Portraits. Produced by Pat Ferrero. 16 mm, 30 minutes. New Day Films, 1980.

Quilting Women. Produced by Elizabeth Barrett and Appalshop, 16 mm, 28 minutes. 1980.

A Stitch for Time. Produced by Peacequilters Production Co., 1987. Videocassette.

Historical and Theoretical Texts about Quilts and Quilting

Clearly, this book takes as its project contributing to the historical and theoretical discussions of quilts and quilting; thus, many of the texts listed in Works Cited are critical to those interested in quilt scholarship. Listed below are other volumes that use an historical or theoretical lens to view quilts. Frequently interdisciplinary in nature, sometimes incorporating a feminist or Marxist framework to position their arguments, these works occasionally use specific quilts or quilt patterns as a way of illuminating their discussion. Other texts listed here trace the general history of quilting in the United States, providing an overview for quilt study. Some, such as those texts edited by Jeannette Lasansky and Joyce Ice and Linda Norris, bring together a variety of essays that consider aspects of quilt culture. Generally, titles of these works indicate their focus. Readers are also encouraged to consult the work of Colleen Makowski, whose annotated bibliography on quilts is invaluable in providing further information about texts published prior to 1983.

Bacon, Lenice Ingram. *American Patchwork Quilts.* New York: Bonanza, 1980.
Bank, Mirra. *Anonymous Was a Woman.* New York: St. Martin's 1979.

Benson, Jane, and Nancy Olson. *The Power of Cloth: Political Quilts, 1845–1986.* Cupertino, Calif.: Euphrat Gallery, 1987.

Binney, Edwin, and Gail Binney-Winslow. *Homage to Amanda.* San Francisco: Kiracofe, 1984.

Bishop, Robert, and Patricia Coblentz. *New Discoveries in American Quilts.* New York: Dutton, 1976.

Brackman, Barbara. *Clues in the Calico: Identifying and Dating Quilts.* McLean, Va.: EPM, 1989.

Christopherson, Kay. *The Political and Campaign Quilt.* Frankfort: Kentucky Heritage Quilt Society, 1984.

Colby, Averil. *Patchwork Quilts.* New York: Scribners, 1965.

———. *Quilting.* New York: Scribners, 1971.

Cross, Mary, ed. *Women's Work: A Study of Quilts.* Portland, Ore.: Columbia-Willamette Quilt Study Group, 1984.

Davis, Carolyn O., Margaret Rooker, and Lynn Stacey, eds. *Pioneer Quiltmaker: The Story of Dorinda Moody Slade 1808–1895.* Tucson, Ariz.: Treasure Chest, 1990.

Fox, Sandi. *Small Endearments: Nineteenth-Century Quilts for Children.* New York: Scribners, 1985.

———. *Wrapped in Glory: Figurative Quilts and Bedcovers 1700–1900.* New York: Thames, 1990.

Hall, Carrie A., and Rose G. Kretsinger. *The Romance of the Patchwork Quilt.* New York: Bonanza, 1935.

Johnson, Mary Elizabeth. *Country Quilt Patterns.* Birmingham, Ala.: Oxmoor, 1977.

Ice, Joyce, and Linda Norris, eds. *Quilted Together: Women, Quilts and Communities.* Delhi, N.Y.: Delaware County Historical Association, 1989.

Lasansky, Jeannette. *Bits and Pieces: Textile Traditions.* Lewisburg, Penn.: Oral Traditions Project, 1991.

Linsley, Leslie. *Quilts Across America: The Making of the Great American Quilt Banner.* New York: St. Martins, 1988.

Lipsett, Linda Otto. *Pieced from Ellen's Quilt: Ellen Spaulding Reed's Letters and Story.* Dayton, Ohio: Halstead, 1991.

———. *To Love and to Cherish: Brides Remembered.* San Francisco: Quilt Digest, 1989.

McKelvey, Susan. *Friendship's Offering: Techniques and Inspiration for Writing on Quilts.* Martinez, Calif.: C & T, 1990.

McKendry, Ruth. *Traditional Quilts and Bed Coverings.* New York: Van Nostrand, 1979.

McMorris, Penny. *Crazy Quilts.* New York: Dutton, 1984.

Makowski, Colleen L. *Quilting, Nineteen Fifteen to Nineteen Eighty-Three: An Annotated Bibliography.* Metuchen: Scarecrow, 1985.

Martin, Nancy J. *Threads of Time.* Botthell, Wash.: Patchwork Place, 1990.

O'Brien, Sandra L. *Great American Quilts.* Birmingham, Ala.: Oxmoor, 1988.

Orlofsky, Patsy, and Myron Orlofsky. *Quilts in America.* New York: McGraw, 1974.

Pershing, Linda. "'She Really Wanted to Be Her Own Woman': Scandalous Sunbonnet Sue." In *Feminist Messages: Coding in Women's Folk Culture,* edited by Joan Newlon Radnor, 98–125. Urbana: University of Illinois Press, 1993.

Roach, Susan. "The Kinship Quilt: An Ethnographic Semiotic Analysis of a Quilting Bee." In *Women's Folklore, Women's Culture,* edited by Rosan A. Jordan and Susan J. Kalcik, 54–65. Philadelphia: University of Pennsylvania Press, 1985.

Safford, Carleton L., and Robert Bishop. *America's Quilts and Coverlets.* New York: Dutton, 1972.

Schabel, Elizabeth Smith. "The Historical Significance of Patchwork Quilt Names as a Reflection of the Emerging Social Consciousness of the American Woman." *Tennessee Folklore Society Bulletin* 47.1 (1981): 1–16.

Strauss, Lucy. *Artists' Quilts.* California: Hultas, 1982.

Swan, Susan Burrows. *Plain and Fancy: American Women and Their Needlework, 1700–1859.* New York: Holt, 1977.

Von Gwinner, Schnuppe. *The History of the Patchwork Quilt: Origins, Traditions, and Symbols of a Textile Art.* Translated by Edward Force. West Chester, Penn.: Schiffer, 1988.

Webster, Marie. *Quilts: Their Story and How to Make Them.* New York: Doubleday, 1915.

Weissman, Judith Reiter. "Anonymous Beauty: Quilts, Coverlets, and Bedcovers: Textile Treasures from Two Centuries." *Clarion* (Spring 1981): 24–39.

Woodward, Thomas K., and Blanche Greenstein. *Crib Quilts: And Other Small Wonders.* New York: Dutton, 1981.

Journals and Serial Volumes Concerning Quilting

The number of journals that focus on quilt scholarship has increased significantly over the past two decades. Those listed below should be considered as representative of journals concentrating on the history of quilts and theories of quilt culture; one, the *Quilt Digest,* ceased publication in 1989. Journals like the *Quilt Journal: An International Review* and volumes such as *Uncoverings* are interdisciplinary, employing quilt research from fields such as economics and anthropology. Not included here are periodicals that are instructional in nature, although such texts are often invaluable aids for considering specific quilters and their work, or specific quilt patterns. One listing, *Uncoverings,* represents the compilation of papers presented at the annual American Quilt Study Group meeting: volume 13 is forthcoming. That group's publications list includes the table of contents for each of the twelve volumes currently available; additionally, *Uncoverings* is indexed in *Clothing and Arts Textile Index, America: History and Life, Bibliography of the History of Art, Historical Abstracts, MLA Directory of Periodicals, MLA International Bibliography, New Books on Women and Feminism,* and *Sociological Abstracts.*

Quilt Digest. San Francisco: Kiracofe and Kile, 1983–1989.
Quilt Journal: An International Review. Louisville, Ky. 1992–.
Quilter's Journal. Mill Valley, Calif.: 1983–.
Quilter's Newsletter Magazine. Wheatridge, Colo.: Leman Publications, 1969–.
Uncoverings: Research Papers of the American Quilt Study Group. Vols. 1–12. San Francisco: American Quilt Study Group.

Literary Texts Concerning Quilts

It is clearly beyond the scope of this bibliography to include every dramatic, poetic, or fictional work that incorporates images of quilts or their makers. Several such works, like Toni Morrison's *Beloved* and Joyce Carol Oates's "Celestial Timepiece," are discussed at length in the preceding essays. The additional texts listed here devote significant attention to images of quilts, and thus should serve as useful points of discussion for readers interested in studying the ways in which quilts have been incorporated into American literary culture. The anthology edited by Cecilia Macheski includes fictional, poetic, and dramatic works along with songs written since 1845, and thus will be invaluable for those concerned with this aspects of quilts, their makers, and their manufacture; the collection of early short stories concerning quilts, compiled by Cuesta Ray Benberry and Carol Pinney Crabb, is equally important for those exploring quilts as they operate in fiction.

Acosta, Teresa Palomo. "My Mother Pieced Quilts." In *Festival de Flor y Canto: An Anthology of Chicano Literature.* Los Angeles: University of Southern California Press, 1976.

Alcott, Louisa May. "Patty's Patchwork." In *Aunt Jo's Scrap Bag.* Vol. 1. Boston: Roberts, 1872. 193–215.

Benberry, Cuesta Ray, and Carol Pinney Crabb, comps. *A Patchwork of Pieces: An Anthology of Early Quilt Stories 1845–1940.* Paducah, Ky.: American Quilters' Society, 1993.

Fisher, Dorothy Canfield. "The Bedquilt." In *Women and Fiction 2: Short Stories by and about Women,* edited by Susan Cahill, 35–43. New York: New American, 1978.

Glaspell, Susan. *Trifles.* 1916. Rpt. in *The Norton Anthology of Literature by Women,* edited by Sandra M. Gilbert and Susan Gubar, 1388–99. New York: Norton, 1985.

Hall, Eliza Calvert. *Aunt Jane of Kentucky.* Boston: Little, 1907.

Levin, Larry. "The Quilt." In *The Morrow Anthology of Younger American Poets,* edited by Dave Smith and David Bottoms, 398–99. New York: Quill, 1985.

McPherson, Sandra. *The God of Indeterminancy*. Urbana: University of Illinois Press, 1993.

Macheski, Cecilia, ed. *Quilt Stories*. Lexington: University Press of Kentucky. 1994.

Newman, Molly, and Barbara Damashek. *Quilters*. New York: Dramatists Play Service, 1986.

Smith, Dave. "On a Quilt in the Bennington College Library." In *Cuba Night*. New York: Morrow, 1990. 75–76.

Stowe, Harriet Beecher. *The Minister's Wooing*. 1855. New York: Library of America, 1980.

The NAMES Project Quilt

A quilt in tragically continuous production, the NAMES Project Quilt has been the subject of a number of theoretical and historical articles in the recent past. The works listed below, along with discussions such as Elaine Showalter's, as found in the "Common Threads" chapter of her *Sister's Choice*, Jeff Weinstein's "Names Carried into the Future: An AIDS Quilt Unfolds," Judy Elsley's "The Rhetoric of the NAMES Project AIDS Quilt: Reading the Text(ile)," and Peter Hawkins's "The Art of Memory and the NAMES Quilt" represent ways of "reading" this mammoth text.

Crichton, E. G. "Is the NAMES Quilt Art?" *Out/Look* 1 (1988): 5–9.

Mohr, Richard. "Text(ile): Reading the NAMES Project's AIDS Quilt." In *Gay Ideas: Outing and Other Controversies*. Boston: Beacon, 1992.

Sturken, Marita. "Conversations with the Dead: Bearing Witness in the AIDS Memorial Quilt." *Socialist Review* 92 (April–June 1992): 65+.

Nations Other than America and Their Quilts

While quilt scholarship in America has centered largely on those quilts designed and created in the United States, scholars have considered the significance and history of textiles in nations other than America. As such work continues, and as attention continues to be paid to multicultural issues, texts like those listed below will undoubtedly proliferate. The entries here, moreover, by no means include all of the significant work on the role of the quilt in various nations other than the United States.

Bishop, Robert, et al. *Hands All around: Quilts from Many Nations*. New York: Dutton, 1987.

Burnham, Dorothy K. *Pieced Quilts of Ontario*. Toronto: Royal Ontario Museum, 1975.

Conroy, Mary. *Three Hundred Years of Canada's Quilts*. Toronto: Griffin, 1976.

Dendel, Esther Warner. *African Fabric Crafts: Sources of African Designs and Techniques*. New York: Taplinger, 1974.

Eicher, Joanne Bubolz. *Nigerian Handcrafted Textiles*. ILE-IFE, Nigeria: University of IFE, 1976.

Irvine, Jan. *Australian Quilts: The People and Their Art*. Brookvale, Australia: Simon, 1983.

Liddell, Jill, and Yuko Watanabe. *Japanese Quilts*. New York: Dutton, 1988.

Morishige, Reiko, and Kazuko Mende. *Sashiko: Blue-&-White Quilt Art of Japan*. Briarcliff Manor, N.Y.: Japan Publications USA, 1990.

Nelson, Christine. *Contemporary British Quilt Art*. Pomfret, Conn.: Trafalgar, 1989.

Picton, John, and John Mack. *African Textiles*. London: British Museum, 1979.

Rolfe, Margaret. *Patchwork Quilts in Australia*. Richmond, Australia: Greenhouse, 1987.

Specific Collections / Exhibitions

It is beyond the scope of this bibliography to include catalogs from each of the quilt exhibitions hung throughout the United States in the recent past. Moreover, many of those titles are listed in other sections of this bibliography, such as Regional Quilts or African American Quilts. Those texts listed below, then, are included here because they discuss general collections that are not defined by their relationships to regions or to ethnic groups. Further, they offer important perspectives, including historical discussions of quilts and their makers, that transcend specific exhibitions. Lisa Turner Oshins's text offers a relatively full guide to those collections extant in the United States and Canada. Jonathan Holstein's recent text, with its foreword by Shelly Zegart, includes critical information on the history of quilting in the twentieth century.

Bowman, Doris M. *The Smithsonian Treasury of American Quilts*. Washington, D.C.: Smithsonian, 1991.

Holstein, Jonathan, with a foreword by Shelly Zegart. *Abstract Design in American Quilts: A Biography of an Exhibition*. Louisville: Kentucky Quilt Project, 1992.

Macneal, Patricia M., and Maude Southwell Wahlman. *Quilts from Appalachia: Exhibition Catalogue*. University Park, Penn.: Palmer Museum of Art, 1988.

Oshins, Lisa Turner, with commentary by Barbara S. Bockman. *Quilt Collections: A Directory for the United States and Canada*. Washington, D.C.: Acropolis, 1987.

Peck, Amelia. *American Quilts and Coverlets in the Metropolitan Museum of Art*. New York: Metropolitan Museum, 1990.

State Collections / Projects and Texts Concerning Regional Quilts

An on-going interest in the history of state quilts and their makers has produced a quantity of texts dedicated to exploring the significance of regional quilts. Many of these volumes result from various state projects, undertaken by quilt researchers and scholars in each of the United States; such projects have resulted frequently in public exhibits of state quilts. Other texts listed here, as well as those noted in the first half of this bibliography, represent the work of individuals interested in documenting the history of both quilts and the states in which their makers lived and worked. As the titles illustrate, some of the works focus on quilts constructed during a particular time period, while others extend their consideration to quilts currently being made. Listed below are representative texts, but the continued work of state project participants guarantees that further volumes are forthcoming. Also cited here are those texts dedicated to exploring the significance of quilts emerging from regions such as Appalachia and the South. Most of the texts listed include illustrations of the quilts to which they devote significant attention and discussion.

Adkins, Jacqueline M., and Phyllis A. Tepper. *New York Beauties: Quilts from the Empire State*. New York: Dutton, 1992.

Arkansas Quilter's Guild. *Arkansas Quilts*. Paducah, Ky.: American Quilters' Society, 1988.

Barber, Rita Barrow. *Somewhere in Between: Quilts and Quilters of Illinois*. Paducah, Ky.: American Quilters' Society, 1986.

Bishop, Robert, and Elizabeth Safanda. *A Gallery of Amish Quilts: Design Diversity from a Plain People*. New York: Dutton, 1976.

Boyink, Betty, and Milly Splitstone. *Michigan Quilters and Their Designs*. Ann Arbor, Mich.: Boyink, 1983.

Brackman, Barbara, et. al. *Kansas Quilts and Quilters*. Lawrence: University Press of Kansas, 1993.

Bresenhan, Karoline Patterson, and Nancy O'Bryant Puentes. *Lone Stars: A Legacy of Texas Quilts 1836–1936*. 2 vols. Austin: University of Texas Press, 1986, 1990.

Carter, Hazel. *Virginia Quilts: First Search for Virginia-Made Quilts, Beginning in Northern Virginia*. Vienna, Va.: Continental Quilting Congress, 1987.

Clark, Ricky, George W. Knepper, and Ellice Ronsheim. *Quilts in Community: Ohio's Traditions: 19th and 20th Century Quilts, Quiltmakers, and Traditions*. Nashville, Tenn.: Rutledge Hill, 1991.

Cleveland, Richard L., and Donna Bister. *Plain and Fancy: Vermont's People and Their Quilts as a Reflection of America*. San Francisco: Quilt Digest, 1991.

Crews, Patricia Cox, and Ronald C. Naugle. *Nebraska Quilts and Quiltmakers*. Lincoln: University of Nebraska Press, 1991.

Fox, Sandi. *Quilts in Utah: A Reflection of the Western Experience*. Salt Lake City, Utah: Salt Lake Art Center, 1981.

Frost, Helen Y., and Pam Knight Stevenson. *Grand Endeavors: Vintage Arizona Quilts and Their Makers*. Flagstaff, Ariz.: Northland, 1992.

Goldman, Marilyn, and Marguerite Weibusch. *Quilts of Indiana: Crossroads of Memories*. Bloomington: Indiana University Press, 1991.

Haders, Phyllis. *Sunshine and Shadow: The Amish and Their Quilts*. New York: Universe, 1976.

Hammond, Joyce D. *Tifaifai and Quilts of Polynesia*. Honolulu: University of Hawaii Press, 1986.

Harnden, Jane Amstutz, and Pamela Frazee Woolbright, eds. *Oklahoma Heritage Quilts: A Sampling of Quilts Made in or Brought to Oklahoma before 1920*. Paducah, Ky.: American Quilters' Society, 1990.

Havig, Bettina. *Missouri Heritage Quilts*. Paducah, Ky.: American Quilters' Society, 1990.

Heritage Quilt Project of New Jersey. *New Jersey Quilts: 1777–1950, Contributors to an American Tradition*. Paducah, Ky.: American Quilters Society, 1992.

Holstein, Jonathan, and John Finley. *Kentucky Quilts 1800–1900: The Kentucky Quilt Project*. New York: Pantheon, 1982.

Horton, Laurel. "Economic and Cultural Influences on Germany and Scotch-Irish Quilts in Antebellum Rowan County, North Carolina." In *Arts in Earnest: North Carolina Folklife*, edited by Daniel W. Patterson and Charles G. Zug, III, 89–101. Durham, N.C.: Duke University Press, 1990.

Katzenberg, Dena. *Baltimore Album Quilts*. Baltimore, Md.: Baltimore Museum of Art, 1981.

Kettering, Terri. "'Bear's Paw,' 'Philadelphia Pavement': Quilts of the Mid-Atlantic Region." *Journal of Regional Cultures* 2 (1982): 128–38.

Lasansky, Jeannette, ed. *In the Heart of Pennsylvania: Symposium Papers*. Lewisburg, Penn.: Oral Traditions Project, 1986.

Laury, Jean Ray. *Ho for California: Pioneer Women and Their Quilts*. New York: Dutton, 1990.

Lewis, Alfred Allan. *The Mountain Artisans Quilting Book*. New York: Macmillan, 1973.

Lohrenz, Edna, and Anita Miller Stamper. *Mississippi Homespun: Nineteenth-Century Textiles and the Women Who Made Them*. Jackson, Miss.: State Historical Museum, 1989.

Luster, Michael. *Stitches in Time: A Legacy of Ozark Quilts*. Rogers, Ark.: Rogers Historical Museum, 1986.

MacDowell, Marsha, and Ruth D. Fitzgerald. *Michigan Quilts: One Hundred and Fifty Years of a Textile Tradition*. East Lansing: Michigan State University Museum, 1987.

Marshall, Martha. *Quilts of Appalachia: The Mountain Woman and Her Quilts*. Bluff City, Tenn.: Tri-City, 1972.

Ramsey, Bets, and Gail Trechsel. *Southern Quilts: A New View*. McLean, Va.: EPM, 1991.

Ramsey, Bets, and Merikay Waldvogel. *The Quilts of Tennessee: Images of Domestic Life Prior to 1930*. Nashville, Tenn.: Rutledge Hill, 1986.

Twelker, Nancyann Johanson. *Women and Their Quilts: A Washington State Centennial Tribute*. Bothell, Wash.: Patchwork Place, 1988.

Williams, Charlotte Allen. *Florida Quilts*. Gainesville: University Press of Florida, 1992.

Yabsley, Suzanne. *Texas Quilts, Texas Women*. College Station: Texas A&M University Press, 1984.

◆ Notes on the Contributors ◆

SUSAN BEHUNIAK-LONG is Associate Professor of Political Science at Le Moyne College in Syracuse, New York. She has collected hundreds of quilt slides, which she uses during her public lectures on quilts and women's history. She is currently at work on a manuscript that traces how women voice their politics and engage in political activism through quilting.

SUSAN E. BERNICK is a philosopher. She teaches at Furman University in South Carolina. Her interest in quilts was sparked during her graduate work in aesthetics at the University of Minnesota. The relationship of quilts to art, and thus to aesthetics, has given her a model for how philosophy can and should connect with the world.

AUDREY BILGER is Visiting Assistant Professor of English at Oberlin College. She researches and writes on eighteenth-century women novelists and has articles forthcoming or published in *Women's Studies: An Interdisciplinary Journal* and *Women's Writing: The Early Modern Period.* She is currently completing a book-length study of feminist comedy entitled *Laughing Feminism: Comic Strategies in Frances Burney, Maria Edgeworth, and Jane Austen.*

ANNE L. BOWER has been Assistant Professor of English at Ohio State University–Marion since 1990. She enjoys teaching American and African American literature, fiction surveys, and composition. Her research sometimes relates to pedagogical issues, though the focus involves the intersection of literary and nonliterary texts: novels and letters, poems and quilts, autobiographies and cookbooks. Currently she is editing a book that explores the discourse of fund-raising cookbooks.

VIRGINIA B. BROADDUS is a doctoral candidate in English at West Virginia University. Her interests lie in the fields of American studies and feminist theory.

JUDY ELSLEY is Assistant Professor of English at Weber State University in Ogden, Utah. She completed her doctoral dissertation at the University of Arizona on quilts as textile texts and has written a number of articles on quilts as metaphor. Elsley also writes autobiographical essays. Her collection of pieces on living in the American West, *Getting Comfortable: A Woman in the West,* will be published by Jumping Cholla Press in 1994.

VAN E. HILLARD is Assistant Professor of the Practice of Rhetoric in the English department and Assistant Director of the University Writing Program at Duke University. He has written about the rhetoric of art and photography and about the teaching of writing.

MARGOT ANNE KELLEY is Assistant Professor of English at Ursinus College in Pennsylvania, where she teaches American literature. She is interested in relations among literature, science, and culture. Currently she is exploring the concept of complexity in various contexts. Of course, she quilts—and has recently finished a sampler that includes a Sister's Choice square.

PAGE R. LAWS is Associate Professor of English and Director of the Honors Program at Norfolk State University. Coeditor of *Variations on Humankind: An Introduction to World Literature* (Kendall-Hunt, 1991), Laws has also contributed to *James Baldwin: In Memoriam* (MAWA Press, 1992). She has written articles for *American Theater* magazine, *Wellesley Magazine,* and national newspapers, including the *New York Times,* the *Wall Street Journal,* and the *Washington Post.* She is also a consulting dramaturge for the Virginia Stage Company, a regional theater.

CATHY PEPPERS is a graduate student in English at the University of Oregon. She is at work on her dissertation on the usage of goddess and cyborg discourses in feminist theory and contemporary women's novels.

NORA RUTH ROBERTS is a doctoral candidate at City University of New York and teaches English at Medgar Evers College in Brooklyn. Her dissertation, "Three Radical Women Writers: Meridel Le Sueur, Tillie Olsen, and Josephine Herbst," is forthcoming from Garland Publishing. In addition to a half-dozen academic articles, Roberts has published short stories and poetry in numerous publications.

CHERYL B. TORSNEY is an associate professor in the Department of English at West Virginia University, where she teaches American literature and literary theory. The author of *Constance Fenimore Woolson: The Grief of Artistry* (University of Georgia Press, 1989) and the editor of *Critical Essays on Constance Fenimore Woolson* (G. K. Hall, 1992), Torsney is currently working on a study of Henry James.

♦ Index ♦